WAR DOGS

Keith Cory-Jones was born in 1940 in Bristol, where he still lives. His career to date has included such diverse activities as sales and marketing, antique dealing, exhibition promoting, military equipment distribution and a lengthy spell as a photographer, before settling for writing as a full-time occupation. This book was completed despite intricate communication problems with country-hopping mercenaries who phone him in the dead of night with mortars playing in the background, and the unwelcome interruptions from Kelly, his boxer dog who strongly objected to her walk periods being delayed.

To Judith

For whom every day is a battle . . .

WAR DOGS

British mercenaries in Bosnia
tell their own story

by

Keith Cory-Jones

arrow books

This edition published by Arrow Books Limited 1997

1 3 5 7 9 10 8 6 4 2

First published in the United Kingdom in 1996 by Century
Random House UK Ltd, 20 Vauxhall Bridge Road, London SW1V 2SA

Arrow Books Ltd
Random House UK Ltd, 20 Vauxhall Bridge Road, London SW1V 2SA

Random House Australia (Pty) Limited
16 Dalmore Drive, Scoresby, Victoria 3179, Australia

Random House New Zealand Limited
18 Poland Road, Glenfield
Auckland 10, New Zealand

Random House South Africa (Pty) Limited
Endulini, 5a Jubilee Road, Parktown 2193, South Africa

Random House UK Limited Reg. No. 954009

A CIP catalogue record for this book
is available from the British Library

Papers used by Random House UK Limited
are natural, recyclable products made from wood grown in
sustainable forests. The manufacturing processes conform to
the environmental regulations of the country of origin

ISBN 0 09 918482 6

Printed and bound in Great Britain by
Cox & Wyman Ltd, Reading, Berkshire

Glossary

66:	lightweight and disposable anti-tank rocket launcher
AK-47:	Kalashnikov assault rifle (see also *Klash*)
APC:	armoured personnel carrier
Arkanoci:	Arkan's men (Serb nationalist militia commander)
Armbrust:	portable anti-tank system with no backblast
basha:	single square sheet of material used for sleeping shelter
beasting:	military slang term for a beating
bergan:	military term for rucksack
berm:	tank entrenchment
big four:	minimum information given to the enemy (name, rank, serial number and birth date)
bivvy:	waterproof sleeping bag cover or term for settling down for the night (to bivvy down)
blow and go:	detonate explosives and depart in haste
brew-up:	hot drink
BSA:	Bosnian-Serb army
camo:	camouflage face paint or combat clothing
cam up:	to apply face paint
Chetnik:	Serbian irregulars (general term)
chinstrap:	army term for a state of exhaustion
chopper:	helicopter (general term)
claymore mine:	area protection anti-personnel mine
COP:	covert operations vest
CP:	checkpoint
Danner:	brand name for expensive and very desirable military boots
DEA:	US Drug Enforcement Administration
DPM:	disrupted pattern material (camouflage)

E&E:	escape and evasion
ethnic cleansing:	racial or religiously motivated killing
FFD:	first field dressing
FIBUA:	fighting in built-up areas
flak jacket:	upper-body armour
FRAG:	fragmenting
gat:	weapon (American underworld use; from Gatling gun)
gig:	a contract or mission
GPMG:	general purpose machine gun
GSG-9:	German special forces
HEAT:	high-explosive anti-tank (explosive detonates at critical distance before impact and penetrates armour plating)
HEP:	high-explosive plastic
HESH:	high-explosive squash-head (explosive spreads on target surface before detonating)
Hind:	Soviet attack helicopter/gunship
HOS:	extremist Croatian militia
Huey:	US helicopter used extensively in Vietnam
HVO:	Bosnian-Croatian militia
ID:	identity document or card
JNA:	Yugoslavian national army
keffudle:	soldier-speak for a conference
Klash:	Kalashnikov assault rifle (see also *AK-47*)
klicks:	kilometres
LUP:	lying-up point
mag:	weapons magazine containing ammunition
Makarov:	Soviet pistol
merc:	mercenary soldier
MG-42	pre-1945 German 7.92 machine gun
MiG:	Soviet fighter/bomber
MoD:	Ministry of Defence
Mortar:	Light, portable infantry support weapon
NVA:	night-vision equipment
OP:	observation post
PE:	plastic explosive
phos:	phosphorus grenade
pinkie:	long-wheelbase Land Rover
porridge:	period of confinement or capture
RPG-7:	hand-held rocket launcher

RPK:	AK-47 with larger and longer barrel
Rupert/Rodneys:	term used by the lower ranks for an officer
RV:	rendezvous point
SA-80:	automatic weapon in current use by British army
SAM:	surface-to-air missile
Serbo-Croat:	language in general use in former Yugoslavia
shemagh:	type of shawl used by people in the Middle East
shoot and scoot:	attack and get out fast
Skorpion:	Czech 7.62mm machine pistol
sneaky beaky:	slang term for covert operation
SOP:	standard operating procedure
SPG:	self-propelled gun
squaddie:	soldier
stag:	sentry duty
stripes and pips:	visible indication of commission/authority
T-55:	Soviet tank; entered production in 1944
T-72:	Soviet tank; entered production in 1972
tab:	fast march over a long distance; often with full pack
tiger stripe:	method of applying camouflage paint to skin
TMA-2:	Yugoslavian-manufactured plastic-bodied mine
Trislander:	light aircraft requiring minimal take-off/landing area
UN:	United Nations
UNPROFOR:	United Nations protection force
White Eagles:	Chetnik group of irregulars known for their brutality
Zolya:	rocket launcher

Chapter One

... and for the price of a plane ticket you find yourself in some hostile country; where even your 'friends' treat you with suspicion and you know, only too well, that you are expendable!

No way was this decrepit old Trislander, with its misfiring engines producing puffs of smoke, oil and occasional flames, going to be able to land intact on that short piece of corrugated earth beneath us.

I knew it, the men around me knew it, but the pilot – a veteran crop duster from Indiana, USA – simply didn't seem to understand the problem as the plane just kept going down, lower and lower; clipping branches with its spinning wheels as he aimed through a minimal gap in the tangled trees.

The ground was coming up fast now and the pilot sweated hard; peering as if hypnotised through the filthy, bug-splattered windscreen. His gum-chewing jaws had ceased their rhythm whilst he held his breath; juggling levers with the precise abandon of a true professional. Suddenly he exhaled and leaned back in his sheepskin-covered seat as his feet did a little tap dance on the foot pedals. We were going in.

The impact was violent as he dropped the crate vertically from about ten feet, braking immediately and causing the plane to snake frantically and for a moment uncontrollably over the rough ground. No room for any mistake; the forest was straight ahead and getting closer, fast. We weren't going to make it, and I'd left my rosary at home!

The stench of burning rubber from the locked tyres filled the aircraft, and in a gut-wrenching moment it skidded in a tight arc and shuddered to a gasping halt. We'd arrived ... Just another day in the life of a mercenary on his way to work.

Silence and more silence. No one spoke, no one moved, not even a sigh of relief. It was a time for patience. The action would, no doubt, come later.

The soft drone of a distant vehicle started the darting eyes.

Everyone looked at everyone else, questioning with no voice. Friend? Enemy? How would we know until it was too late?

A battered Range Rover pulled into the clearing, followed by an open lorry filled with tough-looking men who dispersed before the vehicles had stopped, surrounding the aircraft with grim expressions, cocked weapons and itchy fingers. We looked out of the windows, searching for a familiar or friendly face; seeing nothing to calm our churning stomachs.

Kit chuckled. 'It's OK, lads, they're friendly. Just a welcoming committee.'

The tension evaporated like steam from a kettle as we clambered out to back-slapping, handshakes and bear hugs.

This was the Republic of Albania, whose ethnic groups claimed descent from the ancient Illyrians, Greeks and Romanians. In 1967 the country closed all mosques and churches, banned organised religion and declared itself to be the 'first atheist state', but the fact remains that 70 per cent of the population are active Muslims, sympathetic to the plight of those being persecuted in neighbouring Yugoslavia and willing to assist anyone prepared to fight for their cause.

Albania is a land of erratic mountain ranges, gnarled, twisted ravines and thick, impenetrable forests, an almost ideal spot for the start of a covert recce into war-torn Yugoslavia by the small group of mercenaries – assisted in these early stages by our Albanian Muslim 'friends'. I had just come along for the ride, to take a few pictures, write a few words – and was rapidly beginning to wish that I hadn't!

We stood and watched as the old aeroplane coughed and restarted its engines to begin a futile attempt at ungluing itself from the bumpy ground. It roared and whined, rattled and revved, starting its staggering run-up to take-off. After what seemed only about a hundred metres it was away; climbing steeply, almost vertically, clear of the threatening trees. The pilot looked back over his shoulder in triumph. His shining-teeth smile said it all.

We all climbed into the already overladen truck, our destination unknown, to begin the bumpy, dusty, scary trip. Through villages, over skinny mountain trails, across bridgeless swollen rivers until finally, and not a moment too soon, civilisation appeared in the guise of a group of military-type huts in a clearing. The convoy slowed and we knew that this was home for a while.

We clambered down from the lorry, throats parched, eyes filled with prickly dust, hair matted, coughing and spluttering – glad to be anywhere as long as the ground wasn't moving. The group that had met us moved off without a word, and we were left alone to contemplate; but not for long. A tall, grey-haired man with an upright military bearing emerged from one of the huts with two companions, his hand outstretched in welcome. A brief handshake and Kit, our group leader, was led back to the hut, leaving the rest of us once again in silent contemplation.

Studiously avoiding eye contact, I casually gazed around at my resting 'comrades', none of whom – with the exception of Kit – I had met before. They were a mixed bag – a 'wild bunch', more like raggedy-assed outlaws of the American West than soldiers. The style of dress was varied and interesting, if a little weird, with personal preferences obviously much more important than any resemblance to military convention. Camouflage prevailed from a wide range of countries: US tiger stripe from the Vietnam era and British NATO DPM dominated, with a little Italian, German and Russian thrown in for cosmopolitan effect. One member was dressed dramatically in black from head to foot. 'Looks intimidating, dunnit?' he commented, adjusting his rather fetching over-the-shoulder shotgun belt. Berets with SAS, Para and Foreign Legion badges, and of course the inevitable bandannas, adorned shaven heads. Bodies bristled with grenades, and numerous pouches carried whatever the owner felt was necessary for his comfort and survival. It was easy to imagine we were on a film set, waiting for the director to cry, 'Roll 'em!'

Pete was lazing against a wooden crate, pale, taut and muscular. He obviously kept himself very fit but was tense and not inclined to small talk. He must have been about forty-five years old, but it was difficult to be sure. He moved young but his eyes were stagnant pools of decay.

Jim was the talker, chattering on endlessly to bored faces showing no sign of interest. 'Well I says to him, sod off, I'm not paying that. So he says, what will you pay? I says, twenty bucks and he says, OK. So I bought this Rolex. It's the real thing . . . Look!' Nobody was taking any notice of him, but off he went again without taking a breath. 'How much bloody longer do we have to wait?' He was very twitchy as, still yakking, he passed cigarettes around.

Steve declined with a curt 'Enough ways to die without those things.' He was a strong, proud man, composed and together. No doubt very capable in an emergency. His sand-coloured beret bore the insignia of the SAS – not that that proved anything, of course.

Kit was unflappable. He smiled a lot and never stopped moving. For a big man he was light on his feet and could easily keep up with the whippets of the group. Originally from Newcastle, he'd been around the block a few times, learning about war the hard way, with a warm gun and little else. Kit had become a friend in the past few months, and was trusted and relied upon by all. He'd been in this dodgy 'volunteer' business for a long time and was respected by the men under his command. An essential ingredient for a mercenary leader: stripes and pips didn't mean a damn thing with this lot . . . believe me.

Then there was the kid – they called him 'Sprog'. Everyone liked him; perhaps because he didn't play the tough-guy role like most of them. The kid came from Warrington and was about eighteen years old. This was going to be his first taste of action and he was trying hard, but seemed totally confused about everything; especially why he was here.

Mick was standing apart from the rest of the group. Full of manic self-pity and explosive language, he was bitter about something, anything – everything. It was difficult to warm to him, so nobody bothered to try. 'Life's too short to dance with ugly women' was Steve's reason for ignoring him.

Nigel wandered back from the tree line where he'd been relieving himself. He was the odd one out, well educated and from a wealthy background. Apparently a month ago he had been caught reading the *Times* by one of the group, but was converted now and took the *Sun* – because the paper was softer. He used to be an officer in the Guards until something went wrong and he left in a hurry. Now he was a mercenary . . . nobody knew why.

There was an older guy who for obvious reasons was known as 'Pop'. He was a little mature for a mercenary, late fifties, maybe early sixties. Pop had seen it all and just didn't care any more. He waited, sipping dark rum from a GI water bottle, eyes flitting around the forest perimeter, just in case . . .

Four of the team kept to themselves. No names were given.

They were Australian Croats and had returned to the mother country 'just to help out'. An exception to the rule that only money can buy loyalty.

It was an odd feeling to be simply a 'spare part', with no practical function, and although the 'professionals' were amiable enough, there was always a degree of suspicion and doubt in their eyes. Some were open in their conversation, others guarded and hostile.

It was not a comfortable wait, and I was grateful when Kit returned with our Muslim contact. It appeared that the function of our team was to undertake a recce of Mostar airfield. The objective was simply to check out the movement of military aircraft and personnel. Engagement was to be avoided, if possible. It was a 'sneaky beaky' recon operation, loved by all, judging by the smiles and nudges.

Happy days were here again. My companions were now electrically charged by the news, travel weariness and boredom long gone. Apocalyptic events were about to take place and the group was metamorphosed – action and excitement were the very life blood of the mercenary soldier. That was what it was all about . . . and the money, of course.

Weapons were selected from the back of a covered jeep. Maps were pored over, with great emphasis being placed upon the trig points which clearly indicated mountainous terrain. Escape and evasion techniques were discussed and argued about. Money in the correct currency was allocated, together with maps, radios and compasses. Everyone was apprised of the purpose of the mission. Kit made it clear that the whole exercise was covert. The Bosnians and Croatians were allies at this time, both fighting the Serbs, but they were unaware of our objective and would therefore be just as big a threat to its success as the JNA. 'So be careful, lads,' was his pointed recommendation.

As most of the journey would be taking place after dark, one man in four was assigned passive night-vision equipment, 'Big one' and 'Big two', products of the famous German optical company, Leica. This type of equipment uses a single image intensifier tube to amplify naturally occurring residual light from the moon and stars, and because the goggles can be strapped to the user's head, the hands are free at all times for more important things. Infrared systems are for use inside a building and are rarely employed in external situations where their location can very easily be detected and tracked, with unpleasant results.

The meeting was now coming to its natural close. The intense focus of the men had begun to wander and serious questions were being replaced by the usual banter of men anxious to get on with it.

Kit sighed in a resigned manner and looked around the group. 'You're just a bunch of fuckin' assholes. If you mess this up, I'll shoot you myself.' He said it with a smile, but you could never be sure with Kit.

The forest was dense, dark, forbidding; thick with sounds and then, in an instant, silence. Leaves dripped with perspiration in the struggle to breathe clean air; smells invaded the nostrils like musty unwashed clothes. The dazzling flicker of laser-like shafts of daylight soundlessly blasted holes through the canopy of rotting vegetation, temporarily blinding anyone foolish enough to look upward.

If I concentrated, listened carefully, I could feel the invisible life surrounding us, hear the trees growing and the pulsating hearts pumping blood through the veins of thousands of insects, reptiles and animals. Tree trunks, vines and horrible twisted, sticky growths grabbed at us with threatening gestures as we sliced a trail with our swinging machetes.

'You've got to look through the foliage,' I was told, 'not at it.' I never learned how, but my more experienced colleagues had trained and finally mastered this essential woodland fighter's art.

All this – and a human enemy too.

Twenty-six boots mulched a trail through the droppings of a million animals as we tramped single file for about two hours, until dusk turned rapidly into inky darkness and spooky sounds. A suitable clearing was located and we bivvied down for an uncomfortable night. With adrenaline now used up, weariness took over, and within minutes the camp was silent as we slept with apparent disregard for the enormous snakes, spiders and bats which I was convinced were waiting to devour us.

We were awakened in the damp, chilly morning by the comforting sound of the Rolling Stones' 'Jumping Jack Flash' all tangled up with machinery noises. It took a while for us to figure out that the music wasn't coming from our camp. Even though we were brain dead, logic prevailed. 'Don't move,' someone hissed. Nobody moved. Kit and Steve, by some unspoken signal, slid away towards the sound and disappeared into the undergrowth. Within minutes they returned, grinning from ear to ear. 'It's all right, children, our transport has arrived.'

No more than 150 yards from where we had slept was a narrow road, cut through the forest and invisible from the air. The music was coming from the radio of what can only be described as a vintage farm lorry, being driven by a young boy hardly big enough to see over the steering wheel. He looked about eight years old and by his broad smile we could tell it was all a bit of a joke to him. The radio continued to blast out its message of joy as he beckoned us into the back, which was full of pig shit, chicken feathers and other disgusting things which we all tried hard to ignore. The smell was unbelievable. After a while, Pete located its source.

'Oh Christ,' he moaned wearily, I'm sitting on a dead sheep, and the bloody thing is crawling with maggots!'

As there was no room for him to move, the rest of the journey was spent trying to stop them crawling all over him. To help pass the time everyone joined in the hunt. They move fast, those little white wriggling buggers.

It was an easy trip to Pulaj. Our rendezvous point on the Albanian–Yugoslav border was close to a convenient estuary where, according to Kit, Muslim contacts would be waiting for us. I did wonder why we had taken such a tortuous route to the coast, but when I asked, Kit told me to mind my own business; in a friendly way, I hasten to add.

Our new mode of transport was lying there waiting for us in all its World War II glory: a battered old ex-Royal Marine 'rigid raider' – a steel-bottomed inflatable boat – with a pitifully small, rusty outboard motor which looked destined to cause trouble. The craft, measuring some sixteen feet by six, was hardly big enough for the group, but otherwise ideal for the task.

Kit had calculated that it would take about three days for the coastal trip, then a fast 'tab' to reach our destination at Dugi Rat, about fifteen kilometres east of Split. The whole boat trip would take place only at night; during the day we would come inland and rest up. It would be fatal to travel in the craft by daylight. We would make an excellent target, with little opportunity of evading attack from the shore or the sea, and if hit carrying all of the spare fuel required, we would stand a nil chance of survival.

It was still very early in the morning, and the world was poised and expectant as we tried to make small talk over coffee with the three Albanian contacts. They told us how grateful they were that we would be fighting for them against the hated Serbs, voices rising in hysteria as they glared at one another, then finally running out of conversation and mumbling to themselves. The mercs, most of them experienced in this type of thing, showed little emotion. The simple fact was that they didn't really give a damn. Muslims today, Africans tomorrow . . . whoever paid the best.

Our biggest problem at the moment, and one that needed immediate attention, was Pete: he stank! With the odd maggot still dropping from the folds of his clothing, and bits of flesh and skin welded to his new Para jacket, he was a mess and something of a liability. If we could smell him, so could anyone, therefore it became necessary for him to be the first to have a dip in the Adriatic. This and a thorough soaping made him just bearable to be around, although for the next week, even with your eyes closed, it was possible to tell when he was within ten feet.

We had a lot of time to kill before nightfall. Ever since the plane had landed east of Shkodra, we had all been subjected to a series of stops and starts, and here was another one. Small irritations could become big ones under such circumstances, if not dealt with or avoided. So we played cards, drank gallons of tea and listened to lunatic conversation. The planned helicopter flight from Split to Mostar became the main target for the banter, especially as this appeared to be something of a Mickey Mouse operation – judging by the logistics so far. Volunteers to kick-start it were selected by the size of their boots, or by who had experience with radio controls, and comments about the probable mental or visual limitations of the pilot were endlessly thrown around until everyone fell silent, realising that the best course of action was sleep; who knew when the next opportunity might come?

Chapter Two

They do not solicit sympathy or expect gratitude.
Nor do they seek respect, honour or fame. Life is
simple for the mercenary ... Full payment for
services rendered – on time! And you can forget the
flags, medals and trophies.

Kit woke us at dusk as a slight sea mist offering excellent cover
began to engulf the shore. It was time to 'cam up'. Some did it
themselves, others let a partner cover the areas of the face that
would shine in the moonlight. No one spoke. We were finally on
our way. The raider was slid into the sea and we all clambered in
as it settled in the water, a little low for safety. Someone
murmured, 'I hope the bloody sea ain't rough,' voicing everyone's thoughts at that moment.

The coast of Yugoslavia, between our departure point and our
destination, has about six lighthouses to protect its shipping.
These were an obvious hazard to us, and great care would have to
be taken when we came within range of the powerful beams. Kit
selected Molunat as our first lying-up point. This meant passing
lighthouses at Ulcinj and Budva, and two at the estuary of Boka
Kotorska. All went well on our first night at sea. The engine
behaved itself, and the first day was spent on a shale beach
surrounded by steep cliffs, with no chance of a surprise attack
from the land. For which we were all extremely grateful.

By now we were well into Yugoslav waters, which presented
another problem. Serb patrol boats made continuous passes over
this area, and moved quickly. At the speed our overladen craft
could travel we would stand no chance of outrunning or
outshooting them, so avoidance was the only weapon we had, a
sobering thought as we tried to make ourselves comfortable on
the gravel and pebble beach.

We all awoke at different times throughout the day, and for
different reasons; by mid-afternoon everyone was up. Unnecessary moving around was frowned upon, so murmured conversation seemed the only way to pass the time. Kit, however, had other
ideas.

'Don't just sit there playing with yourselves. Strip your fucking weapons and don't forget the copper slip.' He glared at Mick, Pete and Sprog.

'Copper slip?' Sprog mouthed silently in Pete's direction.

Pete threw a plastic bottle of lubricating solution to him without a word, and started checking his own AK-47 magazine to make sure that it contained only twenty-nine rounds instead of its full capacity of thirty – leaving an empty space at the bottom for dirt and general debris to collect.

'After you've done that, check your water bottles and see that the fucking radio batteries are fully charged. Then make sure your FFDs – first field dressings – are kept in the same place on all of you. I don't want to be hunting around for them if you get hit.'

After an hour of feverish activity, Kit still wasn't satisfied. 'Let's see your morphine and syringes; check your boot laces for wear and replace them with paracord if they're iffy.' Then, turning to Sprog, 'Get rid of that bloody chiming wristwatch.'

Sprog took the watch off and started to tie it around his neck with paracord, like the other men.

'No. When I said get rid of it, I meant ditch the bloody thing. If it starts chiming at the wrong time we're all in trouble.'

Sprog looked at him in dismay, but thought better of starting an argument, burying the watch in the shingle without saying a word.

Kit drew us together for further advice on the rest of the trip, pointing out that the next phase was likely to be the most hazardous. We would soon be entering the stretch of water known as 'bomb alley', on our way past Dubrovnik, an area of constant bombardment from the offshore Serb fleet and retaliation from inland Bosnian artillery. Muffled booms of heavy artillery opened up in the distance as he finished the lecture with a smart-ass 'I told you so' expression on his chops.

The rest of the day drifted past with only a small rockfall to break the monotony. Just for a moment there, we thought that we had been sussed from above: weapons were cocked and hearts started pumping as we craned our necks to look up the vertical cliff face, expecting the worst. We had nowhere to run on that small shale beach, not even a boulder to protect us. We froze: nothing happened. Jim started to giggle with relief; Steve told him to shut up, then everyone started to laugh as a large bird flew out from a ledge about halfway up the cliff face.

Daylight merged into dusk, and as night-time approached we started to organise ourselves for the second phase. Kit was very quiet, gazing out to sea, checking the sky and looking at his watch. We were all ready to go, but there was a problem. It may have been an ideal night for lovers, with a full moon and twinkling stars, but for a group of mercenaries on a 'sneaky' mission in enemy territory, it was most certainly a no-no.

Bomb alley was no place to be on a night with such visibility, and Kit wisely – we all agreed – decided to stay put. We did what all good soldiers do on such occasions: we got our heads down.

The early-morning rain awoke us this time. Some of the men had had the common sense to bring Gore-Tex waterproofs; those less organised had to make do with bashas to keep out the downpour.

It was a miserable way to spend the day, which seemed to go on endlessly. Manic Mick had obviously decided that Sprog was going to be his entertainment for the day, and kept throwing pebbles in his direction and needling him mercilessly until we'd all had enough.

'For fuck's sake, leave the kid alone,' Pete spat at him.

'Mind yer own fuckin' business.'

Sprog moved away from Mick and crouched by Pete for support.

'Gutless little bastard. If you want to be a soldier, you've got to be a man first.'

'What, like you?' Sprog muttered.

'What was that?'

Sprog turned to face him defiantly. 'I said, *like you!*'

'Yeah, that's right, virgin. Like me.'

'What have you ever done that's made you a man, apart from killing unarmed people in Africa?' Sprog knew he'd gone too far, but he couldn't back down now.

Mick leapt to his feet, his face contorted in fury. 'You cheeky little git, I'll have you for that.'

'Sit down, Mick, and shut up! You asked for it, now leave him alone or we'll break your fucking legs and leave you here to rot.' Steve had slowly edged between them, towering over Mick and staring at him menacingly. The combined force of everyone's malevolent glare finally did the trick, and Mick sank into a moody, face-twitching silence for the rest of the day.

As darkness fell, the downpour continued unabated. The

temperature dropped dramatically and the very real possibility of hypothermia became a serious threat to our soaking-wet bodies. Sprog and Pop had already started to show signs; shivering uncontrollably, with vacant expressions and difficulty in concentrating on the most simple tasks.

'Exercise is what you need; a bit of paddling will do the trick,' Kit said as he rubbed his stiffening hands together before joining us to drag the raider over the slippery pebbled surface into the cold, unwelcoming waves. The conditions were ideal for concealment, and would no doubt reduce any serious activity at sea from the Serb frigates and the inshore artillery.

The little engine did its best to get us out from the shore, aided by some furious paddling. It spluttered for a few heart-stopping moments, but with a few friendly words of encouragement – most of them with four letters – it manfully beat in time to our fluttering pulses as we hugged the coast to Cavta, looped away from Dubrovnik and chugged back inshore to Lopud, the first of many small islands. We had survived bomb alley unscathed and could watch with detached awe the sky being illuminated by the spasmodic bombardment.

The next and final lying-up point was going to be one of the small islands between Dubrovnik and Split. We had an almost infinite choice of temporary resting places, although some care was required. Many of the 'landlords' would be Serbs and would not take too kindly to having us as guests. Everyone was pleased to set foot on shore once again; sailors we weren't. We were cold. We were wet. We were tired. The raider was dragged ashore, which wasn't easy, as by now it was full of water. Nobody cared any more. It was nearly daylight and time for some desperately needed shuteye. Most of the group slept through the entire day, waking only to the smell of cooking. Not the smartest thing to do under the circumstances, but hot food can make all the difference to morale, and on some occasions the risk is justified. We stuffed ourselves with sausage and beans, anxious to be on our way, and still chewing dragged the boat into the sea. We were now only a bob and a weave away from Dugi Rat as we slipped around the eastern side of Hvar island. The lighthouse at Sucuraj, a potential hazard, was non-operational. Perhaps a casualty of the offshore bombardment – a bit of luck at last.

We followed the coastline tightly, passing what had once been holiday beaches at Tucepi and Baska Voda. Even in the darkness it was possible to see the deep craters in the sand and odd bits of suspicious metal lying about, where only a year ago children had laughed and played whilst their parents lay soaking up the sun.

The raider chugged around the final bit of coastline, entering the cove at Omis. Kit whispered, 'Cut the engine, we'll paddle the last few kilometres. No talking.' The prearranged truck was waiting for us and we were greeted without warmth by four heavily armed, shemagh-adorned Muslim soldiers, complaining in an agitated manner that we were a day late.

We tried a quick burst of '*Kaka ste?*' – How are you? – but only got stony silence in return before the little guy with the scar over his left eye started rattling on and gesturing at his watch. Nobody was in the mood for criticism and it all got a bit heated as we dragged our tired, stiff bodies over the rough ground to the truck and slumped into the back. As we were covered by a tarpaulin, we could hear them muttering at us in the now familiar phrase, '*Ye benti peca matarina*' – roughly translated as 'Piss off, motherfuckers.' The vehicle lurched away, its crunching gears only adding to their irritation.

The trip was about twenty kilometres, just about bearable under a tarp with twelve men who hadn't washed for a week. Even after three days at sea, Pete's relationship with the decomposed sheep was still apparent, and revolting in such close proximity.

Our arrival at Split airfield was met with great excitement. We were ushered into a small hut on the perimeter and offered meat and beans mixed together in a large encrusted pot, with great hunks of bread to soak it up and a vicious rocket-fuel drink of rakia to help wash it all down. The Muslim people are unable to keep anything secret, and within moments, heads were popping through the doorway of the hut to look us over.

The rakia, combined with weariness, started to take its toll, and we would have loved to have been able to get our heads down, but it was not to be. The pilot had arrived and was anxious to show us his new toy, which, much to our delight, wasn't the relic we'd feared. A Soviet Mil Mi-8 HIP helicopter stood on the runway, fully armed with eight pods of 57mm rockets. The only flaw in its immaculate bodywork was an exquisite line of ventilation holes, running from the pilot's cockpit side window along the cabin, stopping just before the external fuel tanks at the rear. Another few inches and the helicopter would have been just a flaming ball in the sky. We clambered in, spreading ourselves loosely around the twenty-eight-seat chopper as Zlatco, our pilot – renamed 'Zippo' by Jim, because, like the lighter, he seemed very reliable – gunned the massive five-bladed rotors.

The helicopter had been pre-warmed, and as soon as the blades dropped into their 'whump whump whump' rhythm he quickly climbed away, savagely veering east to our intended landing point somewhere in the Valley of Imotski. His enthusiasm for the task of flying us over this treacherous territory knew no bounds as the HIP dipped and climbed over the mountains and forests below, hugging the tree line in an attempt to avoid detection from the radar at Mostar. We drew a little small-arms fire over the front line of Imotski which sounded like someone hammering on the outside of the chopper – in all probability from Croats, unaware that they possessed a helicopter. Zippo told us in his fractured English that only three days ago they had used SAM missiles to knock out two of their own MiGs, captured from the Serbs a few weeks before at some cost to life. Zippo was very philosophical about it, muttering, 'Ah, the fortunes of war,' before tailing off into silence once again.

The trip was mercifully short. Fifteen minutes of roller-coaster ride after a meal and the rakia could have been something of a problem for our already sensitive stomachs. But before anyone could embarrass themselves, we had dropped into a small clearing, hovering a foot above the ground. Zippo was gesturing wildly for us to disembark through the already open doors – he wasn't going to hang around and risk damage to his new toy.

The Valley of Imotski – no man's land. The heavy rain would help us by covering the sound of our arrival, but it was still wise to get clear as fast as possible. The area was technically unoccupied, but groups of Chetniks were known to roam here, doing just about what they damn well liked. 'Evil people,' was Kit's comment. 'Big hairy bastards, like mountain men. Really evil.' The Chetniks – or White Eagles, as they were called by the locals – were responsible for most of the massacres taking place, and were feared and hated by just about everyone in the country.

Without further discussion we gathered our gear together and legged it for about seven kilometres, following the contour of the hills to avoid detection, finally locating a suitable lying-up point for a breather and to check our position on the map. It was decided that we should 'basha' out at this point for the day and get some much-needed rest. We were about thirty-five kilometres from Mostar airfield, and it was going to be busy from now on, with no time to relax until the recce was completed.

The following night we moved about twenty-three kilometres, dropping Jim, Nigel, Mick and Pop at the first lying-up point, each with a radio and spare batteries.

'Check the radios first and let me see you do it before we go. Communication is vital and don't forget it.' Kit was insistent.

Mick, still not over his recent humiliation, growled a reply. 'We all know what to bloody do, Kit.'

Pop banged the radio on the heel of his palm. 'Bloody light's flickering.'

'Give it here,' said Nigel. 'It's probably a dodgy connection.'

He examined the battery, scraping the connections with the blade of his Swiss army knife, and tossed it back to Pop. 'It's OK now. Seems like some sea water got in, so keep your eye on it.'

Kit gave them a sweeping glance before grabbing his bergan. 'OK then, if everything's checked, we'll move out.'

We'd all cammed up ready and moved stealthily forward a further eight kilometres to discuss the overall plan, making this the RV – rendezvous-point. It was agreed that the E&E – escape and evasion – plan, if necessary, would be a bluff attempt at convincing our captors that we were the UN and had lost our bearings. We had all been allocated 'liberated' UN armbands, and Kit had made sure that the team was now carrying European FN rifles, instead of the preferred AKs, to substantiate the story. The major flaw in this plan was that we would also be carrying explosives, grenades, timers and claymores, not exactly what you would expect a peacekeeping force to have in its possession. Ah well, no plan is perfect. Ask General Custer . . .

Three of the four Australian Croats and Sprog were left at the RV. Instructions to protect the area with claymores were given, and a code of two radio clicks for incoming, and a reply of three if safe to do so, was agreed.

The close observation of Mostar airport would be undertaken by Kit, Pete, Steve and Ivan – the fourth Australian Croat, who, like his comrades, was a deserter from the Australian artillery.

Mostar airfield, used as a civil and military base, was situated south-west of the town and just off main route seventeen, leading to the coast. We were approaching it from the west side and had heavy woodland to contend with, plus the distinct possibility of mines and perhaps roaming Serb patrols. The night was cold and progress agonisingly slow. Everyone wanted to get to our destination as quickly as possible. Get it over with and get out. Sounds – any sounds – made us flinch, pausing until the source was located. We would move forward on our toes like military-booted ballet dancers, tense, looking down for trip wires, up and back for the enemy, occasionally getting slapped in the face by branches springing back, wanting to strike out in frustration. We must have had about two kilometres to go to the end of the tree line when Ivan froze, wobbling on one leg, the other poised in the air.

'Kiiit!' he breathed in a drawn-out gasp. 'I can see some string.'

There it was sure enough, the dew lying white upon its surface, a length of cord far too thick to be invisible, leading to an unsophisticated but effective booby trap. A wooden spike had been driven into the ground with about three inches protruding above the earth, and the charge, rather like a larger version of the old pineapple grenade, was attached to it. The thickness of the trip wire had saved us this time.

From here on in, we would have to be ultra-cautious. Kit chose not to disarm the booby trap, marking it with a small piece of white tape instead. Should patrols be checking their traps, to find them disarmed would give away our presence. We found only one other, and this was dealt with in the same manner.

We approached the tree line with some relief and were met by the unexpected smell of cooking. Steve moved ahead to check the source, whilst the rest of us kept well back. He returned within minutes with the glad tidings that there was a Serb post dug in outside the perimeter, fortunately some way from our position and no immediate threat. Kit and Ivan left us at the tree line, taking passive night-vision equipment, grenades and their FNs, crawling out into the exposed ground between the woods and the perimeter fence. Thankfully the immediate area was long grass, making their initial foray difficult to detect.

As they disappeared into the night, we settled down to wait. It was nearly three a.m. when they returned; two hours had passed surprisingly quickly. Kit was excited, we could tell. He said nothing at that point, merely beckoned us back into the woods, covering the same route as before to enable us to remove the white tape from the trip wires and cover our tracks. When we arrived at our RV he couldn't stand it any longer.

'Would you fucking believe it, there's three bleedin' gorgeous MiG-21s on the runway, all tooled up. We've got to give it a go.'

'I thought this was only supposed to be a close OP recce, Kit?' Pete reminded him. 'We're not getting paid for taking out MiGs, are we?'

'Yeah, I know, but it's so easy. Although there's a load of mines around the place and probably some roaming patrols in the woods, the actual perimeter fence is unguarded.'

'What happens if it all goes wrong?' Pete said flatly.

'It won't fucking go wrong, you miserable sod. The MiG-21s are only about fifty metres inside the perimeter fence, fully armed and ready to go, with loaded twin-barrel GSh-23 cannon and bloody vicious-looking AA-2 Atoll air-to-air missiles. It's a fucking gift, man!'

It was decided that it would be worth our while to take a pop at them. The pompous military terminology for this objective would be 'a target of opportunity'. Kit just thought that it was a bloody great idea.

But there was a problem. Due to an oversight on the part of our beloved leader, or a sodding great cock-up, depending upon your viewpoint, it was discovered that the lads at the lying-up point, some twelve kilometres back, still had the timers. There was talk of lynching, but it was decided that Kit was more use to us alive than dead . . . though only just.

'So who's going back for the gear then?' Kit looked around at three men suddenly afflicted with deafness.

'It's a fucking long way, Kit. Through all of those mines and the Serb patrols. What's it worth?' Pete was on the hook.

'Booze, bonus, or no stag for a month. Take your pick.'

'How much bonus?'

'A ton.'

'Nah, it's too risky for a ton.'

'OK, my final offer. No stag for a fortnight and a ton.'

'You're on!' Steve jumped to his feet.

'Hang on a minute, I'm doing the negotiating,' Pete pointed out irritably.

'I think you'd both better go, just in case of aggro. Split the cash deal, with the pair of you off stag for two weeks. OK?'

By now, the darkness was evaporating. Speed was vital, and without any further delay Steve and Pete slipped away into the forest gloom, leaving the rest of us to plan the attack for the following night.

They arrived back knackered with the equipment, which had been modified by a friend back in Britain from video recorder timers, with a booster enabling a twelve-volt charge to be transmitted. The units were made waterproof by encasing them in Tupperware containers, and sealing the wire entry holes with Plasticine. Very hi-tech.

Kit had explained the plan of action to us in their absence. The timers would be buried or stashed at the rear end of the jets and set for a one hour forty-five minute delay, allowing us plenty of time to make our escape before all hell broke loose. Thirty kilos of plastic explosives would be used, adequate for the job, he said – without conviction.

Admitting his lack of knowledge of aircraft construction, Kit reasoned that the weakest part of the aircraft was probably the belly. This was where the main charge was to be set, with additional small charges beneath the fuel tanks. The plastic explosive would be held fast by masking tape, which would overcome any tendency for it to fall off in a change of temperature. The charges would be linked by detonator cord to each aircraft. With just one detonator, all of the aircraft should go up at the same moment. Kit was no explosives expert and admitted that it was 'a guessing job'.

It was daylight by now and we all fell into a fitful sleep, waking to the heavenly sound of rain. Nice noisy rain to deaden and cover our tracks.

The final brief was given. Two men stayed at the RV and six went out this time. Four remained at the perimeter to provide back-up if necessary – with limited resources, essentially the twenty-round-magazine FNs and grenades. Kit and Ivan would cut through the perimeter wire, enter the compound and lay the explosives. Everyone cammed up, checked equipment and moved out, faces set in grim determination.

It was an almost ideal set of circumstances as Kit cut through the wire fencing: pitch dark, pissing down with rain and the enemy loath to expose itself to such unpleasant conditions. The MiGs, sleeping menacingly in the torrential downpour, waited to be destroyed. It was a laborious process, taking longer than anticipated. The masking tape would not stick easily when wet, the plastic explosive kept slipping from their hands and it was difficult to find things when they were dropped. There was a moment of panic when one of the hut doors opened and a shaft of light cut through the black compound, momentarily exposing Ivan in its glare.

'Jeezus, that's fucked it,' Pete breathed through clenched teeth, easing his safety catch off in readiness.

We literally held our breath, willing the gods to intervene.

Both men froze as a Serb soldier scuttled across the runway and into another hut, causing yet another blast of unwanted illumination. With both doors open at the same time it would only take a glance in their direction and the game would be over.

The second door slammed as he sprinted back with his head down, carrying a bottle of something. A burst of laughter greeted him as he entered the first hut, closing the door behind him. Darkness again, soft, friendly, safe blackness. We could complete the task and set the timers.

Kit and Ivan slipped out through the fence, tying the previously cut slit with paracord, and joined us back at the tree line, nodding to indicate that all was well. We were in a hurry now; the job was completed and everyone just wanted to get out as fast as possible.

Steve went ahead, slowly picking his way through the undergrowth, the last man removing the white tape from the trip wires. We made no sound as a Serb patrol suddenly appeared to our right. I think we all saw them at the same time, stopping dead in our tracks as they moved past us talking in hushed whispers. We waited. How far would they go? Would they come back? As soon as they were out of earshot, Kit held a brief discussion on whether we should compromise our position by killing them.

'This is a bit fucking dodgy. They're gonna slow down our retreat if we've got to worry about avoiding them, but if we kill them, there's no way we're gonna be able to get away with the UN scam if we're stopped trying to get back through Croatian lines.'

Ivan shook his head. 'It doesn't feel right to kill them. The noise may attract attention anyway.'

'You're right. Let's sit it out for a bit and see what happens.' Kit had dropped back into his military training mode: if in doubt, do nothing.

We waited impatiently for twenty minutes, at which point the patrol returned, passing us in a line on its way back to base. We had made a wise choice.

The RV was approached with the two click, three click code.

Little conversation was necessary as we bundled the gear into our bergans and headed in the direction of high ground some distance away to watch the effects of our work. We had almost thirty minutes to spare as we nestled down low in excited anticipation. Kit checked his watch continuously as we all stared in the direction of Mostar; licking our lips, drumming our fingers, waiting ... waiting. First there was a dull thud, followed by another in quick succession. A pause drifted into a muffled roar, and then it happened.

The explosion was like a hundred separate orchestrated sounds, exquisite to hear, wondrous to behold. Three fully armed jets with full fuel tanks don't go quietly. They light up the night and just keep on blasting. I swear the ground shook as huge balls of flame erupted into the low sky. Oily smoke swirled and mingled with already ominous clouds as the overheated ammunition – sounding like giant firecrackers – cut through the dense forest air. The sheer power of the destruction held us spellbound in frightened awe. It would continue until the jets were simply piles of twisted and charred metal. And all this devastation from a plastic Tupperware box. You'd better be careful next time your wife goes to one of those parties!

I looked across at Kit. He was sweating, the beads of perspiration running down his face and mingling with a look of angelic contentment. The Australians said nothing, simply shaking hands and nodding. Pete muttered a hissing 'yesss!' as Steve gave a mock salute to the dead and dying, inevitable in the midst of that carnage.

We broke radio silence for the first time, contacting our lying-up point with the brief message that we were on our way back.

The tab back to the Croatian lines was uneventful, although great care had to be taken as we got closer. It would have been an annoyance if anyone had been killed by our allies at this late stage of the game.

Now amongst a friendly force, with the past days of tension behind us, Kit suggested that rest and recuperation were called for, and a ride to Split was arranged in a military police lorry. With the help of the Croatian-speaking Australian, Ivan, and a little bit of wheeling and dealing.

We arrived at the prestigious Split hotel where the manager, who seemed to be expecting us, handed Kit a bulky envelope containing thirty thousand Deutschmarks – roughly ten thousand pounds – which were furtively counted in the corner of the reception before being distributed to eager hands. After a quick drink at the shiny, chrome-plated bar, the thirteen of us, raggedy-assed, in filthy clothes, faces covered in cam, moved into six sumptuously decorated rooms on the second floor overlooking the bay, with smartly uniformed UN personnel as fellow guests in the four floors above us.

We stripped off our gear, leaving it where it lay, and padded into the showers, emerging squeaky clean and feeling a whole lot better for the effort. Then one by one we slumped on our beds for a decent kip, with the sound of exploding MiGs still ringing in our ears.

On our second day at the Split hotel we were approached by a wealthy-looking man with an Australian accent, who told us he was from Posusje. He bought us a few drinks and said that some of his friends were very impressed with our latest job and would like to offer us more work if we were interested. It seemed that news travelled fast. But as I said before, the Muslims never can keep a secret . . .

For the next few weeks we all enjoyed life: no guns, mud or sleeping rough in the forest. The UN had a party every Friday night – to which we were not invited. No matter; with a shave and a smart suit we got away with it for a while before we were found out and barred by the 'Rodneys', who expressed their dislike of the riff-raff element invading their festivities by pointing out that we were nothing but opportunists and military effluent, ignoring us in the corridors and moving away from us in the restaurant.

Shortly after, our group began to break up. Mick went first, and was later arrested for killing someone in a bar-room brawl in Tuzla. Three of the Croat Australians had their own battles to fight and left for the front line a few days after him. We were sorry to see them go, but the simple fact was that we were fighting the war for different reasons.

The wealthy Australian came back to see us again, and now Kit was ready to talk to his new friends. The freelance warrior has to look at all options.

He was taken to meet the governor of the town of Posusje, a man in his mid-fifties, of medium height, grey-haired, with an athletic build and a very dominant personality. His name was Drago. Kit listened to what was said through an interpreter. 'He offered me money to go to his town. His exact words were: "For every task you perform, there is money for you." He told me that funding for weapons and equipment was *nema problema*.'

Kit said that he would think about it and came back to the Split hotel to talk it over with the remaining members of the group and some other British and French volunteers who had joined us briefly in their hunt for the most lucrative employment. Everyone was by now getting a little bored and dispirited by their confinement and lack of income.

A few more days passed in idle contemplation and occasional piss-ups in the hotel bar or one of the many pick-up joints in town. The men lounged around, talking in comfortingly regional accents, from Manchester, London, Wales and Cornwall – but what they said and the manner in which it was voiced caused any thoughts of home and normality to be quickly dispelled.

'How do you know which is the enemy?' I asked; both sides wore the same uniform of the former Yugoslav army. They told me that the regulars wore a full uniform, with distinguishing patches, so that wasn't so bad. The worst were the men wearing tracksuits, who were totally unpredictable and either to be avoided or shot without question. In between were the militiamen, who tended to wear part uniform, but were without any command structure or obvious objective. Most of the time no one seemed to know who was shooting at whom or why!

'It's a bloody mess,' Alex from Manchester muttered softly. 'I've been here six months and I still don't know the difference between Serbs, Muslims, Croats or Bosnians, or what any of them are trying to achieve.'

Silent until now, Mark, from the Cornish holiday town of Mevagissey, spoke. 'I've only been here for five weeks. I couldn't get a job at home and always fancied being a merc, so I bought a plane ticket to Split and then hitched a ride to Zagreb. I asked around the place and a taxi driver directed me to the army headquarters at 25 Ilica. I told them that I had no military experience, but that didn't seem to matter. They gave me an old uniform, a rifle, a thousand rounds and six grenades; then I was taken to the front line.'

His voice tailed off and I waited for him to continue, but he didn't. So I asked what had happened at the front.

'I couldn't understand a bloody word that was being said,

nobody spoke English, and on my first recce things went wrong . . .' Mark stopped in mid-flow and looked at the others.

Alex shrugged his shoulders. 'It's OK, tell him,' he said.

'Well, I was sent out with another Brit "volunteer". He was from London, a bit of a cockney clown. We were in single file going through the woods and he was in front, walking along without a care in the world, not with caution, not with care, fooling about with a boogie shuffle walk, waving his AK-47 in the air to imaginary rock 'n' roll music. The track curved and he disappeared for a moment . . . then I heard a "whump" sound, it was sort of muffled and he started to fall. I thought, silly sod, he's tripped over, but he was flying through the air like an enormous doll all covered in red stuff. I couldn't believe it. I yelled out, calling his name, screaming his name, but he didn't answer, he just lay there jerking and spitting and gurgling soft pink milk-shake bubbles. I was terrified. He just stared at me as if I was to blame, but it wasn't my fault he'd stepped on a mine. I stood there, I wouldn't go close, couldn't go close, his legs were gone, his arms were gone. I stopped screaming, he stopped gurgling. It was all quiet. But his eyes still stared at me through his blackened, charred face, his hair and clothes still smouldering. Stupid bastard, my brain told me as I turned around and slowly walked back. I didn't look over my shoulder, not once . . .'

Mark started to sob softly and turned away. Nineteen years old, and the memory will stay in his subconscious forever. He had relived his nightmare as the rest of the men had no doubt relived theirs.

Later, we talked of the atrocities that some of the newcomers had witnessed, this time without the machismo that is an integral part of mercenaries' personal armour, but instead with anger, horror and fear. Even these professionals did not understand the reason for the mutilated bodies with hearts and ribs wrenched out, arms and legs hacked off, eyes gouged with red-hot pokers. It was the way that children had been treated that got to them most.

'Can you fucking believe these crazy bastards? I saw a kid of about six. The same age as my daughter. They'd shoved a grenade in her mouth and pulled the pin. Her pregnant mother was dead by her side with her stomach sliced open and her unborn baby lying by her side in the dirt,' Alex spat.

'Why do they kill the old people? I can't understand why they kill the old people,' Billy, another recent arrival, said. 'I saw one two days ago who'd been garrotted and thrown in a pit. She looked like my granny. The bastards had even taken her false teeth out.'

'Who are they?' I asked. 'Serbs, Chetniks?'

'They're all the bloody same,' Kit replied distantly. 'It's just that some are worse than others.'

Death and injury they accepted, but this! They talked of men who had had their testicles hacked off and pushed into their mouths.

'Why do they do that?' Billy broke in again.

'It's because Muslim men are circumcised and Serb men aren't. So the simplest way to find out if a man's your enemy is to make him drop his pants and have a look at his dick. If it's been skinned, then . . .' Kit tailed off, further explanation unnecessary.

Before or after death? No one wanted to know the answer to this question.

For the mercenaries, every day was different, every week and every month brought tension, boredom, panic, madness. But it was like a drug, the catchword was 'buzz'. If you asked any of them why they did it, they would tell you that 'half the time we don't get friggin' paid'. They admitted that they didn't make good civilians, so what was left? Just the buzz, it seemed, a day's work doing what they liked doing best.

A decision had to be made, but it wasn't easy. Pete, Jim, Steve and Nigel wanted to take the offer. Pop and Sprog weren't so keen. Meanwhile Kit was approached by yet another anonymous character in a grey business suit. This time the deal was a short-term job leading a team in the northern town of Osijek, some three hundred kilometres away from the luxury of the Split hotel. This temporary 'gig' was accepted as a means of earning some fast money whilst mulling over Drago's long-term offer.

Chapter Three

*. . . And few are immune to the 'Genghis Khan'
image of themselves as the invader. Conqueror and
slayer.*

Sprog and Pop had decided to stay behind in Split for a while,
joining us later in Osijek. Their intention was to bum a ride in a
UN chopper out of Split airport – easy to do; most UN pilots were
easily bribed with a CZ 9mm handgun.

Their decision was based upon utter laziness. This breach of
etiquette was discussed in their absence, and in a heated exchange
it was agreed that the matter was serious enough to be considered
'desertion in the face of the enemy' – a grave war crime, and, in
accordance with the rules of warfare (mercenary version),
punishable by a fate worse than death.

Kit had decided that it would do them good, and be a test of
their skill under fire, for the management to discover that the rest
of us had departed without paying the bill. It would be interesting
to find out when we saw them next how they had dealt with the
problem. Anyway, they should have come with us, shouldn't
they?

So, as the seven of us stole out of the hotel in the early hours of
the morning, Pop and Sprog were left snoring in their cots to await
the wrath of the management.

Creeping along the corridor in single file to exit through the rear
window of the hotel like naughty schoolboys, we had difficulty
stifling giggles at the ridiculous spectacle we must have presented: grown men, clad in camouflage gear and big boots,
mincing along on our toes. Getting through the small window
was in itself a test of military ingenuity, as we silently passed
weapons, ammo and bergans to Nigel, who dropped them to a
waiting Ivan. It all went beautifully, and why not? They were,
after all, professionals at getting out of dodgy situations – referred
to in the textbooks as escape and evasion.

We had to do it this way; the bar bill alone would have taken all
of the money earned on our last job!

We tiptoed across the crunchy gravel of the hotel drive and threw our stuff into the 'pinkie' carefully parked on a slope the previous evening in anticipation of the plan. Still giggling, we clambered aboard. 'Everybody in?' Kit whispered urgently. We looked around. Nigel was missing.

'No Nigel,' Steve replied.

'Where the fuck is he? Somebody go and find the useless bastard!'

Steve and Jim slowly uncoiled themselves from their cramped positions on the mound of equipment in the rear and started back towards the hotel just as a shadowy figure appeared carrying a large square object under his arm.

'Where the hell have you been?' Steve hissed at him. 'And what the fuck is that?'

'Nothing,' Nigel replied as he pulled himself into the vehicle. 'Sorry to keep you waiting, lads.' He turned to a smouldering Kit waiting at the wheel and with a supercilious smile, available only to ex-Guards officers, said in his cultured tone, 'You may drive away now, cabby.'

The steering wheel started to buckle under suppressed homicidal inclinations. 'Later,' Kit said, 'we'll have a chat about this later, you stupid prick!'

This was no time for a showdown, so with a gentle push from Jim the Land Rover was rolling and we were away. Leaving Sprog and Pop very much in the shit . . . we all hoped.

Our destination was Osijek, some three hundred kilometres north-east of Split – as the crow flies. But there was a problem. Isn't there always? Just about every kind of enemy imaginable lay in the area of central Bosnia and the chances of us all surviving the trip were slim. So Kit had concluded that the scenic route was best.

We would head west along the coastal road, with the sea on our left and the rolling fields on our right. The downside of this detour would be an extra three hundred and fifty kilometres. With seven men and their gear jammed into the Land Rover, it wasn't funny any more.

The air was heavy with a smouldering ground fog – a consistent feature in Croatia – as we trundled out of town and picked up the main Adriatic road, settling down to a boring, uncomfortable drive to the next town, Sibenik, approximately sixty klicks away. It was still too dark to see anything, so we all simply sat, staring blankly into the solid mass of mist, while Kit, his face tight up to the windscreen, attempted to keep us on the road.

Shhhhiiit! Flump, flump, flump. We all heard the rhythmic sound of flapping rubber and felt the lurch of the Land Rover as its front end slewed drunkenly to the centre of the road. Just thirty kilometres west of Split on the coastal road to Sibenik; a flat tyre and no bloody spare. Not a word was spoken. The resigned expressions said it all . . . it was a bit of a bastard.

Cigarettes were shoved despondently between pinched lips in anticipation of divine intervention. We waited, but nothing happened. The pinkie just sat there lopsided. Collective deep sighs broke the silence as it became evident that someone in this group of lazy sods would have to get up off his ass and do some work. The question was, who?

The ciggy butts were flicked away, curving tracer arcs in the sky, as Kit stared with dull eyes around the desolate countryside. 'Anyone in the AA?' The humour was strained; nobody responded.

We slowly clambered out and looked at the guilty wheel with absolute hate. The tyre was shredded, impossible to repair. Pete passed the information on to an agitated Kit, still gazing at the expansive countryside with little interest in the view. We could tell that his brain was refusing to take it in.

The cause of the blow-out was not obvious; no glass or uneven surfaces were apparent and as we had not been travelling fast at the time, why the hell had the tyre shredded? The answer came quickly as the red-clay roadside started to spit angrily upward. It took a while before the team had logged the reason for its agitation . . . but it was simple once you knew.

We were being attacked by someone, somewhere. Out there in the hills some unfriendly bastards were shooting at us, and we hadn't done a thing to irritate them . . . yet.

There wasn't much cover. In fact there wasn't any bloody cover, so we dived back in the Land Rover as Kit forced it to hobble erratically down the road. Swerving to avoid a hit wasn't a problem; the car had developed its own evasion tactics as it swayed and hopped away from the ever-advancing spray of bullets, its now buckled wheel gouging a deep trough in the dirt.

It's an odd fact that missiles have a different sound when they are after you; ask any soldier and he will tell you the same thing.

They sound vengeful and persistent. Just like a swarm of wasps that have decided that you are the one with the jam tart and they are going to have some. We all felt like that at this moment; exposed and vulnerable. The enemy was invisible but he had decided that he wanted us . . .

The windscreen splintered, and there was a dull thud as a round dug deep into the door pillar. Another one followed, spraying glass everywhere. They had our range now and the small-arms fire might well be followed by mortars. A mortar hit would wipe us out in a second; there was only one thing to do: ditch the Land Rover and run for it. 'Hold on!' Kit screamed as he swung the wheel and rolled the car off the road and through a hedge into an adjoining ploughed field, bringing the Land Rover to an abrupt halt as we scrambled out.

Never one to forget his early training, even in the heat of battle, Kit then uttered the immortal word used in so many famous military manoeuvres: *'RUN!'* Steve pointed to a copse about five hundred metres to the left, which seemed like a good idea. So with heads down we staggered towards it, carrying our weapons and extra ammo across the undulating ploughed field as the purple-red tracers peppered around us, getting closer by the second. Thank God nobody was hit; with all that slipping and sliding over the rough ground we must have made lousy targets, anyway.

Time for a collective nervous breakdown. We were trapped. And they, whoever they were, could now do whatever they wanted until we got ourselves sorted out.

'Follow the tracer.' Our bloodshot eyes watched the graceful curve of the incoming shit until we had sorted the position of our attackers. 'Look! To the left of the farm. In the depression. Can you see it?' Yes, the mist had cleared enough. We could all see it . . . Now what?

'Right, lads. We'll go and do them, shall we?' Kit was smiling. He does that kind of thing.

'Pete, Jim, you two man the AKM. Give us cover. Straight down the line. And lay it on heavy.' Looking at me he said, 'Stay still, keep your head down and shut up!' I could handle that.

'Ivan, you go with Steve to the right. Nigel you're with me. OK, Pete, lie flat on your back and feed . . . Now do it!'

The AKM was set up on its tripod and blasting in bursts of three at the source of the incoming. Boom-boom-boom . . . pause.

Boom-boom-boom . . . pause. Kit and Ivan grabbed some grenades and a couple of 66 rocket launchers, crawling out to go their separate ways in the general direction of the source of trouble.

The onslaught became sporadic as the enemy kept his head low. The men zigzagged across the open ground. Three hundred metres is a long, long way to run – especially with a hangover!

I just had to look up . . . carefully. In time to see Nigel trip and fall to the ground. Within seconds he was up again, hopping and scuttling like a demented rabbit across the uneven earth. He arrived at Kit's side as they both took cover behind a mound of earth. Kit looked over at Ivan and Steve, also safe behind cover. A quick wave and they were off again, darting, diving and rolling in the ploughed field as our AKM kept up its staccato bursts of covering fire.

Sudden silence. A nervous wonder-what's-going-to-happen-next stillness. We should have known. Whump! Whump! Fucking mortars. That's what's going to happen next. Christ! I hate bloody mortars, they just come out of the sky at you and blow bits off your soft, warm body.

Their aim was off. Thank God. Obviously the AKM fire was making them keep their heads low and it was all guesswork, but they could still get lucky.

I looked up again. There was dense smoke coming from the depression. A phosphorous grenade had been lobbed in by Kit or Nigel. That was the signal to stop firing. Kit and the rest of the lads were going in for the kill and didn't want to be hit by our covering fire. The clattering burst of an AK-47 on full auto drifted back to us, followed by a shrill scream that went on and on and on, echoing across the murky countryside as it slowly trailed away.

Pete continued to reload the AKM magazines as we waited blindly for the outcome. Brother, were we in trouble if the lads had blown it!

'Come on, you Geordie git, stand up.' Jim was getting anxious. 'What the fuck are they doing over there?' We could see nothing. The rolling mist had returned like a blanket, muffling all sound and reducing vision to a little over a hundred metres. We strained our ears and three pairs of eyes tried to bore holes into the nothingness. We were getting more than a little concerned when a slight movement to the left caused us to dive for cover.

The figure was unmistakable. Emerging from the spooky grey mist loomed four ghost-like characters from a Wagner opera, led by one Christopher Freeman. They arrived back at the copse looking totally knackered. It was a full five minutes before any of them could give us the story.

There had been three of them. Young, inexperienced and now very dead. They'd been members of the extremist Croatian militia the HOS. 'Cowboys and wankers,' Kit commented. 'They deserved to get it.'

There had been no reason to attack us. We were not their enemy. Kit had tried to explain this to the remaining live member of the group. But he had become offensive and had tried to grab a weapon in retaliation. So he'd had to die with his comrades. 'They won't listen, these kids. All they want to do is dress up in black jumpsuits covered in bloody stupid badges and kill people.' He showed us a British army commando knife and a knuckle duster, taken from one of the bodies. 'Look. Kids' stuff. Straight out of fantasy land.'

We wearily gathered our gear together and headed back to the Land Rover. Nigel was moaning as he limped along, dragging his right foot. Apparently he had been hit in the heel, and although the bullet had passed cleanly through the skin it had ruined his recently purchased American Danner boots. 'They cost me one hundred and fifty quid, guaranteed waterproof. Now they're crap . . . The bastards!'

'Serves you bloody right. If we hadn't been delayed by you at the hotel the whole thing wouldn't have happened.' Kit's logic prevailed and Nigel fell silent.

The Land Rover looked kind of forlorn with its front end buried in the field. It was no use to us now and its demise gave us yet another problem to contend with. Transport for seven men, six weapons, ammunition, seven bergans, claymores and ancillary equipment, and it was still only five a.m.

Somebody had to say it. 'What are we going to do, Kit?' It had to be Jim. He never knew when to keep his mouth shut. Kit didn't answer.

'Kit, I said, what are we going to do?' You could feel the heat.

'I'll tell you what *you're* going to do, my son. You're going to get us some transport.' Jim looked along the straight road in both directions. Nothing. Not a movement, not even a bicycle.

'How?' he asked in a small voice.

'Well, my son, you'll just have to walk back to Split and hire something from Hertz, won't you?'

'You must be joking. There is no bloody way I'm walking back to Split. It's Nigel's fault, you said so yourself. Make him go back!'

Kit shook his head. 'Don't be a dipshit. Can you see Hertz letting you have a car looking like that? Now shut up and let me think.' He sat down and let out a sigh. Things were not going too well and the sky was getting lighter. Soon the main coastal road would be busy with all sorts of people – some might even be friendly.

'Somebody make a brew.' Ivan foraged in the back for the cooking gear and dragged out a square cloth-covered bundle; the cloth slipped to the ground, revealing an elaborately framed painting.

'What the hell is this?' The question was directed at Nigel. It was the parcel he had carried out of the hotel.

'That, dear boy, is a painting.'

'I know it's a bloody painting, you sherbert. What I really meant was, what is this bloody painting doing in the back?'

'It's mine.'

'You mean you stole it from the hotel.'

'Well . . . I liberated it. They obviously didn't know what it was. Otherwise they wouldn't have hung it in the corridor.'

'OK, smartass. What is it then?'

'It's a Renoir. An original, worth thousands of pounds.'

'Bollocks! Who the fuck is Renoir?'

'A French impressionist painter.'

'You mean you jeopardised the whole trip for this piece of rubbish?' Kit got to his feet and walked over to Ivan, looking at the picture with some interest. 'Look, we haven't got time for this now. Chuck it in the back. If he's right we split the money. If he's wrong . . .' The threat was left hanging in the air as the sound of a vehicle approaching took precedence over the proceedings.

It was a BOV-M, an armoured patrol vehicle, available to the federal army, the Yugoslav militia or anyone else who could steal one. This one might have been sent out to check on our recent firefight, or perhaps was just on early-morning patrol. Whatever the reason, it seemed wiser to keep our heads down and hope that the crew didn't notice the hole in the hedge. The APC lumbered past without so much as glance from the observer and sped on its way in the direction of Split.

Our brew was ready and the business of the painting was forgotten for the time being – it's all a matter of priorities. At this

31

moment the most pressing consideration was transportation. We still had a long way to go and hitch-hiking was most definitely not an option.

Steve looked at his watch for the tenth time. We had been waiting for over an hour. A few small cars had passed, Renaults, Fiats and the inevitable VW Golfs. None was large enough for our requirements.

'How about another brew?' It was Nigel this time, no doubt feeling bad about his role in placing us in this predicament.

'Oh, go on then,' Kit replied in a resigned voice. 'Only one sugar, I'm slimming.'

Everyone was thoroughly pissed off by now and it showed in the pile of dog-ends littering the field, and in our twitchy behaviour. It wouldn't take much for someone to start a punch-up. Thank God Mick wasn't with us any more. He'd been a surly bastard at the best of times and would have been unstoppable by now.

Kit drained the last drop of his tea and climbed to his feet.

'Look, we're going to have to leave the Land Rover, so sort out the gear and leave anything we don't need. Pete, you come with me. I'm sick of waiting around like a vulture. Let's go and get something.'

Pete grabbed his AK. 'Forget the gat. We'll stand out if we carry guns. Let's go. If we're not back in an hour ... wait. Forever if necessary.'

They slipped through the hole in the hedge as the rest of us started to sort through the gear. Less than a minute later they were back, smiling. 'There's a non-military lorry coming from the direction of Sibenik. It's ours. I don't care how you do it, but get that bleedin' lorry.'

It was easy. Six men in DPM, faces covered in camo cream and brandishing automatic weapons, will tend to focus anyone's attention, even in Croatia. The lorry driver stopped. Steve waved a gun in his direction, indicating our wish for him to exit the vehicle. He did so, very quickly, and knelt in the road expecting the worst. I guess this sort of thing happened all the time. They dragged the frightened old guy into the field and threatened him with the internationally understood finger-slicing-the-throat sign. He nodded his head, and was still nodding it as Pete tied his arms and legs with paracord whilst we threw our gear, including the painting, in the back and drove away in his rusty old lorry. We were on our way once again.

There was a cold wind blowing from the sea and it soon became pretty uncomfortable in the open back as we tried to cover ourselves with the bergans and some sheets of plastic. Kit, Steve and Pete kept looking back through the cab window with self-satisfied smirks on their ugly faces as we lopped off the klicks on the final stretch of the road into town. We were all bloody hungry by now. Nobody had eaten, washed or shaved since last night, and a proper break in a civilised place was very appealing.

That was before we saw two bloody great rock-filled trucks blocking the road. It was the ZNG – paramilitary national guard – well tooled up. They would no doubt be very interested in an old lorry overflowing with weapons, ammunition and six foreign soldiers of no fixed abode.

Kit pulled to the side of the road. We needed to get a story going, and fast. Kit got out, and under the pretext of checking the load started telling us what to do – apart from panic, that is.

'Look, lads, we've got to stop, there's no choice. We'd never batter our way through those lorries, and even if we did they've got MG-42s. They'd cut us to pieces. I'm going to bluff it out. If it goes wrong, you're on your own, OK?' He got back in the cab before any of us could reply. It didn't matter. What could we have said?

The last few hundred metres were the worst. Click, click, click. We could hear the safety catches coming off as we approached the checkpoint. The lorry hissed to a halt and Kit, together with the Croat-speaking Ivan, climbed out of the cab, their faces wreathed in warm, friendly smiles.

'*Dobro jutro*, gentlemen. *Da li govorite engleski?*' Kit was formally polite as he tried out his limited Serbo-Croat, withdrawing his ID card and a letter from the governors of Zagreb which explained our role as 'volunteers'.

The ZNG guys didn't seem in the slightest bit interested in the paperwork as they climbed over the truck, examining the bergans and equipment. 'Down!' The order was barked by the one with the most badges. We obliged, and huddled in the road. Our furtive eyes locked on to the menacing machine guns. 'Where are you going?' The question was addressed generally. Nigel started to answer but was cut up by Ivan, who replied in Croatian. The officer smiled – a good sign?

'*Da!* The women, eh!' The smile disappeared. Sod it! I'd thought things were looking up.

'Why have you so much equipment and so many weapons if you were only in Split for the women?'

Ivan didn't pause for a second as he rambled away, laughing and gesturing at the rest of us standing there without a clue about the direction or the content of the conversation. We smiled back at the officer.

The two soldiers had completed their examination and returned to the captain. They went into a huddle. The atmosphere had suddenly become tense. Kit looked around at us all, his expression clearly saying, 'Cool it.'

As the captain returned to our group it became apparent that his manner had changed, yet again. He stood in front of Steve and looked him up and down, focusing on the pistol in his belt.

'Ah! A Skorpion. Nice pistol. It is new, is it not?' Steve looked at the officer and then at the rest of us, a resigned expression on his face. He handed the gun to the officer without a word. It was wheeling and dealing time.

Two of the soldiers worked their way around us like professional pickpockets at an outdoor market, pointing at wrists and hands with murmured demands concealed as comments. 'Nice watch . . . good ring . . . pretty chain.' All were handed over with ill-concealed contempt. It was over in ten minutes. We had been picked as clean as oven-ready chickens.

We all felt like shit as we climbed back on the truck. Losing the stuff didn't really matter. None of us would carry anything of value in a battle zone anyway. It was just the knowledge that we had been treated with disrespect that rankled.

The incident was not mentioned again. Everyone seemed embarrassed about the whole episode, and there was little conversation as we arrived in Sibenik without any further problems.

The newer part of Sibenik suffers a little from ugly high-rise apartments and an air and sea-polluting aluminium smelting plant. But it's a quiet town . . . at this time of the morning anyway. And that was all that mattered just then.

A big breakfast of eggs, sausage and some kind of ham at the Restaurant Mornar on Ulica Vlade Perana, and a wash and shave made us all feel a hell of a lot better. Not difficult in our current state of low morale. We ate and cleaned up fast, anxious to be on our way to the next town, Zadar, about sixty kilometres west.

Zadar was, according to Kit, 'like the OK Corral'. A comforting thought, and one that we could have done without.

'All aboard for the magical mystery tour.' Jim was cheerful as we walked back to the lorry, parked out of the way at the rear of the empty vegetable market. We obviously didn't want to draw any more attention to ourselves than was necessary.

The tired old engine finally started with a moan of anxiety, anticipating the long drive ahead to our ultimate objective, Osijek. A few gear crunches from Pete and we were off again, heading out of town on the Ulica Borisa Kidrika and feeling a whole lot more human.

Soon we were outside the town and on the open road once again. 'Keep a sharp lookout. Scan the hills and the road ahead. We don't want any more surprises.' Kit didn't need to give us this advice. Nobody wanted another working-over like the last one.

The wind had now dropped and the last of the ground mist was evaporating rapidly, leaving us with a bright, crisp morning. The clear air had exposed the sparkling sea and the clean, open countryside. Large roadside signs still displayed messages to overseas visitors: 'Welcome to paradise', 'Enjoy our beaches', 'Come back again'. The sun shone on the beaches of Murter, Drage and Biograd, which lay to our left bordering the peaceful Adriatic Sea. Not so long ago the now shrapnel-scarred motel at Pirovac had been full of happy tourists and happier Croats. Would they ever return?

Who could forget this genocidal war? The tourists might. But when your local postman runs around with a blazing Kalashnikov, killing women and children, and the dentist organises nighttime raids on the homes of the old and infirm, how can things ever return to normal? Yugoslavia is dead and so are most of its people. Just look into their eyes!

As Zadar appeared on the horizon we congratulated ourselves on an uneventful trip. There had been sounds of sporadic firing on occasion, but always in the distance; nothing had occurred to threaten our current good humour.

We knew it couldn't last. On the approach to the outskirts of the town two ominous-looking Ladas were parked across the road. A smoking Simca lay in a ditch with its engine still running. We could just make out some tracksuits lounging against the cars, cigarettes hanging from their arrogant lips. This was trouble for sure, and Kit, who was in the back with us this time, clicked off his safety catch and told the rest of us to do the same. It was too late. As we approached, six more tracksuits appeared from the roadside ditch to our left and right. This was an ambush, and we were in it.

The lorry slowed to a halt at the checkpoint and we could now see that the driver of the Simca was still in his car. He was alive, just, and covered in blood from dozens of bullet holes. It was all over for him as he waited for the end to come.

The tracksuit boys were jumpy. 'Papers!' Kit did his friendly smile act once again and handed them the ID and documents. 'Out!' We all gathered by the roadside in a group.

This time it was different. They were agitated, in a hurry. We were obviously professional soldiers, a problem to be disposed of, fast.

The leader was about twenty-two years old and spoke English with an educated accent. Conning this guy wasn't going to be easy.

'What is your business here? *Gdje idete?*' Where are you going?'

'We are from the UN,' Kit replied.

They sniggered and told us to turn out our pockets. 'Hurry, hurry!' They were strung out, probably on something.

'You have few possessions for members of the United Nations,' the leader commented sarcastically. 'Are you poor people? No jewellery. Cigarette lighters. Watches.'

His sneering manner was beginning to piss Kit off as the abuse continued and he started to jab him in the chest. Nigel and Steve were edging slowly back to the lorry when we were all told to kneel down. This was getting silly. The lorry was full of weapons. They knew it, and we knew that they knew it. They also knew that if push came to shove we would go down fighting. These men don't like fighting – just killing. There's a big difference.

'Catholic or Muslim?' The leader was off again, cocking his AK-47 as he waited for an answer to the irrelevant question.

'Fuckin' atheist.' Steve had had enough. The point of no return had been reached. The tracksuits looked to their leader for guidance. The next move was his.

None of us actually heard the trumpets as the cavalry arrived in the guise of a German TV van, closely followed by a car full of American journalists. Within the space of a few seconds the road was full of cameramen and guys scribbling in notebooks. We were suddenly forgotten in this photo-opportunity. The tracksuited militiamen preened themselves, looking suitably tough for the camera. They became expansive when asked what they considered their role to be in this war. They were eager to impress the world with their importance. We were simply grateful and slipped away with our tails between our legs once again.

Kit was right. Zadar wasn't a town you would want to stay in for a bit of peace and quiet. Splintered glass and bullet casings littered the road, as staccato bursts from automatic weapons, crackling like a Chinese dragon dance, echoed endlessly in the narrow alleys. We could see shadowy figures, armed to the teeth, crouching behind burned-out cars as our lorry lumbered through the side streets on the way into the centre of town.

From our position in the exposed back of the truck, we were aware of rooftop snipers watching our progress with weapons cocked, waiting for a steady target. We covered them as best we could, any moment expecting a grenade to land in our laps. 'Sod this,' Steve growled in my ear as the steady beat of a GPMG opened up from a building to our right.

Kit hammered on the window, gesturing to Pete. 'Get the fuck out!' he yelled, as Pete did his best to make the old lorry do wheelies down the narrow stone streets.

Avoiding the overturned and burned-out cars was an impossible task. Ramming them out of the way was easier but not very comfortable for those in the back, as we were thrown from side to side, making it impossible to track any would-be snipers on the roofs. The whole thing was unreal, like one of those dream sequences you see in out-of-focus existential French films. Our lorry was being ignored as wild-looking people appeared suddenly, as if from nowhere, legs apart, AK-47s firing wildly from the hip at empty shop doorways. Seconds later, others would leap out and fire back, hosing the area indiscriminately as yet another window exploded, spraying glass upward like silver confetti. Nobody wore uniforms or identification of any kind. How did they know who they were firing at? This was Dodge City, and these bloody Croats were gun-crazy.

The lorry lurched twice and headed for the front of the Archaeological Museum. I just caught the sign saying 'Closed on Mondays' as Pete wrestled us back into a straight line again. We looked behind and saw the cause of the bump; two crushed bodies lay in the road.

My attention was distracted by three men thirty-five metres directly ahead in the town square. They were kneeling in the road, pointing a long tube at us and trying desperately to aim it at the bucking lorry. Kit and Steve saw them at the same time and scrambled to a standing position on the swaying floor, opening up with their AK-47s as we thundered towards the square. The whole thing happened very quickly. A sudden whoosh and the air was sucked away as a rocket screamed over our heads. Seconds later, an explosion came from behind us and debris filled the air from a gaping hole in the town's library. Our lorry struck the three men responsible, throwing them like dolls into the gutter.

'Foot down. *Go, go, go!*' Kit screamed wildly as Pete started to slow. 'Turn right and just keep going.'

It seemed that the east side of town was the battleground for today. We hurtled through the winding side streets and out of the town gate, past the archaeological ruins and the mosque. On the outskirts, things became quieter and it was possible to slow down and drive at a less frantic pace as we approached Murvica. Even the buildings weren't as badly damaged as those we had recently passed. But there were no people . . . anywhere.

We were back on the main E65 now, heading north-east for a while through the slightly damaged towns of Policnik and Posedarje until we reached a fork in the road. If we turned right at this point, the road would take us to Karlovac, a mere forty kilometres from the Croatian capital of Zagreb and all the comforts of home with Kit's friend, Tony Abranovich, a colonel in the Croatian army. It was not to be. We turned left. The coastal road was still the safer route. Avoiding confrontations was our objective.

The old lorry was starting to cough a bit, steam coming from its nostrils in short, sharp bursts. Soon we were going to have to ditch it and borrow something else.

Steve was driving now, and as the weather had become warm and pleasant the rest of us were in the back, soaking up some winter sun. The coastal road was fairly straight at this point and it was possible to see many miles ahead, making another surprise ambush or road block unlikely.

We had passed the flat, elongated island of Pag and were

staring out to sea at the rocky outline of Rab island when, with a gigantic hiss of displeasure, the lorry shuddered to a halt, steam pouring from the engine compartment. We were all very relaxed about the whole thing as we climbed down and watched Nigel lift the bonnet and cautiously remove the filler cap. There was little we could do until the engine had cooled.

'Nigel, you and Pete stay with the truck,' Kit ordered. 'You lot, come with me.' He walked the few metres to the beach and took off his boots and socks, rolling up his trousers. 'I'm going paddling. Come on, race you to the sea.'

With that, he was off and running. The rest of us, caught up in the silliness of it all, followed him, chortling, into the waves. We splashed around like kids for about twenty minutes, feeling the anxiety of the past hours lift. It was bloody cold but it didn't seem to matter.

We returned to a muttering Nigel and Pete, who were obviously a little put out at being excluded from this brief moment of pleasure.

The engine had cooled enough for them to examine it in our absence and they had detected a burst hose, repairing it as best they could with the military version of the all-in-one tool kit: wide black 'gaffer' tape. The radiator was filled with water from our canteens as Kit climbed in, eyes lifted skyward in prayer. He turned the key . . . The engine started, running a little unevenly . . . but running.

We moved off slowly, knowing that the repair was only temporary. A new set of more suitable wheels would be needed, and very soon.

The scrubby, desolate but heavily industrialised island of Krk to our left marked the last twenty-five kilometres before we would arrive in the busy and potentially hazardous seaport town of Rijeka. Kit decided that we would skirt the town on this occasion and turn eastward, getting back as quickly as possible on the main E65 leading us into Zagreb. It wasn't quite as simple as it appeared. An autoroute link was under construction, creating havoc with our map-reading. Many of the smaller roads no longer existed. The whole area was a mass of huts, thick, oozy mud, and abandoned earth-moving equipment. None of the vehicles was suitable for our needs – a great pity.

We finally joined the main road at the village of Gornje, about a hundred and thirty kilometres from Zagreb. Between us and our first major stop was Karlovac, the scene of some vicious fighting in the past months. There was no way to avoid it!

It had been a long day. We were hungry, dirty and worn out by the unpredictable events of the past nine hours. The mental picture of Pop and Sprog still living the life of gentlemen in the Split hotel was unbearable. With a bit of luck they had been thrown out or arrested. Even this thought was no consolation as the lorry trundled on.

We were about three kilometres away from the village of Lokve when Ivan drew our attention to a weathered sign off to the left saying 'Autocamp' – holiday camping site. Empty now and a little overgrown, but still looking attractive to our tired eyes, it was set amongst the trees with an adjacent lake and a few log cabins. Close by were the restaurant and grocery store, now fallen into disrepair.

We looked at Kit like puppy dogs begging for a bone. It was pathetic, but it worked. 'OK, let's bivvy down for the night and start early in the morning. We may need our wits about us in Karlovac.' Then he added: 'Check it out first. Every cabin. Every hut. Every bloody thing, mind you!'

Pete, Nigel, Jim and Steve went to work, approaching the buildings stealthily, peering through windows first and then entering with AKs on auto. You can't be too careful. Mercenaries are anyone's target in most war zones, and especially in Croatia. Kit, Ivan and I waited, keeping our eyes and ears tuned for the slightest sound or movement as dusk settled in.

The men returned to the lorry looking very laid-back about it all. 'It's OK, the place is clean.'

Kit decided, however, not to make use of the buildings. He reasoned, against some opposition, that it was wiser to sleep outdoors, amongst the trees, in our bivvy bags. Just in case someone came back after dark. The necessary gear was unloaded from the lorry and we all relaxed, wandering over to the lake to watch the fish swirl and jump as they came up for their evening snack of flies.

'Anyone fancy some fresh fish?' Kit was staring at the silver back of what looked like a trout.

'How the hell are we going to catch enough fish for seven of us? It could take hours,' Nigel commented.

'No . . . minutes. If you don't mind getting wet.'

'Oh yeah. What are you going to do? Tickle them out?'

Kit took a grenade from his webbing, pulled the pin, and with a graceful overhead lob threw it into the centre of the lake. A distant muffled roar preceded an enormous cascade of water. Within seconds tranquillity returned as the smooth surface was restored.

'Fuckin' hell!' Jim, who had been lighting a fire, stood with his mouth open in wonder. 'That's what I call direct action; and to think I used to sit for hours by the canal at home.'

About three dozen fish floated to the top, awaiting collection by an equally impressed Nigel, already removing his smock for a swim.

Watching Nigel sweep the area, grabbing at the slippery fish, gave the lads some much-needed entertainment. Cries of 'Round 'em up, cowboy!' and 'Plonker' filled the air as he was directed to each fish, plucking them out of the water and dropping them into his knotted string vest.

He arrived at the bank triumphant and deposited his catch at our feet. Some had only been stunned by the blast and were now wriggling in a desperate attempt to escape. These were dealt with and carried to the smouldering fire.

Nigel peeled off his clothes and spread them by the fire as Pete and Ivan set about making a feast of the trout.

'How would you like them cooked, sir?'

'Would you care for a starter?'

'Perhaps sir would like a house vino or a glass of *pivo.*'

The banter continued throughout the meal, the past three hundred kilometres of terror and frustration temporarily forgotten in the pleasure of the moment.

We all helped clear away any signs of our presence and settled down for the night in our bivvies, spread out over a wide area. A guard had been selected by the 'short straw' method of democracy. Steve had lost this time and would do the first four hours. Pete would follow. We were all on our chinstraps by now. Sleep came quickly and was undisturbed.

A thick layer of the dreaded Croatian ground mist shrouded everything when we awoke. From our prone positions it was impossible to see anything. Even Jim, sleeping only about three feet away from me, was invisible, though easy to locate by his gentle snoring.

Movement to my left made me instinctively sit bolt upright. Stupid move. Kit and Ivan were already up and boiling water for coffee. They looked odd, with the bottom part of their bodies lost in the mist. Slowly the rest of the lads woke and crawled out of their bags to a welcome warm drink served up by a serious-looking leader.

'Now listen, lads. The next major town is Karlovac. It's only a few kilometres from the Serbian lines . . .' His voice tailed off until we could barely hear it. 'It's going to be rough, but there's no way we can avoid it. Check your weapons and ammo and keep your wits about you. We'll have to play it by ear. Now load up and let's move out.'

The old lorry didn't like the cold, wet mist. The engine groaned as it tried to turn over, and our hearts sank into our stomachs. On the fourth attempt it coughed and sprang into life, burbling and missing a beat from time to time as we pulled on to the main road. It was still only five a.m., and roadblocks – manned mostly by part-time soldiers who liked their kip – were unlikely to cause any problems for a few hours. Which was just as well, since the mist would make them impossible to see anyway.

The early-morning cold sliced through us all as we sat huddled in the open back. Foot-stamping and hand-rubbing had little effect as we all gradually turned white and then blue.

'Let's get the sleeping bags out.' Jim, at last, was using his head. We unrolled and snuggled into them.

'Course, you're in dead trouble if you've got to get out fast.'

'Shut up, Nigel. Just sit there and freeze your balls off if you don't like it,' said Pete from the depths of his Buffalo bag.

'I was merely pointing out that tactically it's an unwise procedure.'

'You can be a right pompous git sometimes, Nigel.'

Nigel fell silent. A few minutes later he crawled sheepishly into his bag. He was right, of course, but at this moment we didn't want even to consider the possibility of another roadblock.

Kit must have sensed our discomfort as he leaned out of the cab window, turning his head back in our direction. 'We'll get a decent motor in Karlovac, with a heater. Trust me. There's bound to be something lying around.'

It was eighty kilometres to Karlovac, through vast areas of exposed countryside, along endless stretches of straight road offering the sniper a clear line of fire. There would be dangerous bends with unknown conclusions, and the Serbian artillery on our right. We needed something to take our minds off the bitter cold and the feeling that we all looked like rats in a barrel. We really needed a lesson in Serbo-Croat from Ivan . . . didn't we?

It was straight out of *The Sound of Music*. 'Now repeat after me,' he said in a singsong voice.

We looked at him dumbly. 'Oh, sod that, Ivan. Not now, for Chrissakes!' Pete was not amused.

'You will be grateful. It is good to know another language.'

'French, German, Italian, maybe. But not Serbo-Croat.'

'The knowledge could save your life, my friend.'

Jim turned to the irritated Pete. 'He's right. None of us knew what the bloody hell was being said at the checkpoints. Did we?'

Our silence was taken to be acceptance of the impending lesson, and we continued the trip reciting conversational Croatian in unison.

We had driven through the towns of Kupjak and Skrad, with their familiar streets of burned-out and looted houses. Old women shrouded from head to foot in black, like spectres of death, spat and screamed hysterically at us as we passed, collapsing in anguish and frustration as the stones they threw had no effect upon our progress. Because we wore a strange uniform, we were the enemy. In Croatia, everyone is the enemy.

As we approached Bosanci, the stillness of the countryside was being methodically replaced by noise, muffled at first, but becoming distinctively aggressive. Karlovac was now a mere twenty kilometres away.

Sounds of heavy artillery fire register in the stomach and the bowels before the brain.

With Ivan's short language course we were now slightly bilingual, but had mixed feelings about the benefit this might bestow upon our chances of survival as the distinctive howl of a low-flying MiG fighter/bomber heading for Karlovac reverberated in our ears, making us cower in the back of the lorry like beaten dogs.

We were heading into a proper war zone this time. That was what we'd come for . . . wasn't it?

Chapter Four

The men live in a twilight mercenary reality whilst away from home. A world defined by myth and splintered militarism. Ideological motivation is not a prerequisite for the job . . .

A smouldering yellow-grey haze hovered menacingly over the city of Karlovac as our clapped-out lorry crept cautiously along the rubble-strewn streets. The incoming Serbian cocktail of heavy artillery, T-55 tanks and a rocket onslaught from MiG fighter/bombers had gutted the front-line buildings on the east side of the town. An acrid stench of cordite burned our throats as chaos stared back at us, our tired minds refusing to take it all in.

Waxen-faced bodies lay everywhere. Many had obviously been there for days, judging by the degree of decomposition and the interest shown by packs of starving dogs. A pile of thirty to forty tattered and bloody corpses was stacked untidily against the fractured wall of a restaurant. Vibration from the next bombardment would bring it crashing down, burying the bodies . . . yet again.

The first line of that old Animals song, 'We gotta get outta this place', jammed itself firmly in my mind and ran round and round. I tried to avoid thinking of the second line, 'If it's the last thing we ever do'.

The lorry stopped. Kit and Steve clambered out. The rest of us climbed down, stiff and awkward, to join them by the roadside. Ragged people walked past, glancing at us with blank, zombie-like stares as they carried their few possessions – to God knows where – in prams and wheelbarrows.

A British Warrior patrol car slunk alongside. Its observer gave us a casual once-over and then sped away, uninterested.

'We don't need this. It's not our problem. If we detour around the west side of town and park somewhere we'll miss most of the crap.'

Kit wasn't interested in any discussion on the matter. He, like the rest of us, just wanted to get out. So without another word we all climbed back into the truck and continued weaving through the narrow, debris-littered streets. After about twenty minutes of dodging rubble we pulled up and Kit got out again. 'Steve, you come with me. The rest of you, stay put. Don't get out of the truck.'

They moved quickly away, disappearing into an alley in the direction of the front line, taking their pistols but leaving their AK-47s behind.

The intermittent crackle of small-arms fire somewhere close by caused us to scrabble for our weapons. An instinctive reaction born of suppressed panic. The noise ended abruptly and we returned thankfully to the waiting game.

'Fancy a drink? There's a bar over there.' Nigel pointed to a slightly damaged pizzeria just as a man staggered out and began to weave his way in our direction, collapsing almost immediately before shaking convulsively and lying still in the gutter.

'Two sheets to the wind,' Jim said.

'It's three sheets to the wind actually,' Nigel corrected him.

'Whatever . . . He's pissed out of his skull anyway.'

'So would you be if you had to live in this fucking place,' Pete added.

We lapsed into silence, closing our eyes for a semi-snooze while we waited for Kit and Steve to return.

'Look . . . look!' Pete nudged me awake, nodding his head toward the man's body and pointing to a group of about a dozen rats now slowly approaching the inert figure. They snuffled around him for a few minutes, then two of the larger ones started to crawl over his body, while another moved around to his head and began to lick his mouth. Sucking the alcohol-based saliva, no doubt.

They were nosy little sods, scrambling in and out of his pockets and up his trousers. Some were already nibbling away at his grotty old boots. The rat at his mouth was a big bastard, black and shiny, about the size of a cat. He appeared to be in charge of the operation; the rest just seemed to follow him, keeping a little way behind at all times.

Blacky soon got tired of sucking at the man's mouth and moved on to his nose, nibbling at the nostrils with a lot more enthusiasm. We could see blood and bits of flesh being torn away.

'Christ! They're eating him . . .' Jim choked back his excitement.

The whole thing was getting a bit sick now and we knew that we should stop it, but nobody did.

As we watched, the rest of the rats started to crawl over the body, and in minutes the man's nose and the right side of his face were eaten away. The creatures seemed suddenly to get bored, moving to his hand and starting again. Within seconds the bloody face had attracted large blue flies, unperturbed by the rats – I suppose there was plenty for everyone.

The rats were slowing down. The feverish activity had ceased and they began to wander away with fat little bellies to sleep it off.

As we watched, a dog appeared from an alley nearby and sniffed at the body. For a moment our interest was renewed. The dog cocked its leg up on the fly-blown face, and the hot liquid steamed into the gaping wound that was once a cheek. Then the man moved.

We looked at one another, guilt etched upon our faces, as Kit and Steve, driving a new-looking Land Rover with Karlovac Brigade stickers, pulled up, blocking our view of the body.

No time to think . . . thank God.

They both leapt out of the vehicle. 'Shift the gear over, fast.'

We stood in a line, passing equipment from one to another. Within a few minutes the lorry was empty, Nigel ensuring that his genuine Renoir was stowed away safely.

'Everyone in? Lets go.'

With another Serbian bombardment ringing in our ears we headed north-west. Away from the town. Away from the battle. Away from the sight of that body, quivering and jerking into consciousness.

'Anything happen while we were away?' Steve asked.

We stared at one another with hooded eyes. Pete spoke. 'Nah, bloody boring.' He quickly changed the subject. 'You took your fuckin' time getting some wheels.'

The memory would linger. Best not to prolong it by discussion.

'Where did you get the motor?' Ivan asked a beaming Kit, who had switched on the radio – an added bonus.

'We had to wander about a bit. It's a right mess at the front. Fucking M-84 tanks everywhere, most of them blown to hell. Some silly sod had left this motor with the engine running. It was a gift. Is he gonna be pissed off when he gets back.'

Kit chortled merrily and started singing along with the gypsy music on the radio. He was flying at the moment, high on adrenaline. We all felt relieved to be able to move fast and in some comfort at last.

The 'blitzkrieg' of Karlovac continued as the MiGs swooped

low, cluster-bombing the town. Shells whistled their fluttering chorus overhead, always followed by the dull thumps which precede an explosion. Mortar fire and artillery retaliated, but seemed ineffective in slowing down the incoming barrage.

Groups of soldiers – many volunteers – manned heavy weapons hidden from the air in graveyards and bushes. Some waved at us as we passed. Many would die this day, a long way from home.

'We've got to avoid the main highway now,' said Kit. 'It's about fifty kilometres to Zagreb and a bit of peace and quiet. We'll go through the back roads and head for Plesivica.'

We were soon on the secondary road to Ozalj, after which we turned north-east through twisty but relatively safe lanes. All was calm again, although the battle at Karlovac continued at a muffled distance.

'I'm spitting feathers.' Pete reminded us that we hadn't eaten or had a drink for hours. 'What about a brew, Kit?'

'Yeah, sure. Why not? I think we're out of the shit by now anyway.'

We had just passed Krasic and were approaching some ruins of apparent archaeological interest – judging by the entrance cost. It seemed like a nice tourist-like place to stop and enjoy a cup of tea, amongst the silent pine forests and fast-running streams. Under different circumstances it might well have been.

Folk music was playing softly from the radio as we slumped around the Land Rover, letting our minds wander over the events of the past twenty-four hours. It seemed crazy in retrospect: the changes of fortune; the tension and torment; even the occasional high points – mostly from simple relief at surviving.

How did these men who lived their lives in the murky world of mercenary soldiering manage to retain their sanity? Did the things they saw and did affect them in the lonely hours? Did dark doors open in their minds?

I had asked Kit about this some weeks ago. He had denied having any regrets or hauntings. Later, he admitted to nightmares – on occasions. He also admitted to almost always pissing himself in firefights. 'You canna help it,' he had told me without embarrassment. 'You don't know you've done it until afterwards.'

We washed the mugs and filled our canteens from a nearby

stream of clear spring water, then made ourselves comfortable again in the comparative luxury of the Land Rover.

'Hang on a minute, Kit. Don't you think we should remove the Karlovac Brigade stickers?' Nigel was on the ball. We'd forgotten them.

'Whoops!' Kit grinned. 'Yeah, you're right. Rip 'em off, will you? It could make things awkward with the police in Zagreb.'

The stickers came off easily and within minutes we were away on the final thirty-five-kilometre run into the capital city of Croatia.

The last bit of the trip was over some difficult off-road terrain. The four-wheel-drive Land Rover was a godsend. Many of the smaller lanes and cart tracks were not shown on our maps and we had to resort to the compass on several occasions, often cutting through fields and farmyards. Much to the dismay of the farmers, who probably thought that they were being invaded.

Our first sight of Zagreb was the Sava river, as the ornate shopfronts and Viennese-style buildings of the town began to appear around us. The city had a time-warp feeling about it – lost somewhere in the 1920s, with Mount Medvednica dominating the northern skyline. It was easy to feel that we were arriving at our holiday destination; until Kit broke the spell.

'Right, lads. You can cut out the sightseeing. Our first port of call is the army headquarters at 25 Ilica. We've got to see my friend Tony Abranovich. He's a colonel in the army. You'll like him. He's a little dumpy fella with a ginger beard – looks a bit like Bob Hoskins.'

The military headquarters were in a large grey building only a short distance from the Trg Republike – Republican Square. The building was austere on the outside but with a spacious and impressive interior, where we were quickly approached by two armed military policemen who insisted upon searching us and removing all weapons before asking our business.

The tall, aggressive one spoke first. 'You . . . are . . . *engliski*?'

Ivan was outside, guarding the Land Rover, so it was down to Kit.

'*Da. Ja sam engleski. Zao mi je. Ne razumijem Croat.*' Yes. I am English. I am sorry. I don't understand Croat.

Kit was trying his best, as Jim whispered the immortal words, 'Didn't he do well!' in his best Bruce Forsyth voice.

The shorter guard smiled and in perfect English replied,

'Trying to speak our language is important, even if you get the odd word wrong. Now, what can we do for you?'

'My name is Freeman and these are my men. Is it possible to see Colonel Abranovich, please?'

'For what purpose do you wish to see the Colonel?'

'He is a friend. We have come a long way to meet him.'

The guards walked a few yards away and went into a huddle. The short one returned as the other walked briskly to the bottom of the grand stairway.

'My colleague will see if the Colonel is available. Please wait here.' He guided us into an adjoining room.

In less than two minutes a small man wearing an American bomber pilot's jacket, with a Browning pistol at his hip, bounced into the room. A huge smile spread across his face as he saw Kit waiting for him.

'Ah, Kit my friend. It is good to see you again. Come, we shall take coffee.'

He ushered us out into the hall and we followed him down a flight of stairs leading to the canteen. Coffee was ordered as Kit and the Colonel swapped stories, Tony Abranovich bursting into high-pitched laughter from time to time.

The good-old-boy stuff continued for about an hour, while the rest of us amused ourselves playing with the pinball machines until we became aware that the conversation had taken a serious turn, now being conducted in conspiratorial whispers. We slowly drifted back to the table. Too late. The deal had been completed.

Colonel Abranovich stood up. 'I will arrange rooms for you in a local hotel.' To the rest of us he said, 'I shall, no doubt, meet you again before you leave. Meanwhile, I wish you a pleasant stay in my city.' He turned back to Kit and with a meaningful smile said, 'No trouble, mind you. I do not control the police, and they are very strict.'

We were left to drink more strong, black, stomach-churning coffee and stare at the ornate ceiling for some time, before a sergeant returned and in poor English tried desperately to explain to a confused Kit the whereabouts in the western part of the city of our hotel.

The high-rise Panorama Hotel in Trg Sportova was an ideal 'crash' for a bunch of unwashed, unshaven slobs. Not too particular, and not far from the centre of town and the night life –

still active in spite of occasional attacks from Serb jets and the odd terrorist bombing.

The sergeant had warned us about sniping. Apparently old women of Serbian descent were often seen crouching in the windows of their flats taking pot shots at passers-by in the street, regardless of their nationality. He also pointed out, glancing at our DPM clothing, that they had a preference for those in military uniform.

All of this was as nothing compared with the horrors of the past few days. We checked the windows facing the army headquarters as we left, though. You can't be too careful.

The feeling of being on a Continental holiday continued as we merrily unloaded equipment and weapons, carrying them a little self-consciously through the lobby and into the lift.

Although it was still only late afternoon, weariness descended on us quickly. Pete and Ivan couldn't stop yawning, and any decisions that had to be made were best left until later. We democratically tossed a coin for bedrooms – two with a view and two without – and lay down on our beds, dirty boots and all. The gentle cursing from Jim in the next room became a lullaby as sleep took over.

'Wake up, you lazy sods!' The bedroom door crashed open. The morning light filtered through our window and with it the sounds of early-morning city traffic, a comforting noise that meant civilisation. It was seven o'clock. We had slept for thirteen hours.

We were up, washed and dressed in our clean camos within ten minutes as an agitated Kit ran round checking on things. God knows what he was checking, but his early military training made it a compulsion.

'Are you all ready for breakfast?' he yelled across the hall. Stupid question. We trooped down to the restaurant, famished.

Ivan asked us what we wanted and ordered in Croatian from a hovering waiter. The normal Yugoslavian breakfast of coffee and rolls with butter and jam or honey was not what we had in mind, and our insistence on *slaninu sa jajima* – bacon and eggs – caused something of a problem to the young waiter, who disappeared for well over twenty minutes while another kept us going with strong coffee.

The greasy bacon and runny eggs arrived, piled high on a large plate. We dived in, ignoring the white blobs of congealed fat. It was worse than Kit's cooking – impossible but true.

Back in our rooms, feeling slightly sick, we were summoned to a keffudle in Kit's room and told of the arrangement with Abranovich.

The man who had contacted Kit in Split had done so at the request of the governors of Osijek, on the recommendation of Colonel Abranovich. We were to have three days' R&R in Zagreb. Then we would meet an American contact, who would take us to the town of Osijek and introduce us to the commander, a Spanish ex-journalist named Eduardo Florez who was responsible for the defence of the town. Wages had been agreed at a converted rate of one hundred pounds a month – plus the odd bonus. Kit looked at the men. 'Is that OK?'

They looked at one another and Pete spoke. 'Not much choice, have we?'

'Yeah, you've got a choice. Don't accept it and go home.'

Kit was not happy with the deal either but there was little he could do about it. No doubt he had tried his best to up the ante, but there were a lot of mercs coming to Yugoslavia and it was a buyer's market at the moment.

'It's only for a short time, lads. Then we're off to Posusje; maybe I can get a better deal for you there. Let's have a show of hands.'

Ivan's hand was the first up. He wasn't here for the money: this was a debt he felt he owed his mother land. Slowly the rest of the men raised theirs. Although they would not easily admit it, money was a secondary consideration to excitement, comradeship and just simply being in a battle zone. As Jim at his poetic best put it: 'It makes you feel alive. Much better than nine to five.'

'Agreed, then?' Kit looked round.

'Yeah,' they all replied in quiet unison.

'Right. The next three days are yours. Relax. Take in the sights and don't get into any punch-ups. I'm going shopping. Anyone want to come?'

Few of us had been to Zagreb before, so we opted to accompany Kit on this first trip into town, keeping a sharp lookout for old women in windows.

Areas of the city were pockmarked with shell fire from marauding MiGs, but the inhabitants seemed oblivious to the damage as they walked the leafy squares and narrow cobbled passageways about their daily chores with a relaxed, unconcerned manner.

We dived in and out of bars, sampling local beers and wines,

51

which did little to settle our stomachs after that breakfast. Ivan caught a passing tram and went off on his own to look up a relative living in the upper town of Gorji Grad, and Pete, feeling more nauseous than the rest of us, decided to sleep it off on a park bench and join us later.

As it was Friday, the Dolac market was in full swing, and Jim decided that he would go and nick something. We asked him what he wanted. He replied, 'Anything,' as he walked away standing out like a sore thumb in his DPM gear.

The remaining four of us wandered around Nama – a large department store – for a while, before deciding that it was time to try some food at further risk to our digestive systems. We looked at menus in the windows of restaurants, finding that food was expensive in most of the better-class places, and finally opting for the Kaptolska Klet in the northern part of town.

The menu was in Croat and the waiters busy with local customers, so we looked for familiar phrases, not wishing to make any mistakes with this our first main meal. Heading the list of food was something Kit recognised, *zagorska krumpirska juha* – hearty potato soup. It seemed safe enough. We ordered it.

An enormous bowl turned up at our table. It smelt good, and though it looked a little dodgy, we attacked it with vigour, leaving little but breadcrumbs on the red checked tablecloth.

Although it was cold when we left the restaurant, the sky had become a clear, unclouded blue, and it was possible to see the mountains in the north without difficulty. Even in these few short hours it was easy to forget why we were here, as we basked in the winter sun in yet another spacious, flower-filled garden on our way back to the hotel.

'Fancy some exercise?' The hotel was set amongst tennis courts, swimming pools and other sports facilities. Kit liked to keep fit.

Steve was keen. Nigel wasn't. I was of non-combatant status; it means lazy. With this lack of support the exercise fanatics decided not to bother at the moment either, so we went back to the hotel for a doze and to await the return of Ivan, Jim and Pete.

Pete was in his room when we arrived, looking rough. His skin was yellow and he was doubled up in pain, sweating heavily as he lay moaning on the bed. The breakfast, or something, had really upset him. It wasn't like Pete to exaggerate a condition. If anything he would play it down.

Kit looked at him anxiously. 'You gonna be all right?'

Pete opened his eyes. 'Yeah. Sure. It's just that bloody breakfast. Never could take greasy food.' He leapt up and ran to the bathroom, retching horribly.

'Shiiit! That's all we need right now.' Kit picked up the phone. '*Da li u hotelu ima doktor?*' Is there a doctor in the hotel?

He turned to us. 'There is a doctor here. He's coming up now. Go and get Pete into bed.'

Pete looked ashen as he hobbled back to bed and collapsed.

'The doctor's on his way, my son. You'll soon be right as rain.'

A sharp knock on the door and the doctor walked in briskly, heading straight for the bed. '*Na sta se zalite?*' What's the trouble?

Kit spoke. '*Govorite il engliski?*' Do you speak English?

The doctor nodded and started to examine Pete, taking his temperature and pressing his abdomen as Kit explained the symptoms.

'It is not serious,' he said finally to a relieved Kit. 'No food or drink for twenty-four hours. Give him this.' He handed Kit a bottle of liquid, waving away an offer of payment. 'Colonel Abranovich will settle my bill. Phone me again if his condition deteriorates. He should be well by the morning. Good day.'

Ivan and Jim arrived almost together and came into the room looking anxiously at the bedridden Pete.

'Has he been shot?' asked Jim.

'No, he hasn't been shot, you prick! It's just a bad stomach upset.' Kit was feeling a little tense after what could have been a minor disaster.

We left Pete to sleep and went downstairs to the lounge for a chat and to learn of Jim's futile attempts at stealing from the market.

'The bastards wouldn't take their eyes off me,' he whined. 'I stood no chance. Anyway, it was a bloody food market. Nothing worth nicking.'

We decided to spend the rest of the day rubbernecking around the city by tram car. We bought twenty-four-hour passes, which gave us unlimited travel for thirty dinars. There were a lot of laughs, and the occasional odd glance at my uniformed colleagues, who were acting like demented kids, hollering at passing girls, jumping on and off trams and other such irresponsible acts resulting from a temporary freedom from anxiety.

As dusk approached, the lights of the city began to change the appearance of the pink and grey buildings. Steve reminded us that we had a sick colleague back at the hotel who might need some help, so we changed trams once again, leaping off almost outside the Panorama.

Pete was sitting up in bed, looking a lot better. The medicine seemed to have worked. The pains had decreased and he was no longer being sick. In fact, he was a little pissed off at missing the day. 'Where are we going tonight, Kit?' He tried to smile.

'You aren't going anywhere, sunshine. You're ill. Maybe tomorrow, we'll see.'

Pete didn't argue. It was all a bluff anyway. He was where he wanted to be, for the moment.

Ivan turned on the radio and tuned it to VHF 90.5, Radio Zagreb. English-speaking programmes were broadcast on this station every day except Saturday. We settled down to hear the news and in a moment were brought swiftly back to harsh reality, with reports of Serbian attacks on towns and villages to the south and further Chetnik atrocities on helpless women and children.

Looking out of the balcony window at this fairy-tale town, it was, once again, impossible to believe that this beautiful country was being torn apart from inside.

Jim, ever sensitive to the plight of others, broke the spell. 'Are we going out on a piss-up tonight, lads?'

'Dunno. Who wants to go out?' Kit didn't seem too keen. He looked around for a response. Nobody seemed eager to leave Pete alone again, so we agreed that tomorrow night we would paint the town. Tonight we would stay in, play cards, watch TV . . . and tell a few lies to one another.

Our evening of domesticity passed pleasantly enough. At midnight we turned in, sleeping soundly as the city grew quiet around us.

The unmistakable sound of a low-flying MiG woke us as it screamed into a fast climb. An explosion followed, then another, and the hotel shuddered. The war was back. It had followed us into our dreams.

Steve and I ran to the balcony overlooking the city, watching early-morning workers dive for cover as another jet came in on a tight curve, hurling its silver-canistered cluster bombs as it blasted away with its cannon; kicking up the asphalt in neat little lines along the main street in pursuit of scurrying citizens.

The rest of the guys joined us, struggling into their clothes as incoming rockets whistled overhead. Crumph! A building was hit less than two hundred metres away. A muffled explosion followed as windows blew outwards and crimson flames stretched upwards, immediately blackening the once crystalline-white stonework.

As we watched, the whole side of the structure collapsed. People with arms waving in panic – as if trying to fly – followed the debris downward as it piled up on the pavement below. There was no movement from the bodies as they lay silent and hideously contorted. No fear or pain on their slackened faces gave any indication of their thoughts in those last few moments of terror.

The attack had only lasted for a few destructive minutes, and now the jets had gone, leaving clean white trails of smoke in the sky and an eerie silence hanging over the city. A lonely bell began to ring from a local church as the people came slowly from their homes and shelters to pick up the pieces once again.

Zagreb had few defences in the early days of the war and was a soft target for Serbian air assaults aimed primarily at the radio station on the mountain peak of Sljeme, with the odd diversion intended to weaken resolve and create fear within the community.

'What shall we do?' Pete had struggled out of his bed and was staring over our shoulders.

Kit shrugged. 'It's not our war, I keep telling you that! We are here to do specific things for sums of money. We do them right and we get paid. We do them wrong and we get killed. The fuckin' Croats don't care about us. It's their problem, not ours.'

Ivan spoke. 'I've got to help them, Kit.'

'Sure, I understand that, Ivan. You're different, these are your people. Go and give them a hand if you want to.'

'Do you mind if I go and help?' Jim was already putting on his boots.

Kit turned to him. 'You're joking? You've never helped anyone in your bleedin' life!' His voice rose as he stared at Jim incredulously.

'I just want to go. That's all. Is it OK?'

Kit shook his head resignedly. 'Yeah, sure. Anyone else for the Florence Nightingale detail?'

'We'll go,' Nigel and Pete volunteered. Steve nodded his head affirmatively.

As Kit looked at them one by one, his face creased into a grin.

...gnificent fuckin' seven. We're all a bunch of prats. Come

...next four hours were spent loading dead and injured bodies into lorries and ambulances and clearing roads of brick and stonework. We were harassed by the plague of cameramen and journalists drawn like flies to areas of devastation, but the Croat people were warm and friendly to us; obviously grateful that foreigners were prepared to be so generous with help in an emergency. No one seemed shocked at the attack on the town, and the whole thing was treated with a strange detachment. They all knew that much worse was happening elsewhere in their country.

The final count was fifteen dead and twenty-three wounded. Two buildings badly damaged and about twelve slightly. It could have been worse. Tomorrow it could well be.

An old lady of about eighty came up to us and touched my arm. As I looked down at her watering eyes she spoke in a soft, wavering voice.

'*Ja se sovem Katya. Milo mi je da sam vas upoznao. Hvala vam na pomoci.*'

I turned to Ivan for a translation. He put his arm around her frail shoulders and told me that she had said, 'My name is Katya. I'm very pleased to meet you. Thanks for your help.' It was enough.

'Come on, lads. We've done our share. You'll ruin our image if we keep this up. Fuckin' mercenaries, my ass. You're a bunch of pansies.'

Kit had finished his coffee, supplied by a team of firemen, and was anxious not to hang around and become more of a target for the journalists and cameramen. Questions required answers. He was already on the run from the police at home and didn't want his picture spread all over the British daily papers.

We got to our feet as Colonel Abranovich approached. 'Thank you for your help, gentlemen.' He turned to Kit. 'I would like to see you at our headquarters later, if you can spare the time. Your contact has arrived and we must make arrangements.'

Kit agreed to meet him later in the day, after a long soak in a bath. We waved goodbye to the few remaining members of the rescue teams and returned to our hotel for a well-earned breakfast.

We all perched on the edge of Pete's bed. He had recovered

quickly, but the thought of another meal of greasy bacon and eggs had reminded him of the need to eat.

'I just can't face it,' he said in a mournful whisper.

'Try something else then,' Steve suggested.

'Like what?'

'Scrambled eggs. They can't mess those up. Can they?'

We all decided to play it safe, ordering *kajganu* and *vocni sok*, with *preprzen hieb* and *marmaladu* – scrambled eggs, fruit juice, toast and marmalade. It arrived fast and properly cooked. I guess they were prepared for us this time.

For the rest of the day we loafed around the hotel, having a risky lunch brought to our rooms. Ivan and Nigel went off for a swim in the local pool. Kit went to meet Abranovich on his own.

The occasional wail of an ambulance punctuated the normal sounds of the city as time drifted lazily by. Radio Zagreb reported the earlier incident in a bored, monotonous tone, pointing out that citizens should remain alert for further attacks. Clever, these media people.

Kit returned after about three hours and seemed a little preoccupied for a while. When asked if there was anything wrong he assured us that there wasn't. He said he was just mulling things over in his head, but none of us was convinced.

We were to meet an American guy called John Fontain at a jazz club run by Bosko Petrovic – a local vibes player – at nine o'clock that evening. Arrangements were to be made with him for our trip to Osijek.

'Let's clean up and go and have a few beers first. See the nightlife. Then meet the Yank.'

We sprang into action, shaving and covering ourselves with some disgusting aftershave purchased from the Nama department store on our trip around town yesterday.

'Take your pistols.' It was almost an afterthought. Kit was sliding his 9mm CZ inside his shirt.

'What do we need guns for? It's not a war zone, Kit,' Nigel started to whinge.

'Don't argue. Regardless of what you may think, for us it is a war zone. So do as you're told and take your fuckin' pistol. Hide it, mind you. But take it.'

Nigel muttered something inaudible as he grabbed his Browning, stuffing it in the rear of his waistband. The rest followed suit, staring at Kit's back as if he'd lost his mind.

Polished and sparkling, we left the hotel and headed, high on anticipation, for the centre of town and a night of sublime pleasure at anyone's expense. Lock up your daughters, the boys are back in town.

Calo, our hotel waiter, had told us that the best area for a good night out was Tkalciceva. Feeling lazy, we waved down a passing taxi – pointless really, it was only a few blocks away.

We piled out of the Mercedes cab into neon-painted darkness and the welcoming glow of nightclubs offering escape from reality. Hordes of animated people jostled one another as they prowled the streets, laughing, joking and having a good time. Amongst the noise and gaiety of overflowing discos, bars and knocking shops it was easy to forget that the hoarding covering shop-fronts and offices was concealing the unsightly scars of cluster-bomb damage.

First stop was a bar opposite the cathedral – Gostionica Badanj. It was crowded and noisy, just the sort of dive for us to relax in. No pretence. No dress rules. No aggro. That was, until an English-speaking student type wandered over from his group of loud-mouthed friends to accuse Jim of being a hired killer with no interest in his country apart from earning blood money at their expense.

'You English?'

'Yeah, that's right, pal.'

'Not the UN though.' His eyes narrowed as he waited for an answer.

'Well, sort of . . .'

'How do you mean, sort of?'

'Well, we're here to keep the peace for you lot.'

'You are mercenaries, yes?'

'Volunteers!' Jim tightened.

'It is the same thing. Predators, jackals, feeding on the grief of my people.'

Jim had heard it all before. If you earned your living as a mercenary, this kind of needling was par for the course and, like politics or religion, impossible to debate amicably – especially in a noisy bar. On this occasion Jim tried to avoid trouble, wandering away from the source of aggravation and instead trying to engage an attractive girl in conversation. The mouthy student followed him with two others, obviously intending to use Jim's attempt at social intercourse as justifiable reason to continue the altercation.

The whole thing was starting to look nasty, as voices were raised and one of the bigger men pushed Jim against a table, sending bottles and glasses crashing to the floor. Jim clambered to his feet, his hand diving to his boot. In the dim light we saw the glint of a blade, held rapier-fashion in his clenched hand. Jim always carried a Gerber boot-knife and would not hesitate to use it if provoked. With three men having a go at him, that was enough provocation for anyone!

Kit, Nigel and Ivan were standing by the bar, laughing and joking with the locals; they had so far been unaware of the incident. The loud music and overcrowding had masked the raised voices until the crash of the table drew our attention. They looked over and saw Jim climb back to his feet. He was staring across the room with an expression on his face that we had all seen many times before . . .

'Oooh, Christ . . .' I couldn't hear but could lip-read Kit's words as he strode across the room, his massive twenty-stone frame creating a wake of bruised bodies. Nigel and Ivan followed him, with the rest of us close behind.

'*Proverite, molim vas, gume?*' Kit thundered at the student.

The Croat looked at him in astonishment, then stared at his friends.

Ivan whispered urgently in his ear, 'Kit, you've got that wrong. You have just asked him if he would like his tyres checked!'

A second went by as Kit tried to find the right words, not knowing that the man spoke English better than he did. When language failed him, he hit the Croat low, causing him to let out a blast of air and fall to his knees in agony. The room became quiet, apart from the sound of Michael Jackson on the juke box.

One of the other men hesitated for a moment, then swung at Kit and missed, sprawling on the floor with his friend as the other held up his hands in a gesture of capitulation.

'If you get up we'll hammer you,' Kit yelled at the two men, before turning back to the bar to finish his drink. They stayed down until we left . . . ten minutes later.

It would soon be time to meet the American at Bosko Petrovic's jazz club. We walked on this occasion, to clear our minds and laugh at the fracas in the bar. It was a mild event by normal standards of bar-room punch-ups. But if Jim had used that knife, everything would have gone down the toilet.

The cool sounds of jazz filtered through the night as we

approached the club, and a nice relaxed atmosphere greeted us as we entered. The doorman let us in free, no doubt as a result of the military uniform.

A quick scan around the place soon revealed our contact, unmistakable in his badge-covered USAF flying jacket and 'Strike Force' baseball cap. He was in his early forties, very fit-looking, with a Hollywood-craggy face, cropped grey hair and a cigar. He was even chewing gum!

'Hi. You must be Freeman.' A Californian drawl, no less.

Kit looked him over and took a sharp intake of breath.

'Oh aye, canny lad,' he replied in his best Geordie, reserved for those he is about to take the piss out of. 'An' you must be Fontain.'

'Colonel Fontain, actually. But we're all friends here. Call me Johnny, or "Groundhog" if you prefer. I was a jet-jockey in 'Nam. They called me that 'cos of my low-flying tactics.'

Steve moaned softly as Groundhog climbed to his feet, vigorously shaking hands with us whilst asking our names.

'Just so's there's no misunderstandin', the US Government is neutral at the moment. Officially uninvolved. I'm an adviser to the Croatians. Independent. You understand what I'm saying?'

We nodded seriously; it seemed the only thing to do.

'OK, guys. Now here's the game plan. We leave Zagreb at 0600 hours. Day after tomorrow. The sixteenth. OK so far?'

'You mean Monday?' Kit was playing it dumb.

Johnny didn't answer. Nothing could stop him now.

'You follow me on the back roads and I'll take you through the Serb lines without any problems. Then when we get to Osijek, I'll introduce you to the commander of the military installation. OK?'

We nodded dumbly, fascinated by this asshole cartoon character.

'Any questions, guys?'

Questions! This jerk was on full automatic. He didn't want questions, just the opportunity to talk.

'Get some beers inside you, guys. This is gonna be a long night.'

He was right! We got the whole bit: stories of the USAF's 8th Tactical Fighter Wing in Vietnam; the Tet offensive; low-flying air strikes over the Mekong Delta. We were in a time warp of nostalgia as our minds numbed in defence. He went on and on as the soft, cool music percolated through his thick cigar smoke until all we could see was his mouth moving hypnotically.

At midnight the band stopped playing and the bar closed.

Johnny invited us back to his hotel to continue our one-sided chat. There was no way we could take any more, so we made our apologies and trooped back to our rooms – brain dead.

Sunday morning passed in a sleepy haze. We missed breakfast, which at least saved us the trouble of making further decisions on the delights of Croat cooking. At two p.m. a sergeant from the military headquarters appeared, asking Kit if he would go to see Abranovich about some weapons. Three of us tagged along and were once again welcomed with great courtesy by the Colonel, who enquired about our meeting with John Fontain.

We didn't want to talk about John Fontain . . . ever.

Kit spent some time with the Croatian soldiers, demonstrating some recently obtained weapons of which they had no practical knowledge. He was surprisingly patient when some of them were unable to grasp the intricacies of assembly, lovingly separating the components, explaining their function yet again.

We returned to our hotel a little later than anticipated after detouring around the town for the last time. The few days' R&R had passed quickly, but I suspected that Kit wanted to be on the move again.

The evening was spent packing, and it was only ten thirty when we hit the sack. Tomorrow at six we would be back in Vietnam again with Colonel Groundhog. We needed our sleep.

It was a familiar feeling, stealing out of the hotel in the morning darkness. This time, however, our bill was paid, so it wasn't nearly as much fun.

The Land Rover was loaded quickly and Kit returned to our rooms for one last check under the beds where the armaments had been stashed. Check, check, check and check again. The soldier's motto.

At six a.m. precisely a matt-black Cherokee four-by-four pulled up and a wide-awake and grinning Colonel Fontain hit the streets running.

'Hi there, guys. Ready? OK, let's move out.' Then, as an afterthought, 'You look kinda crowded in there. Anybody wanna ride with me?'

Hell would freeze over first. Kit came to the rescue.

'That's good of you, Johnny, but for insurance reasons the men have to travel together with me. It's in the policy.'

Bless his lying little soul.

We crept out of Zagreb by the back door, with one last glance at a city lost somewhere between yesterday, today and an uncertain tomorrow. It was peaceful at the moment in dawn's early light, but the scars remained, hidden from sight. Until the next wave of shiny silver canisters fell from the sky.

Chapter Five

We're not all killers ... Some of us really care ...
Especially if the money is right.

The huge brake lights of the black Cherokee blinked at us through
our mud-splattered windscreen as the Colonel confidently
weaved through the damp and solitary streets, often darting into
dark alleyways barely wide enough for the vehicles to pass
through undamaged.

Within thirty minutes we were clear of the town and entering
the open suburbs. He turned and waved, indicating that we could
speed up a little as we neared the main road, soon to pass over the
Zelina river. He had kept up a steady pace, about thirty metres
ahead of us, occasionally checking in his mirror to see that all was
well.

Nigel, who was in the back with us, located our position on the
map and told us that the first major township was Bjelovar. He
pointed out that we would travel through about eight villages
before we reached it, each one a potential hazard from marauding
bands of Chetniks or the unpredictable militia. Even the local
police could cause trouble.

A convoy of white-painted UN vehicles – the safest colour in
Bosnia – passed us, heading into Zagreb with supplies and
assistance. In preparation for the next attack, perhaps?

We had been travelling for about an hour and had gone through
five villages. Each one had been visited at one time or another by
people with a tendency to destroy anything in their path. The
reversed 'C' sprayed on the walls of the looted, burned-out
houses left us in no doubt. The Chetniks had deposited their
calling card.

Johnny waved out of his window, pulling off the road and
stopping in a cloud of red dust. He gave the terrain a professional
once-over before walking the few metres back to our vehicle, a
cigar clenched firmly between his teeth.

'OK. So far, so good,' he mumbled through a cloud of smoke.

'We're gonna stay on this road until we reach Bjelovar. Then we're gonna head north for a while and pick up the main road heading east. After that it's gonna get hairy. Especially when we reach Nasice, about forty kilometres east of Osijek.'

He stared at us as if to detect any sign of concern. He was unlucky. The men had been there, done it. I had learned to hide any visual signs of trepidation.

'Any questions?' He pulled a nice-looking nickel-finished Colt 38 super-automatic from his shoulder holster and checked the nine-round magazine, slipping it in and out with a practised movement. 'Keep your eyes peeled, guys. Soon it'll be party time.'

'Any chance of a brew?' Jim asked in a flat, bored tone.

'I don't think that's a good idea, son. We're kinda exposed here. Maybe later.' He turned, checking the hills again, and strode back to his car.

'Fucking plonker,' Pete muttered at the receding figure.

The Cherokee pulled away at speed, its rear tyres throwing stones back at us. It was as if Johnny was showing his displeasure at the English weakness for a cup of tea.

We had to accelerate quickly to catch up with the speeding Colonel as he drove rapidly through the villages of Haganj, Zabno and Rovisce, all showing the usual signs of destruction. Many of the houses were still burning. Some, with crosses painted on them, had been left completely untouched, clear indication of ethnic cleansing by a recent raiding party of Chetniks.

No checkpoints so far, and good progress was being made as we entered the outskirts of Bjelovar. There a funeral party gathered protectively around a grieving woman, who was beating her chest hysterically as she wailed in grief for her dead husband being buried in a makeshift grave between a disused factory and an upturned tank. The men stared at the retreating scene impassively, hardened to the reality of war and the sight of other people's suffering.

As we slowed down to negotiate still smoking craters and untended bodies in our path, an old crippled woman in a wheelchair pushed herself into the middle of the road and stopped. We screeched to a halt only a metre away from her.

Pete started to laugh. 'Silly bitch, she could get herself killed doing that.' He started to get out to push her to the side of the road.

'Wait! I don't like the look of this,' Kit muttered as he clicked off his safety catch. 'It doesn't feel right.'

Within seconds of his remark the burning, hissing sound of incoming rounds peppered the road ahead, stitching neat ventilation holes along the side of our Land Rover, narrowly missing five ducking heads. The old woman, helpless and alone, had been a decoy.

We could see nothing from our confined space and had that rats-in-a-barrel feeling again as Steve gave the car some wellie, almost climbing over the slow-moving Cherokee in his haste to get the fuck out of the place.

The Colonel, seeing us about to mount him, accelerated away, leaving us a good hundred metres behind to face the snipers who were now coming out of the buildings to attack us head on, lobbing grenades at our vehicle with gay abandon. We were in no position to retaliate, apart from the odd shot from the open side window. Not very accurate and not very effective in a speeding vehicle.

'*Stop!*' Kit screamed as the rounds started to find their target. Steve braked hard and slewed into an arc, bouncing off the wall of a house. We were out and running before forward momentum had ceased, diving headlong behind anything we thought would protect us from the whining bullets.

'Anybody see them?' Kit crawled along his wall and cautiously lifted his head.

'No. Nothing.'

Silence. Except for our still-running engine.

'Well, we can't stay here. Pete, you go through the garden and around the back. I'll do a runner across the road. Give me some covering fire. Ready. *Go!*'

Kit leapt to his feet and hurtled across the unprotected road as Pete disappeared behind the house. Ivan, Jim and Nigel poked their AK-47s above the wall, spraying the area as best they could.

A dull sound of gunfire from further down the road made Ivan and Jim stop their haphazard shooting and listen.

'Sounds like a shotgun. Who the fuck uses a shotgun?' Nigel cocked his head in concentration.

'It's a semi-auto – it's got to be to sustain that rate of fire – and it's coming our way.'

Boom . . . boom . . . boom . . . boom . . . boom. Somebody was busy out there, and it wasn't Kit or Pete. They had an SA-80 and an AK-47. So who the hell was it?

The shotgun sounds continued, with occasional AK-47s replying in their familiar staccato bursts. The firefight was taking place some distance away from our position by now, and rather tentatively we lifted our heads, waiting for them to get blown off, but it didn't happen. Sheepishly, we climbed to our feet, feeling that we had been invited to a party and had arrived at the wrong house.

The five of us stood there feeling like spare pricks as the noise continued, moving closer by the second. We looked at one another and Steve took the initiative, suggesting that we should move slowly along the back of the houses in the direction of the firing. It seemed like a sensible idea, the alternative being just to wait there and wonder what the hell was going on around us.

In single file, with our heads very firmly low, we inched along the rear of the houses, tripping over the grotesque figure of a naked body with a rope around its neck and a circle with four reversed 'C's carved on its chest. I stared down at the figure in dumb horror. The man's face was contorted with pain as his sightless eyes gazed at me. His toothless mouth was filled with lumps of bloody flesh, torn from his groin.

'Keep moving,' Steve hissed. I kept moving.

A shadowy figure appeared, running at speed across our line of sight. Ivan had seen him first and had raised his weapon, letting off a few rounds as the man looked at us in momentary dismay. The Chetnik was in the wrong place at the wrong time. His punctured body hit the ground and lay still. We looked at the corpse of a man about twenty years old, wearing jeans, a Mickey Mouse T-shirt and gold earrings. Just a kid, who should have been at work in an office or factory. Not playing soldiers. Not killing people for fun. Not lying dead with five rounds of lead buried deep in his chest.

'Let's move.' Steve led us closer to the sounds of battle as an AK and an SA-80 opened in unison; we guessed that Kit and Pete were now participating in the fray. The shotgun still kept blasting regular bursts of fire. This boy sure had rhythm.

We moved more slowly now and could hear voices as we turned into an alley and were confronted by the backs of two men crouched behind a pile of mattresses. Their sixth sense must have warned them, too late, that they were in trouble. As they twisted to face us a hail of automatic fire from four weapons cut them literally to pieces and threw bits of torn flesh into the road.

'Now what?' Nigel whispered to an unsure Steve. 'Do we go on? Wait? Piss ourselves?'

'Shut up, Nigel. Move back.'

We did as we were told and cleared the alley, waiting for someone else to make the next move. It didn't take long.

First we saw the barrel of a shotgun, followed by the dapper shape of Colonel Fontain, looking furtive as he went into the unknown. Kit and Pete were close behind, tense and ready.

We breathed again and Steve called out to them. 'Fontain, it's us. You can unbuckle your gunbelt now.'

So the Colonel wasn't a complete prat after all. He had driven on for a while, parked and returned to help us out. And done a bloody good job of it. Now we would have to pay the price.

'I guessed you guys could do with some help. There were about twenty of them at first; some ran away when it started to become a shootin' war but a dozen or so stayed to fight it out. They didn't anticipate an attack from the rear though. Scared the bastards to death when I came in blasting with the Franchi SPAS.'

Yeah, yeah, yeah. Kit closed his eyes. Would we ever live this down? Listening to Groundhog repeat this story over the next few days could be a fate worse than death.

The Chetniks had, it seemed, fled into the hills, leaving Bjelovar for another day. We collected our vehicles and headed out of town, with no regrets and no thanks from the citizens.

With Colonel Fontain riding point, we headed northward through the slightly damaged villages of Kupinovac, Rakitnica and Semovci. No roadblocks appeared to ruin our day any further, and we settled in for a peaceful drive past wooded valleys and sparkling waterfalls.

A sign just before Durdevac pointing to the right directed us to Osijek. Colonel Fontain pulled off the road, indicating to us that we should follow him down a narrow bush-lined lane. He stopped and came to the side of our vehicle, looking serious.

'We're soon gonna be hitting the secondary road into Osijek. Before we get there we go through Virovitica. It's the last town and a major crossroads. So look out for troop movement at the intersection and any other kind of shit like that. Expect trouble at all times from here on in. It reminds me of when I was in 'Nam. We were on the outskirts of Khe San when . . .'

He paused, suddenly realising that this was not the time or place for reminiscing, and shook his head, smiling apologetically.

'Another time perhaps.' He turned to Kit. 'You guys can have your brew now if you like. It's safe here.'

We didn't need another word of encouragement as we all piled out of the Rover and set up the Peak stove. Soon the kettle was boiling and each of us had a hot mug of tea grasped firmly in our chubby little hands. Even the Colonel succumbed to the evil leaf and gulped back a cup of the life-restoring fluid.

When Fontain returned to his vehicle, having some difficulty turning in the tight lane, Kit drew us together. 'He's right this time. The next hundred kilometres are going to be rough. It's a fairly straight, open road. A sniper's dream. A mortar-man's dream. They'll both have all the time in the world to zero in on us, and we'll have nowhere to run or hide.' You could always rely upon Kit to restore your confidence.

The Colonel had finally managed to turn his Cherokee and waited as we did the same to the Land Rover. Then we followed him back to the road heading for Virovitica and the long, dangerous trip down the main drag.

Brake lights hastily applied made Nigel hit the anchors, bringing us to a shuddering halt in the middle of the road. The Cherokee reversed back alongside us and an excited Colonel yelled through the window, 'Police roadblock ahead!'

Kit was calm about it. 'No problem. We've got papers from Tony Abranovich, haven't we? We are a legitimate military force going about our duties. Don't panic, Johnny.'

'Yeah . . . Of course you're right, Kit. Jumpy, I guess.'

He restarted his stalled engine and drove on, and we followed cautiously towards the block. A thick chain was suspended across the road and six heavily armed men glared at us as we slowly approached. One of the policemen moved forward waving his hand in the air and mouthing the words 'Stanite ovde.' Stop here.

He bent down and peered through the windows of our vehicles, turning to his men and shouting something in an urgent voice as muzzle flashes lit their faces. They were shooting at us!

We couldn't charge the roadblock, which is common practice under such circumstances. The thick chain would have stopped us dead. Our options were limited, so we did the only thing possible: reversed at full speed and leapt out into a stinking, water-filled ditch.

Kit was hopping mad. 'The stupid bastards!' He turned to Nigel and Pete. 'You flank them. Don't worry about casualties. Shoot the fucking idiots.'

He gave them a few minutes to get clear, then leapt out of the ditch, grabbing a 'trombone' – a rifle grenade launcher – from the Land Rover. Without further discussion he stood up and sent a clear message of disapproval. The two police cars exploded in a bright orange flash, killing four of the policemen outright. Nigel and Pete finished the other two with brief bursts of fire. It was soon over.

The whole thing had been a stupid waste. The policemen had been drinking heavily and were probably pissed out of their skulls. Bottles of *votku*, *konjak* and *pivo* – vodka, brandy and beer – lay everywhere, no doubt liberated from the local bar.

'Drunk and scared. A lousy epitaph,' Steve said wearily as we dragged the bodies into the ditch. 'I guess the Chetniks will get blamed for this too.'

Johnny was surprisingly quiet as he walked back to his car and started the engine. Kit went over and asked if he was all right.

'Yeah, I'm fine. Kit. Guess I'm getting too old for this kind of thing. It gets to me sometimes. Vietnam was a long time ago. I was a young man then . . . I'll be OK. Thanks for asking.'

We could hear the Rolling Stones singing 'Paint It Black' drifting back from his cassette player as he moved away. He was trying for a morale boost from an old Vietnam favourite, we guessed, and warmed to him for admitting a weakness. Everyone's bottle ran out from time to time.

The citizens of Virovitica had heard the sounds of battle, and as we entered the town we were met by empty streets. Kit figured that it was safe to stop here due to the roadblock and flashed his lights at the Colonel, who pulled over and cut his engine. A large bearded man approached us alone from a nearby house; realising from our uniforms that we were not Serbian or Chetnik, he questioned us about the gunfire. Ivan explained in a vague manner that there had been a few snipers in the fields and the problem had been taken care of.

He seemed satisfied with this explanation, shaking Ivan by the hand and inviting us into his home for refreshments, which were gratefully accepted.

His wife fussed around us as if we were honoured guests, bringing loaves of home-baked bread, soup, huge spicy sausages and Zilavka – a dry white wine from Herzegovina. We spent a very pleasant hour with Dina and Antunovic, discussing the sadness of the war – with Ivan translating. But it was easy to work out for ourselves the meaning of the often-repeated phrases '*Sta ovo znzaci? Ja ne razumem.*' What does this mean? I don't understand. They were not alone. We didn't understand either.

All too soon it was time to go, and we bade them farewell with a chorus of '*Hvala vam mnogo*': Thank you very much. We meant it. This was the first bit of genuine hospitality we had received since arriving in Yugoslavia.

'Hope they don't get any repercussions from the police,' said Jim as we were climbing into the car.

'Nah,' Steve replied. 'Like I said, the Chetniks will get the blame.'

We pulled away as the couple waved their goodbyes, and were soon out of town and on the main road heading for Osijek.

The hum of tyres on the flat asphalt road soon produced a hypnotic effect on our weary brains. We had a little more space to stretch out and relax now, as Kit had relented and allowed Steve and Pete to travel in comfort with Johnny, who had become, temporarily at least, bearable.

The road was fairly straight and free from hot spots, so we were able to doze and listen to local music on the radio. We passed through about six villages and two roadblocks, at a cost of eight packets of cigarettes and two bottles of whisky. One of the militiamen at Mikleus had actually given us some water. Strange people, strange war. One minute they shoot at you, the next they invite you into their homes.

We sailed through Cacinci and Fericanci, but became involved in an incident in Moticina where two drunken youths had driven a stolen lorry full of explosives off the road and into a ditch. The lorry had turned over but they had managed to get out unharmed. We arrived just at the point when local people, unaware of impending disaster, were running to assist them. As the explosives detonated, spraying shrapnel into the air, and rounds of ammunition buzzed everywhere, the idiot villagers just stood and watched. Four of them were cut down by flying metal.

We pulled up just behind Johnny, who was screaming at them to move back. I guess they didn't understand the language, although his arm-waving didn't need any translation. Kit and Ivan ran toward the nearest group, dragging them away as yet another explosion blasted balls of flame high into the air. The heat finally drove the villagers back, leaving their petrol-doused friends to burn as we watched, unable to approach the bodies.

The locals stood in small groups, stunned by this stupid accident, and for a moment the cause of it was forgotten in their shock and despair.

Kit and Ivan, both with some medical experience, set about helping those injured, while Colonel Fontain, back to his usual self, took charge of the proceedings.

'OK, you goddam gooks. Make up some stretchers and get these people to a hospital. *You!* Fatso. Get something and put out the fire. Where's the goddam ambulance? Where's the doctor? Jesus, what a bunch of bums.'

Of course nobody understood a word of what he was yelling in his strong Californian accent. They stared at him as if he had gone mad.

A police car, followed closely by a lorry carrying members of the Croatian National Guard, pulled up, and assuming that there had been some form of attack, pointed their weapons at the supposed culprits. Us.

It took a few minutes of Ivan's time, and the letter from Colonel Abranovich, to convince the police that we were innocent, and they backed off, listening to the reason for the mayhem. Then they screamed off, sirens blaring, in the direction taking by the fleeing youths.

We did all we could to help the injured, covering the charred dead in bodybags found in the back of Johnny's Cherokee, and were once again treated to a meal by one of the villagers, in his home at the top of a hill overlooking the village. Meanwhile the youths had been captured by the police some way out of town, and it was discovered that they were making a living by stealing arms and selling them to the highest bidder. In all probability they would be shot for this, and who would argue?

Before leaving the village Johnny, who had returned to his role of Groundhog, gave us yet another pep talk.

'OK, you guys, now listen up.' He paused for dramatic effect.

'After we pass the next town of Nasice, it's a straight run into Osijek. No bends. No cover. No fucking nothing. As you're aware, Vukovar fell to the Serbs a little while ago, so the whole area to the north, above the river Drava, and the south-east is open to them.

We've got to get through the net and into Osijek, and it's not gonna be easy.'

We'd all got the picture way back and Kit wasn't interested in any further discussion. He took a deep breath.

'Look, Johnny. Underneath all that crap you're a nice guy. But most of us have been here longer than you, and we know all of this stuff. The bottom line is that we play it by ear, like we always do. Now jump in your car like a good colonel and let's get the fuck out of here.'

The Colonel started to speak but thought better of it, striding back to his Cherokee, gunning the engine and hurtling out of the village. Steve and Pete were left staring after him.

'Sod it,' said Steve with feeling as he turned to Kit. 'What did you want to say that for? It was a bloody sight more comfortable riding with him, and some of his Vietnam stories were interesting.'

'Yeah. You could have left it till we arrived in Osijek,' Pete added morosely.

'Bollocks! If you don't want to walk, then shut up and get in. We've got to catch the bugger up now!'

It took about twenty minutes before we caught sight of the smoking rear end of the Cherokee. Johnny was still giving it some boot. Our speedometer showed ninety-five mph, and we still couldn't catch up with him!

'This is stupid,' said Kit, as Johnny, seeing us in his mirror, started to pull away.

Kit flashed the lights. Johnny didn't slow. Kit tried again, and this time the brake lights flickered and stayed on as the Cherokee slowed and finally came to a halt.

Kit got out and walked to the car, and opened the door. We couldn't hear the conversation but it took a good ten minutes before he returned looking pleased with himself. He climbed back in with us, turning to Pete and Steve.

'If you want to ride with him it's OK now. I've sorted it all out.'

'How did you do that?' Pete asked.

'Easy. I apologised. He's a good guy, but he lives in the past and can't get it out of his system.' And then, thoughtfully, 'Maybe we'll all be like that someday . . . Anyway, go and ride with him. He needs the company and we need the space.'

Johnny waved back at us before pulling away, and we followed close behind at a fast but steady speed of about seventy, while listening to the BBC World Service on the short wave. Sarajevo was getting it today, and the city's main street had been dubbed by the media 'sniper alley'. Those guys loved to tag and glamorise everything; it made better copy.

Slowing only slightly as we passed through Nasice and Jelisavac, we were forced to stop once again at a roadblock just before entering Koska. It looked professional this time, with two APCs and about a dozen uniformed men, thankfully Croatian regulars, who warned us in no uncertain terms that the road ahead was open to continual attack from artillery, mortar fire and, especially past Bizovac, highly trained Serbian snipers. We were advised not to continue.

Kit and the Colonel went into a brief huddle and came over to the rest of us with serious expressions and words of great wisdom. We were filled with awe at their military ingenuity.

Kit spoke first. 'Right. Now here's the plan. It's pretty complex, so listen closely.' He waited until we were silent and attentive.

'We shall leap into the vehicles with great enthusiasm in front of these inexperienced Croat soldiers. Then we shall drive like bastards from hell into Osijek, without getting hit by any of the Serbian mortar or artillery fire. Then we shall stop for a cup of tea. Is that clear?'

'That sounds easy enough,' Nigel replied drily.

'What happens if we do get hit?' Jim added his bit.

Kit gave him a stony glance. 'I learned my soldiering in the British army and the Foreign Legion. Johnny was taught military tactics in Vietnam by the US army. How can you doubt our skill at formulating military decisions? Anyway, sunshine, after due consideration there is no ... other ... fucking way.' He smiled apologetically. 'Sorry, lads, just keep your heads down.'

Johnny silently nodded in agreement as Kit thanked the Croats for their advice, explaining that we had a job to do and that it was in Osijek. After gulping down a quick thick black coffee we were on our way, with sweaty palms and churning stomachs.

The vehicles swiftly gathered speed, reaching about a ton. The Cherokee ahead could have managed a little more, I guessed, but we were loaded up with equipment and slower anyway. Too soon the village of Bizovac appeared on the horizon.

'Keep your eyes peeled for shooters,' yelled Kit as he put his foot down and hit the main street, hurtling through it in a blur of smoking buildings and staring villagers. We were through, and back on the main road, in minutes.

Only fifteen lousy kilometres left when the familiar 'crump, crump' of advancing mortar shells fell around us. Kit swerved instinctively as earth was thrown against the windscreen and a shock wave smashed against the side of the car.

'We're fucked. They've got our range already,' he screamed, battling to keep the weaving vehicle on the road.

Johnny wasn't faring much better as mortars fell thick and fast around his bucking Cherokee, which looked in danger of turning over as we steadied up and shot past him. He tried braking, without success, skidding and spinning around, momentarily stalling his engine.

The mortars stopped and we could hear the flooded Cherokee engine refusing to start again.

'Shit! Shit! Shit! What'll we do, Kit?' Jim was yelling. 'We can't leave them.'

'We can't go back either. We'd be sitting ducks,' Kit replied through gritted teeth.

A black cloud of smoke from the Cherokee's exhaust solved the problem. The engine had finally started, and with a burst of speed the Colonel was soon up with us. He was revving the engine like a madman as he overtook us again in a cloud of oily smoke and sped ahead, rolling from side to side, almost out of control.

The sickening crunch of mortar shells started up again, the side windows of both vehicles splintering as we swerved to avoid the advancement as best we could at this speed. This time they were punctuated by small-arms fire from close by, ripping past us with sounds like tearing canvas. With little opportunity for evasive action on these straight roads, we just kept on going. Some of the men swore, some prayed. It served the same purpose: kept the mind occupied until we were out of range. It took forever.

The rear end of the Colonel's beautiful Cherokee had been ripped away by one of the blasts and was flapping in the breeze. We could see Pete and Steve looking stunned but unhurt in the back as they turned to look at us.

The whole attack had taken somewhere between five minutes and five hours. Whichever, we had all aged ten years and were emotionally drained. We listened to Jim sobbing quietly, whilst he cursed at his weakness. Nobody looked at him or cared. This sort of thing affected different people in different ways. No shame was attached as long as you didn't let your mates down.

We had almost reached the outskirts of Osijek when Johnny waved at us to pull over into a brush-surrounded gully. He clambered out, a little unsteadily, and came back to us. His face was white and he was trembling uncontrollably as he leaned heavily against the battered Land Rover.

He tried a smile. It didn't work.

'I gotta get outta this business.' His voice was shaking as he tried to regain control. 'Look at my goddamn Cherokee.' It was a sorry sight, peppered with small-arms fire, dented by mortar blasts, and the back end hanging by a piece of twisted metal.

He lit a cigar and blew a cloud of thick smoke which hovered below the peak of his baseball cap. A few more deep drags and he stopped shaking, his colour slowly returning to a normal Californian tan.

'If only I could call in some air support. A couple of F-100 Super Sabres or Huey Cobras. We could blow those bastards to hell.'

'Come on, Johnny, you're not in 'Nam now.' Kit said it kindly, not wishing to make matters worse for the shell-shocked Colonel.

Pete and Steve had joined us with blackened faces, both looking shaken up from the hit the Cherokee had taken.

'Hello dere, man. Gimme some skin.' Jim managed to retain a sense of humour with his reference to their darkened features, but they were too far gone to respond and slumped to the ground before their legs gave out.

We all felt fairly safe in the gully, surrounded by dense brush, and it was decided that we should take this opportunity to tidy ourselves up and check the vehicles before making our grand entrance into Osijek.

That was when Ivan got it. No one knew where it came from. Just a single, sharp crack. The bullet hit him in the back and came out of his chest. He spluttered once, fell and stood up again looking bewildered. He stared at us, his eyes slowly moving to the tops of their sockets as he let out a sigh and collapsed across the bonnet. Everyone froze. It wasn't fair. We had thought that it was all over.

'Ivan . . .' Pete's voice trailed away as he rolled the body over and felt for a pulse.

'Anyone see where it came from?' Kit asked, already knowing the answer.

'Could be anywhere, just anywhere,' Steve replied flatly, looking at the pool of blood dripping over the bonnet on to the dusty ground.

'Check out the area before we make another move,' Kit instructed. 'If there's someone still out there I want him.'

We crouched behind the vehicles and scanned the whole zone with binoculars, but not a movement was seen by any of us. Kit placed Ivan's body in the back of the Land Rover, covering him with the Croatian flag that he had always carried in his bergan. His death had shocked us more than anything that had so far taken place, and we were numb with grief as we sorted ourselves out and climbed back into the vehicles after checking the surrounding countryside one more time.

We discussed the incident many times later. There had been no cover for a sniper out there, just flat, unplanted fields for miles and miles. It would have been impossible for a man to have got away without being seen. We would never know the answer.

Colonel Fontain suggested that a possible solution was the old Vietcong trick of burying snipers in the earth, a straw enabling them to breathe until a target came into range. Maybe he was right. It seemed a reasonable assumption. Nothing else worked.

With dampened spirits we arrived in Osijek. There were no banners to greet us, no trumpets to acknowledge our arrival. We were the saviours of the city but nobody cared as we limped through the streets straight into the arms of the local police, who, deciding that we were undesirables, took Ivan's body to the mortuary and locked us in the cells for the night to await questioning in the morning. We were tired and didn't argue. It was as good a place as anywhere to sleep.

A small man with dark hair, an olive complexion and an unsmiling face woke us early, peering through the cell bars as a police sergeant unlocked the door for him to enter. Colonel Fontain strode over to the camo-clad figure and shook hands, turning to us with a grin.

'I'd like you guys to meet Eduardo Florez, Commander of the First International Company of Croatia.' It was five a.m. and a cock was crowing somewhere in the distance. This should have told us something about the man standing before us.

Florez said nothing, merely nodding his head as Fontain did some fast introductions which were received with a deadpan expression through a haze of cigarette smoke.

We were immediately released by the police without any form of apology and taken to army headquarters in a large building on the west side of the town. Boarded and sandbagged against rocket attack, it resembled a fortress, standing almost untouched alongside the badly damaged adjacent buildings.

The Colonel had completed his job, delivering us to Osijek as arranged, and we said our goodbyes with a strange tinge of sadness. As he walked wearily away from us, his hunched, beaten figure bore little resemblance to the Groundhog caricature we had met in Zagreb only a few days before. Even Johnny would admit it now, that Groundhog had evaporated in the damp Croatian mist, somewhere on the road to Osijek. Colonel Johnny Fontain was burned out and heading homeward to the good old USA.

Florez went straight into it, no messing.

'As you already know, my name is Eduardo Florez and I am a Spanish ex-journalist, not a professional soldier.' His English was good, with only a slight Spanish accent.

'I was neutral and objective when I first came here to cover the war, but the neutrality didn't last long – I lost it in the second week. I soon decided which was the good side and which the bad. It's not black and white, of course; I know that. Now I fight for the side of right. I fight for the Croatian people.'

He paused for effect, continuing in a more positive tone.

'These people are being persecuted on all sides by armies more powerful and better equipped than they. But the Croatian people have heart and they will survive with our help.'

Jim whispered, 'And so say all of us.' Florez cut him down with a lethal glare.

'I shall continue. My prime function is to collate information from behind enemy lines and pass it up through the chain of command for others to act upon. Your function is to provide me with this information and to train additional men to fight for the cause against the Serbian oppressors.'

Indicating that we should follow him to a large map of the area, he turned to Kit. 'Freeman, isn't it? I gather from Colonel Fontain that you have been commissioned in the Croatian Army as a lieutenant. Is this correct?'

Kit pulled out a photo ID card which none of us had seen before and put it on the table. It read: 'Darren Abbey. Republika Hrvatska. Vojna Iskaznica. R436467. Rank of zapovjednik voda'.

'A false name, Mr Freeman. Never mind. Your documents are

in order. You will assume the position of second-in-command and the responsibility of training the men up to your standards.' He handed the ID back to Kit.

'Now to the map. Osijek lies south of the Drava river, as you see. To the north we have our front line, which is a few metres from the woods. The Serbian front line cuts through the woods and curves through the zoo on our left.'

'The zoo?' Steve broke in. 'A proper zoo!'

'Yes. The Osijek Zoo.'

Jim had to have his say. 'Do you mean a zoo with lions and tigers and all that stuff?'

'Yes. That's what I mean.' Florez was getting impatient. 'OK for me to carry on?'

'Sorry.' Jim apologised for the interruption.

'The Serbs have many tanks and artillery pieces. In addition they have some air support . . . little, but some. We have none of these things at the moment. Just men who are prepared to die and will do so if they are not properly trained.'

He paused once again as Kit looked over the map with a practised eye.

'Mines. Have the Serbs laid mines?' Kit queried immediately.

'Yes. There are mines on the north side of the river. But we are not equipped or experienced enough to deal with them.'

'OK. That'll be one of our first jobs.' Kit was enjoying this. 'The Serb tanks. What have they got?' he continued.

'Mostly T-55s.'

'Mmmm . . . T-55s. A range of about twelve hundred metres with their 100mm guns. I guess they can hit your front line easily.'

Commander Florez didn't bother to answer this hypothetical question, walking back to his desk to light yet another cigarette as he turned to Kit and said, 'Perhaps it would be wise for you all to familiarise yourself with the town for the rest of the day. I have important things to do right now. We can continue our discussion tomorrow when you have patrolled the area and observed our defences.'

'That suits me fine, Commander Florez. One last thing. Where do we sleep?'

'Oh. Of course, forgive me. You and your men can stay in this building. We have three floors and there are many soldiers sleeping here already. Some are your countrymen. Now I must go. I shall see you tomorrow.'

The map became the centre of attention for the next half an hour as the men discussed tactics and objectives. Jim and Pete, losing interest after about ten minutes, decided to bring the gear in and sort out some living accommodation for us.

The whole building was empty. Everyone was out on patrol, training or at the front, which gave the three of us a great opportunity to look around before Kit, Steve and Nigel joined us on the first floor.

'This fuckin' place is disgusting! Look at it! It's like a pig sty.'

Kit was right. The stench alone made us feel sick. The floors were covered in clothes, beer cans, mildewed takeaway food cartons and rat droppings. Piles of ammunition were stacked up against a wall, making the place a time bomb waiting to go off.

'There's no way I'm sleeping in this shit hole. We'll take that corner over there,' Kit said, pointing at the east window area as he started kicking the clothing and rubbish into a pile away from his chosen place.

'Open the windows and get rid of the stink,' he told Pete. 'Now, you lot, get some water and clean the floor. Then we'll put our stuff down.'

Everyone set to and cleaned up, until the floor was sparkling. Then we laid our sleeping bags in a neat line and waited for the return of the original inhabitants. This could be entertaining.

An hour drifted past as we dozed on our sleeping bags before the silence was shattered by the clatter of heavy boots and boisterous voices. We looked up to see four Croat soldiers standing in front of us, staring at the pile of rubbish that was once their home.

This could be a problem. We didn't have Ivan around any longer to translate for us. We looked at Kit as he searched through his memory banks for a suitable phrase.

'*Dobar dan gospoda.*' Good afternoon, gentlemen. So far, so good.

The largest of the soldiers looked at Kit, measuring him up, then growled, '*Sta ovo znaci?*' What does this mean?

We all understood the question from our brief lesson with Ivan. Kit, however, had run out of replies, so he stood up and tried to look superior. 'It means that I am a lieutenant in your army, my sons, and you are simple privates. So if you want to talk to me get someone who can speak *engleski.*'

He thrust his ID card under their noses. They glanced at it, not obviously impressed.

'*Da*. You are *engleski* lieutenant. We understand. We speak the English . . . a little.'

'Good. Then get this fucking place cleaned up and fast. You're a bunch of bastard slobs. While I'm here we'll do things my way!'

'*Da. Zapovjednik voda!*'

They sprang into action and within ten minutes the whole area was looking clean and tidy. Kit walked around, barking orders like a British sergeant major, insisting that they fold all of their gear in neat little piles at the base of their beds.

Later in the day the rest of the men shambled in, back from perimeter patrols and work parties. They were a mixed bunch of vagabonds, deadbeats and bums, with the occasional committed soldier, distinguishable by his professional bearing and manner, standing out like a flower amongst weeds. There were about fifty of them altogether, gawking at the orderly room in open-mouthed amazement. All were treated in the same manner and ordered to clear their respective areas until they were up to the standard expected.

We spent most of the afternoon wandering around the shell-damaged town. Kit commented incredulously on the locals. 'Look at them! I don't believe it. They're all back out again as if nothing had happened.' He was right. The people of the town were stepping over rubble and twisted metal as they went about their daily routines, ignoring the chaos around them as they bought provisions and stood in groups chattering about God knows what.

We borrowed a jeep later, driving out of town over the last remaining bridge across the river Drava for a look at our front line along the south side of the woodland.

Osijek had taken a bit of a beating last night as we were locked away safe in the jail. Artillery and rocket fire had lit up the night sky for several hours. The police had told us that T-55 tanks had moved into position close to the river on the western side of town but had been driven back by RPG-7-armed Croatian soldiers. The general view was that it was not a serious advance, but merely a test of the defences. The real thing would come later.

The shelling had come to an abrupt halt as the sky lightened. Yet another ceasefire had been called and, for a brief period, maintained.

It wouldn't last, we were assured by a Croatian captain. They never did. This was about the eighth.

We returned to our now spotless home with a clearer picture of the town and the problems which faced its defence. Kit immediately surveyed the map, anxious to get on with the job.

Later in the evening Commander Florez introduced us to several English volunteers. Carl, another instructor, from Liverpool, was lean and permanently mean-looking. He was known to Kit from an earlier period in Zagreb, when they were both with the 102nd Brigade. Dave had the words 'Yorkshire Ripper' painted on his helmet, while a young, fresh-faced, likeable kid named Roy looked completely out of place with these hardened men.

They told us that there were about twenty English-speaking lads in Osijek at the moment. Some British, AWOL from the army or the Foreign Legion, a few Americans and a couple of Australian Croats. Many more were expected to join us within the next few days as the war magnetically attracted men with a desire and sometimes a need for violence and legalised killing.

This was to be the Croatian army's only English-speaking company, and Kit Freeman its chief training officer. A formidable task, but as Kit said over supper, 'I like a challenge.'

Early mornings in Croatia are invariably damp and misty. This one was no exception as we all gathered in Commander Florez's office for an informal operations briefing. The Commander arrived a little late, allowing us the opportunity of listening to the BBC World Service in his absence.

The only news of any interest was the war. The announcer told us in unemotional measured tones that 'Reports from Croatia say there has been renewed shelling of the eastern town of Osijek. At least five people were killed when the town was bombarded overnight. Reuters news agency quoted Croatian police as saying that hundreds of shells and rockets had been fired from positions occupied by the Serbian-dominated federal army and Serb irregulars. The Croatian authorities said that this was the worst ceasefire violation since the beginning of January, when the current truce came into force.'

Not totally accurate but close enough, as small-arms fire started chattering once again from across the Drava river.

'Good morning.' Commander Florez swept in looking agitated. He wore Foreign Legion para wings on the wrong side of his DPM smock.

'Your attention please, gentlemen. Under cover of last night's artillery attack, a number of Serbian tanks managed to progress to the river. They were turned back on this occasion. But we must be vigilant. This was merely an attempt at probing our defences. Further JNA raids will follow. Of this you can be sure.'

His eyes swept the room, alighting on the new man, Kit.

'Have you any ideas on how to deal with this threat?'

Carl looked up, his eyes narrowed. He was obviously not very pleased about the new chain of command structure, feeling a little put out by Kit's position as second-in-command.

'Yes, Commander Florez, I've got a lot of ideas but I need more information about the enemy before offering them to you.' Kit was cautious about making decisions at this early stage. 'I'd like to spend part of the day with a few of my men checking the area. Tomorrow at the briefing I'll give you the information you need.'

Florez pursed his lips before nodding his head in acceptance and lit his fifth cigarette in less than an hour.

'Very well, be as quick as you can. Time is of the essence.'

The briefing became a general discussion, with section leaders detailing the previous day's action with reports on casualties and collateral damage. The Commander looked serious as he gathered his papers and headed for the door, intending to report to his superiors.

Kit caught him as he was leaving and an animated discussion took place out of earshot. Much Latin hand-waving from Florez indicated that he had given in to Kit's wishes. Whatever they were.

'What are you after?' Pete asked as Kit came back, glowing with success.

'I've got us a house,' he replied. 'I can't stand the noise of all that fuckin' snoring and moaning. So I told Florez that I couldn't operate under those conditions and he said that we could take any of the empty houses we liked. As long as it was down by the front line.'

This was great news and we were elated, gathering up our gear in readiness for a change of address as the rest of the volunteers looked on with a mixture of envy and pleasure: without Kit ordering them around they could slip back into their piggish existence.

Carl, Dave and Roy, together with a few other chosen ones, had decided to join us at our out-of-town residence. Now the foreign contingent would have their own centre of operations.

A desirable building was soon located and communications established by linking in the telephone system and liberating two television sets and a video player. Soon the house had all of the conventional reassurances of a home from home, if we overlooked the gaping holes in the roof from the last Serbian artillery bombardment. The original owner was himself a Serbian who had recently been killed by angry Croats, his family fleeing to escape the same fate.

Our small group had expanded considerably and now totalled thirty-two men of mixed nationalities, leaving just enough room in the house for Sprog and Pop, who we assumed still intended to join us at some point; although we had heard nothing from them since leaving them in Split a thousand years ago.

The BBC had moved into our lives a few days earlier, adding some glamour to a boring and uneventful existence. The crew, led by producer Stephen Lambert and co-producer Roger Courtiour, were shooting a documentary for the BBC TV series *Inside Story* – subsequently titled *Dogs of War*. They followed us day and night, sticking cameras and microphones into our faces at all the wrong times, exposing every little human flaw and weakness to the world. Kit Freeman was centre of attention in most of the footage, telling his life story and giving his views on the war in Croatia and the mercenaries' part in it. Carl, Dave and a man named Frenchie were featured artists, with Commander Florez and a few others in supporting roles. The interviewer seemed to enjoy talking to Dave, asking him about his obsession with the Yorkshire Ripper and the Black Panther. Dave, his gold front tooth flashing in the lights, was happy to oblige and with no hesitation told of his wish to emulate these psychotic murderers and kill people, legally, for the buzz.

As we left to recce the immediate area, Kit and Carl had a little 'splat' at one another over the question of which way to aim M-18 claymore anti-personnel mines. A stupid argument developed, even more ridiculous because the mines say quite clearly on the side, 'Front toward enemy'. Carl wasn't having it, insisting that the instruction was wrong. Nothing that Kit could say would convince him, and in the end, exasperated, he cut one in half, showing Carl the position of the 700 steel balls and the explosive charge. This settled the argument once and for all, but created more friction between the two men, which would bubble to the surface in tense moments.

We drove along the banks of the river Drava, past the hospital, and joined the front line at our side of the river, later crossing over at the last remaining bridge to have talks with the Croatians in the trenches as they curved past the edge of the woods. Their attitude to Kit's questions clearly indicated that morale was dangerously low. Many were going AWOL and the ones that had stayed were not confident of their ability to withstand a heavy assault. The simple fact was that they were waiting for something to happen. Today, tomorrow ... sometime. The frightening knowledge that their equipment and armaments were inferior to those of the advancing enemy made their plight even more desperate.

Many of them were simple peasant farmers and children with no military or battle experience. The fear in their eyes was contagious and we were all glad to leave them in their uncertainty. We returned to our new base to have a nice cup of tea while lazing in comfortable armchairs as we drifted into normality: watching football on our liberated televisions as the intrepid Michael Eley, the BBC cameraman, continued to run around the place, merrily sticking his long black lens up everyone's nose.

Chapter Six

. . . It's for the money. All this freedom fighter stuff is crap! We're here for the 'dosh'. Not so a few people can have their independence. I don't give a damn, as long as the money is there. At the end of the day, a war is a war . . .

The shrill yelp of the telephone jarred the tranquillity of our six a.m. breakfast. Carl grabbed at it, too late. Kit got there first, still chewing a faceful of scrambled egg. He listened attentively, with visibly mounting tension, his only verbal response a curt 'Yeah. Yeah. Understood. No problem.' The phone went down hard as he turned to the men, poised in anticipation, and in a matter-of-fact voice gave them the news they had all been waiting for. 'OK, we're in business.'

A red alert had been called as yet another squadron of T-55 tanks was detected approaching the river at a position south-west of the zoo. No one knew if this was the beginning of the big push or just another probe, as renewed artillery fire whistled overhead, creating more casualties somewhere in the centre of town.

Shelling continued steadily as the men dived into their battle gear, hurriedly slapping camo cream on unwashed and unshaven faces in an atmosphere of crackling anticipation. Weapons were feverishly loaded and checked for smooth operation until Kit told them to relax and do the job properly.

'My fucking bolt's jammed!'

'I can't find my ammo!'

'Our Father, which art in heaven . . .'

For some, this was their first action, and many faces were filled with blank apprehension as they joked with one another, smiling with tight lips and rapidly moving Adam's apples which threatened to choke them.

'Has anyone seen my fucking grenades?' Jim wandered around with a little boy lost look.

'There's loads in the truck,' someone told him. He slouched out into the freezing dawn, still in his underpants.

'Shut the bloody door!' Steve yelled after him, as our centrally heated room became immediately cold.

'Yes, Mum.' The door slammed, shutting out the forever damp morning gloom.

The men who were ready silently lined up outside the house. Carl reminded them that this was a real emergency, ordering the guards to return and take up their posts inside the building. Those who remained loaded the waiting lorry with explosives and weapons.

'Now don't drop anything!' he warned, as inexperienced hands fumbled with the heavy gear. 'You! Stay behind. We don't want to lose the fucking cook.'

The phone rang again in short, urgent bursts. Kit grabbed it in his huge paw and jammed it to his ear. 'Understood. OK, out.' He replaced the phone, slapping it with frustration, and stood up, shaking his head.

'Fucking good. Just hold back, he said. There's nothing really kicking off at the moment. No one is allowed on the roads. The police are stopping everyone.'

Commander Florez had informed him that the tanks had turned back . . . another false alarm. The men were instructed by a disappointed Kit to stand down and await further developments.

There was an almost audible sound of deflation as the frenzy of activity ceased abruptly. The men muttered amongst themselves, finally sitting on their beds, looking like boxers who had had their chance of a title fight taken from them by a crooked manager.

'Shit! I was just getting geared up,' spat Dave – the 'Yorkshire Ripper' – as he threw down his AK-47, which bounced on the bed before hitting the floor with a loud clatter.

'You prat!' yelled Kit. 'The fucking safety's off.'

Jim returned from the truck, shivering, his arms full of grenades.

'Ten quid a dozen. Roll up, roll up. Nice and fresh.'

Greeted by a wall of silence, he stared at his comrades with questioning eyes.

'Whassamatter?'

When Nigel told him, he dropped the grenades in disgust.

'Commander Florez is coming here at seven-thirty. So finish your food and then we'll spend half an hour outside, training.' Kit started to hustle them before terminal lethargy took hold. 'Now move it, you bunch of dipshits!'

The attack on the town had ceased, but the dull 'crumph' of mortar fire continued from the front line as the lads shambled out of the house and prepared themselves for the torture that is known as exercise. They ran in groups of three up and down the lane outside, dropping to undertake sit-ups on command with less than total enthusiasm. Kit didn't care about their commitment as long as they did it. He knew from personal experience that the fit fighting man is the efficient fighting man. The lads were surprised that someone of his size could keep up with them, but then Kit was full of surprises.

The final fifteen minutes of the exercise period was taken up by the aptly named 'murder ball', a game with few rules and a lot of physical contact. You just grabbed the ball and ran with it, touching a tin can to score. The opposition's task was simply to stop you. The few rules excluded the use of automatic weapons and hand grenades. Apart from these, almost anything else was legitimate.

A distant siren sounded the all-clear as Florez swept in, his arms full of papers and maps. The men were told to clean up and rest, and the section leaders were summoned to the first briefing of the day.

Kit was told to forget any plans he had made for infiltration behind enemy lines and concentrate upon training the team, as many of the lads would be a liability in their present state of inexperience. He agreed without argument that training should take precedence over a further recce and called the leaders together for instruction.

Carl, whose speciality was explosives, took a small group into the local woods to give them the benefit of his knowledge on detonation techniques, with special attention on the use of claymore mines and how to ensure that they were pointing the correct way! We could hear his curt Liverpudlian voice for a short while as we walked past.

'Now. This stuff is called detonation cord. Right. It's packed with PTM explosive. The average speed of that is seventeen kilometres a second . . .'

As we moved out of earshot Kit repeated his last remark with a smile. 'Seventeen kilometres a second? Wow!'

We sauntered along leafy woodland paths, as if out for a Sunday stroll, while discussing the function and application of facial camouflage; the importance of staying still, not smoking or talking and the different types of hand signals used for communication in the dense woodlands. The inexperienced amongst us were instructed on ambush techniques: how to escape from them, and more important, how to avoid them in the first instance.

Kit made a special point of addressing the Croat members of the group when he said, 'A lot of Croatian soldiers have died unnecessarily in this war because they spend too much time watching Rambo films. War isn't like that. You don't get up and walk away as the credits roll. Forget the bandannas, the ammo belts around your neck and the bloody stupid knives. Learn to be a proper soldier and you may live to tell your family that you fought for your country.'

He turned to the rest of us as they discussed his comments amongst themselves. 'The poor bastards. They're a Mickey Mouse army at the moment, but they've got heart, and that counts for a lot.'

Loud explosions and occasional howls of pain from the nearby wood indicated that Carl was getting enthusiastically stuck in to his favourite occupation of blowing things to hell. A young Croat private stumbled past us, white as a sheet, holding his hands to deafened ears. Kit stopped him to ask if he was all right.

'*Na sta se zalite?*' What's the trouble?

The soldier stared back, looking stunned, pointing to his ear. '*Zlo mi je. Vrti mi se u glavi.*' I feel sick and I feel dizzy.

He was told to return to the house and await medical help, and he muttered his thanks as he lurched away.

As the explosions continued, making it obvious that we were in an area of potential danger, it seemed wiser to move to a safer part of the wood for the survival exercise game of hare and hounds.

'OK, two of you cam up. We'll give you three minutes to disappear. Then we're coming to get you. If we find you before you can get back here, you're in for a good kicking, all right!'

Kit pointed at Frenchie, a Welsh ex-Foreign Legionnaire – so he claimed. 'You and Roy can be the hares. Now go!'

They were off like a shot, soon becoming invisible as the dense wood swallowed them up. Kit counted quickly and the hounds followed, eagerly prodding bushes with their rifle butts and climbing trees for an overview of the terrain. The hares lasted less than five minutes and were told in no uncertain terms what dismal failures they were.

'You're a pair of bloody fairies and wankers! What are you?'

Kit Freeman outside Osijek HQ © Stephen Lambert, Producer,
Inside Story: Dogs of War

Kit and Father outside Registry Office, Newcastle (Kit in Para No. 2 dress)

Kit at Mountain Pine Ridge, Belize, on 60mm mortar course

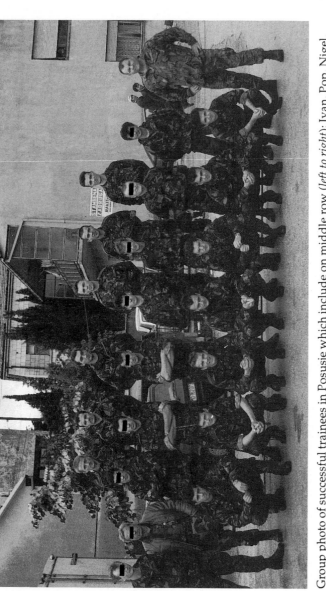

Group photo of successful trainees in Posusje which include on middle row (*left to right*): Ivan, Pop, Nigel, Paul, Mick, Sprog, Drago, Steve, Jeususe, Kit. (Others are local Bosnians who completed the course)

Kit training 'volunteers' in the correct standing position for AK-47 firing

Dave Tomkins (shoulder length white hair) passes on his knowledge of military weaponry to the volunteer force

Training photo – immersion with full kit in Osijek

D.A.F. truck with lid removed by Kit with circular saw; 'Because it did my 'ead in'

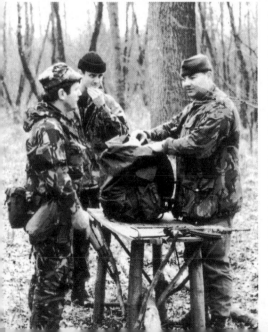

Above: To break the monotony – fun training in stolen dinghy

Left: Kit, Mike Stanton and 'friend' in woodland outside Osijek, preparing for explosive lessons. AK-47, AKMS carried as personal arms

Top right: Re-con operation behind enemy lines – sniper hide located and occupant captured

Right: Claymore mine detected with 'party string'

REPUBLIKA HRVATSKA
VOJNA ISKAZNICA

DARREN
(IME)

ABEY
(PREZIME)

R 436467

Kit Freeman aka Darren Abbey – officers ID used frequently in
tight situations

Serb O.P. 'taken out' by 66s at 35 metres

'We're a pair of fairies and wankers,' Roy and Frenchie repeated in solemn unison before being given a severe 'beasting' by their joyous captors.

Carl and his team joined us later, having completed their basic explosives training, and we all embarked upon the next phase of survival education: the dreaded E&E – escape and evasion. This lively interlude, which involved many kickings for those unfortunate enough to be caught, was followed by CTR – close target recce, also a disaster for the inexperienced soldiers. Finally the hard routine of combat operation in the field was drilled into the men – weapons at hand, belt kit on, all equipment packed away. No smoke, flame or noise. Some basic theory of compass work, map-reading, and night-vision aids was touched but not dwelt upon; most of the men were knackered by now and incapable of absorbing any further information anyway.

It had started to drizzle, making everyone look and feel miserable as we slumped on the wet grass, smoking and waiting for the next cruel joke to be played on us by the instructors. Carl pointed to the lake and Kit nodded his head. Now what?

'OK lads. Now you've rested up a bit, it's time for some boat practice.'

Kit led the men down to the lake where two rubber dinghies were moored. 'Six of you in there and six in the other one,' he ordered, just as Commander Florez appeared through the now heavy downpour, protected by a hooded DPM poncho.

'When I say "Ready", I want you to paddle like hell for the other bank. The winners can get out and the losers continue against another team.'

Kit gave the order and they were off, paddling like madmen for the opposite bank and the chance of a break while some other poor sods went through it.

They were about ten metres from us when Florez asked Kit for something and was given two hand grenades. He pulled the pins rapidly, and with an overarm motion lobbed them high into the air. They landed with dull plops just behind the slower dinghy, exploding almost immediately and creating cascades of water which rocked and nearly swamped the boat. He stood for a moment before walking back to the instructors, where they all doubled up with laughter.

'Oh, he is a card,' Steve murmured without humour. 'Perhaps he'd like a row in the lake and we could chuck grenades.'

Everyone was cold and soaking wet by now so the race was aborted and we returned to the house for some warming soup. Florez stayed chatting with Kit and Carl for a while before disappearing into the woods again on his way back to headquarters, leaving the men from the targeted dinghy to discuss how incredibly amused they were by the grenade-throwing incident, how much fun it had been, and what a joker Florez had turned out to be. Various forms of retribution were discussed; most would have got them shot.

Darkness comes early on rainy nights and after a hard day's work is often welcomed for its comforting release from the fatigue of the day. Men who ply their trade as mercenaries are no different; they also like to veg out after a day at the factory.

The bombardment of the early morning had not been repeated and even the mortar fire had stopped in the afternoon. Now the whole place was silent except for the English-language video of *Commando* that someone had nicked from a damaged shop in town.

With thirty-two men of various dispositions inhabiting the house there were bound to be arguments, some heated, but oddly few physical. In general, everyone got on just fine, making allowances for the odd eccentricities, of which there were many.

If you listened to them talking around the fire in the evenings, never before in the history of military warfare had so many men from élite fighting groups been in one place at the same time. SAS, Foreign Legion, Paras, Delta Force, Selous Scouts, Green Berets . . . we had them all here, with badges and stories to prove it!

Then there was Dave, of course. His needs were simple. All he wanted to do was kill – like the Yorkshire Ripper or the Black Panther – for that buzz. His glazed eyes hypnotised you as he spoke in a steady whisper: 'They had no feeling, no compassion. It's higher than any drug can get you – I think. Having that feeling of taking people out . . .'

The following morning, while the section leaders continued with basic training, Kit and other officers were told to attend army headquarters for a meeting with Colonel Florez. Discussion centred on a proposed covert operation behind enemy lines, to test enemy defences and obtain information on dug-in artillery positions and tank deployment. The meeting went well and Kit was enthusiastic, until Florez made the tactical error of informing him that he wanted his own men to lead the patrol, with Kit and his group merely observers. You could have heard a grenade drop as he made it clear that the new boys would be led by a group of thirty ex-woodsmen named – wait for it – 'Yellow Submarines'. We never did find out why!

In retrospect I think that this marked the beginning of serious friction between Kit and Eduardo Florez. There had been a few occasions in the past days when Kit had bitten his tongue when Florez had suggested something which he knew to be idiotic. But as a soldier, and a good one, he was used to taking orders and did so even if he felt the decision was wrong. On this matter Kit was adamant.

'Don't you think it would be wise to infiltrate with a smaller force?' he suggested.

'No, I do not.' Florez was equally intransigent.

Kit gazed around the room, desperate for eloquence.

'Look, Commander Florez, I have had a great deal of experience in sneaky patrols. Fewer men cause less disruption, are easier to control and are no less likely to succeed.'

Florez was quiet for a moment. It made sense, and he knew it, but he wasn't about to have his authority undermined. Finally he spoke.

'We shall do it my way.' His tone was sharp as he turned back to his papers, indicating that there was to be no further discussion on the matter. Kit had lost the first round.

The rest of the day went by in preparation for the night patrol. Check ... check ... check ... Weapons, night-vision equipment, grenades. Black tape over shiny bits and make sure that nothing rattled. Velcro pouch fasteners were taped over – they may be fast but they're bloody noisy.

We were ready as darkness crept across the river. A silver half-moon occasionally peeped from a cloudy sky as Kit, Steve, Nigel, Pete and I joined the team of thirty ex-woodsmen and climbed aboard the trucks. The BBC crew wanted to come with us, but Kit waved them away with a 'Not this time, lads' as we pulled away heading for the river Drava and enemy lines.

The Croats were a noisy bunch, laughing, joking and gesturing at the British mercs, who sat quietly pissed off and muttering at the rear.

'Buncha fuckin' morons,' was Pete's only comment.

'Maybe he's right. Up to a point,' mused Kit, still smarting from the meeting with Florez. 'People who live in an area can often sense if there's trouble ahead. We may just stumble into it like fucking tourists.'

He fell silent for a moment. 'But he is definitely wrong about the amount of guys he's sending and who's in charge of the operation.'

We reached our front line and disembarked, making final adjustments to our facial camo. The moon kept popping out to look at us from time to time, making Kit even more nervous about the chances of a large group of men advancing through enemy lines undetected.

The leader of the Croats was a small, cocky man with a whippet face and a large moustache, obviously well immersed in his role as partisan fighter. He drew his men around him and began softly to sing their anthem of freedom, or something. Nobody asked us to join in, so we just waited impatiently until they had finished.

At Nigel's suggestion we were tempted to break into the old Beatles song, actually giving tongue to the line, 'We all live in a . . .' but it seemed childish and not in keeping with our image as professional soldiers.

The Croat captain's command of English was poor, and we struggled to discuss our objective in any detail. He was inclined to be pig-headed and arrogant, ignoring any advice offered by a willing Kit as he strode away, instructing his men to separate into groups of ten and search the surrounding countryside for ammunition dumps, tank depots and artillery pieces. If found, they were to be indicated on maps. That was it! Off they scurried, like boy scouts on a badge-gaining expedition.

'I don't believe it!' Kit stood there watching them climb over the defensive mound of earth marking the front line and walk into the pitch black no man's land ahead.

'Come on, let's follow the last lot. At least we can save them from being slaughtered.'

We could hear crunching feet and the crack of breaking branches ahead as we rapidly caught up the final group, whose section leader was a little more co-operative than the captain had been. He listened to Kit's advice, slowing his men down and spreading them out a little as we approached the heavily mined northern zoo area.

Kit had brought with him his most advanced detection device – a can of party string.

'Spray it out in front of you and watch it settle. It makes trip wires easily visible,' he told us.

It worked perfectly, and although not MOD-recognised was bloody effective.

'Step over. Don't cut the wires. With a bit of luck the Serbs will never know we've been here,' he told us. With this herd of buffalo blundering about . . . some chance!

Our ears were strained as we moved stealthily towards the cages. Florez had been telling the truth; it was a proper zoo. Lions and tigers roamed about aggressively, the silver moon reflected in their staring opalescent eyes. We weren't welcome and it was obvious that we had disturbed their slumber as they paced back and forth, hissing and swinging their angry tails at us.

'Hope they don't bark,' Pete whispered.

'Shut up!' Kit breathed. 'Since when have cats barked?'

The ten men around us were doing their best to move inconspicuously, but they just weren't good enough. They stumbled and fell, talked constantly in stage whispers. One lit a cigarette, keeping it hidden in his cupped hand until Kit struck him a glancing blow on his arm. Soon we would be nearing the enemy lines, with little chance that our presence would go undetected. Something had to be done to avoid what looked like the makings of a massacre. The gig should have been easy but it wasn't. God knows what the rest of the plonkers were doing.

We had reached the northern part of the zoo when somebody must have pulled a trip wire. All hell broke loose; an explosion to our right blasted earth high into the air, rapidly followed by concealed muzzle flashes a few metres away. Rounds zipped over our heads like ballistic bees and were followed by rifle grenades flattening the overgrown bushes around us. Then it was daylight as a flare burst and twinkled overhead, illuminating prostrate bodies. The noise was deafening as it rebounded off the concrete walls of outbuildings. An elephant trumpeted. Somebody screamed. Somebody cursed. Somebody hurtled past, his clothes on fire. It wasn't a sneaky operation any more, more like a badly organised firework display. It was time to get out.

'Kit! Where's Kit?' screamed Pete. Our beloved leader was nowhere to be seen.

'Perhaps he's been hit.'

A young Croat of no more than sixteen grabbed Nigel by the

arm, blood pouring from a gaping wound in his side. *'Treba mi doktor.'* I need a doctor.

Nigel did not understand. *'Govorite li engleski?'*

'Da. A doctor . . . It hurts.'

'It's supposed to fucking hurt!' He grabbed the boy and slung him on his back, ignoring his cries of pain. 'Shut up or I'll leave you for the Serbs,' he said.

The game was up. Twenty crashing figures came pounding through the wood to join us in our retreat as yet another flare burst high above, followed by the chatter of machine-gun fire cutting a path through the undergrowth, too far to the left to be a threat.

'Just as well the Serbs are crap,' Kit muttered breathlessly as he suddenly appeared from the wood, catching up with the fleeing mob.

We made it back to the south of the zoo and out of range, only to be met by shrieking monkeys leaping frantically from tree to tree in their enclosures as they tried desperately to get away from this man-made hell . . . just like the rest of us.

Nigel dropped the kid for Kit to look at.

'Tut, tut, tut, and what have we got here?' Kit cleaned off the blood, exposing a deep trough where a bullet had passed cleanly through the skin. 'It's nothing to worry about,' he told the grateful boy as he applied a field dressing to the wound.

Commander Florez wasn't happy with the result of the infiltration attempt and, slightly chastened, agreed that a smaller group should try again the following evening. He didn't notice Kit's little smile of satisfaction as he was leaving, and nobody ever found out who was responsible for pulling that trip wire . . .

The British mercenaries slept late the next day, waking to a bright morning for a change. They sipped coffee and lounged in comfortable armchairs while the birds sang sweetly outside in the battle-scarred countryside, having adapted to the all-pervading smell of cordite and the intermittent sounds of mortars and gunfire. Last night's failure was discussed and they laughed at the memory of the Croat captain as he ran petrified in front of his men all the way back to our line. It was amazing that not one person had been killed with all that shit flying around out there.

Tonight it would be different. It would have to be. Reputations were at stake; a fact that Kit pointed out to the art class who were amusing themselves between patrols by painting symbols on their helmets – Vietnam style. It was a great pity that Johnny Fontain had gone; he would have loved this. Dave naturally went for 'Yorkshire Ripper', neatly printed with a fibre-tip pen. Other popular themes were 'Hired Gun', 'Hell Sucks' and 'Terminator'. It was all kids' stuff, and the older, more experienced guys wanted no part of it.

Steve sat against the side of the house, lazily stirring a can of vegetable soup with a dirty plastic spoon, watching sudden raindrops plop into the food with disgust. The waiting was almost over. Soon it would be time to start work. The kids with their logoed helmets and their talk of killing had depressed him, and he had felt the need to escape for a while.

'You OK?' Nigel joined him, also bored.

Steve looked up, irritated by the intrusion. 'Yeah. I'll be glad when it's over. I hate covert patrols.'

'Me too. All this sneaky beaky stuff gives me the creeps.'

'Yeah, I know. Maybe I'm getting too old for this stuff.'

'Maybe we both are.'

They fell silent, aware that there was nothing further to be said.

'Kit wants us inside to discuss the op. He asked me to come and get you.'

Steve slowly poured the rain-diluted soup away and stood up, following Nigel into the house.

Kit was waiting for them as they entered, maps everywhere. 'OK. You can all listen.' He stared at the rest of the men. 'But don't interrupt! The patrol will consist of five men. Steve, Jim, our friend Marko, because he is a Croat-speaking Australian, and finally Malaria. You all know he is an ex-Spanish Legionnaire.' He counted on his fingers. 'That's only four,' he said smiling. 'Oh, and then there's me, and of course the groupie over there,' pointing in my direction.

He pinned one of the maps to the wall, indicating to the chosen men that they should join him at it.

'We are moving out at one a.m., so it's a good idea if you get some shuteye after the briefing. It's gonna be a long night.'

The chosen men did as they were told and tried to get some sleep amidst the constant chatter and bantering that went on day and night throughout the house. Kit, however, continued to dive in and out of the place, checking, checking, checking, like an old mother hen.

The camouflage-sprayed Lada estate was loaded and waiting

as the men, rubbing sleep from their eyes, jammed themselves in and Kit slipped behind the wheel. 'The magical mystery tour is coming to take you away . . .' he murmured as he released the clutch and the overloaded car pulled away toward the Drava bridge.

This time we avoided the zoo and cut through our lines about two kilometres to the east, once again using the party string technique to mark trip wires. Our passage went undetected and we arrived at the far edge of the wood without disturbing so much as a sleeping insect.

'A piece of piss,' breathed a satisfied Kit as we crawled into the open fields. Black clouds now masked the moon as we headed for a clump of trees to our right and a last minute kefuddle.

'Now you all know why we're here,' Kit whispered as he looked at his map, illuminated by the dim glow of a Betalight. 'It's in and out. No enemy engagement. Just information. Right?'

We followed him as he crawled to the edge of the tree cover, where he stopped and listened, waving to indicate that all was well. We moved out into the open country, getting that prickly feeling at the back of our necks as the cold sweat began to condense on the surface of our skin.

The field was like a swamp after the continuous rain, and the slurping suction of the mud made our movements less coordinated than we would have liked. Very soon we were covered from head to foot in the stuff, making the facial camo cream applied earlier superfluous.

At Kit's signal we split into two groups and, still crawling, moved in different directions, each man carrying his chosen weapon plus L2 grenades and a 66mm disposable rocket, just in case it all went wrong.

We slithered around like crocodiles, manoeuvring over ridges and sliding into gullies. In the total blackness only the whites of our eyes were visible. Kit held up his hand. We stopped and listened. Somewhere close by and to the right he had heard the sound of a man coughing. He indicated a turn to the left and we crawled with difficulty to the top of a large mound of sandy earth, to be confronted by rows of tanks. They were everywhere – T-55s, T-72s. There must have been twenty of the hulking brutes, their huge guns glinting as the quarter-moon slid from behind the clouds for a few seconds.

'Shiitt!' somebody whispered as we dropped low and waited for darkness to return.

'Stay here. I'm going for a closer look.' Kit slid down the mound and disappeared almost immediately. In less than two minutes he was back, breathing heavily – a huge lump of moving mud.

Flashing teeth in his encrusted face showed us that something good had happened out there, but we would have to wait for the details. He looked at his watch and beckoned us away for our rendezvous with the other group.

We had to wait for them in the open. The few minutes seemed like eternity until we heard the prearranged finger-snapping signal. They arrived by our side looking depressed. 'Nothing,' said a disenchanted Steve. Kit looked at him, making a tut, tut sound. 'OK, we go again. This time in one group.' He slid away and the five of us followed in line as it started to rain once again.

We slithered eastward, in the general direction of the zoo, as heavy rain started up again, deadening the sounds of our sluggish progress through the boggy earth. Like so many times before, I was wishing that I had given this one a miss. Not only was it dangerous, it was bloody uncomfortable. They didn't seem to care much, these mud rats, as they moved their hips in unison like synchro swimmers.

All at once Kit stopped, holding up his hand. He had seen something . . . We followed the direction of his pointed finger and sure enough it was possible to make out the rough shape of a building surrounded by stacks of steel barrels. We lay in total silence, listening until the sound of faint voices could be heard, filtering through the beating rain.

As we tried to locate the source, someone struck a match, its orange flame momentarily illuminating a small group of Serbian soldiers sitting on the drums, trying to keep dry under a poncho. They were about thirty metres away with their backs to us, oblivious in their discomfort.

Marko nudged Kit and pointed at himself and at the building, moving his fingers in a walking motion. Kit looked sceptically at him for a moment. Marko smiled and nodded his head, putting his hands together in prayer. Kit stared at him, and with an expression of resignation raised a thumb, indicating his cautious consent. Marko was gone like a snake, without a second glance.

He was good at this, his thin body gliding over the mud without making a sound as he reached the side of the building away from the Serbs and stood up, waving at us. We could just make him out as he peered through the windows and checked the barrels before dropping to his belly and sliding back to our position. He pushed his mouth tightly up to Kit's ear and we were just able to make out the words, 'Ammunition. Fuel.'

'Fucking great. Now we can go home!' The last words came from Jim.

In the pouring rain Kit marked on his map the positions of the tanks, ammunition and fuel dumps. The job was done and we turned to make our retreat with Malaria in the lead position as we headed gratefully towards the wood line. We had covered about two hundred metres and were just standing up from our crawling position when a movement caught my eye, dead ahead. By the time I had given it some thought it was all over. A two-man Serb position, directly in front of us, had been missed on our way in but we had stumbled upon it on our way out. Thank God Malaria was awake!

A Serb soldier, hearing the sounds of movement, had looked up to receive a faceful of AK-47 rounds which literally blew his head off, leaving a smouldering stump where his neck used to be. The other soldier fearfully jumped to his feet with his hands raised in surrender, as Kit, from simple reactive fright, shot him dead with five rounds in the chest. 'Leg it!' Kit yelled as he grabbed their weapons and took off, slipping and sliding on the slippery surface like a pissed ice skater.

We ran like hell towards the inviting trees, expecting a machine-gun burst from the Serb lines to cut us down at any moment, but it didn't happen. What did happen was worse. The earth in front of our running feet suddenly erupted and a dozen angry Serbs appeared from a bracken-covered trench – we had missed these coming in as well!

'Spread out!' someone screamed as the whole area was sprayed with automatic fire. Chaos, total and unrelenting. We all ran around one another like Keystone Cops, trying to avoid being hit by the barrage, making it into the wood to regroup without any casualties. Jim had a rifle grenade with him, and intending to slow down any pursuers he chucked it in their direction – or at least he meant to. In the heat and panic of the moment he must have had a relapse. Forgetting his early training, he used a live round in the chamber to propel the missile, which, finding itself blocked by the grenade, exploded, badly injuring him in the neck and chest. He went down writhing in shock and agony as the rest of us looked on in horror.

For some reason the Serbs did not chase us into the wood. Perhaps they suspected that we might lead them into an ambush. Whatever the explanation, we were able to make it to our own lines without further hassle, carrying a bleeding and very sick Jim on a lashed-together stretcher through our lines and to the waiting car, as the early sun came up like a bright red balloon. It had been a long night.

Jim was worse than we had suspected and was rushed to Osijek Hospital, where there was talk of sending him back to the UK for extensive treatment. Marko had also been hurt in the blast, not realising it until we were back home and he found his shirt covered in blood. It was not serious, needing only a good clean-up and some stitches.

Most of the details regarding the engagement were kept from Florez. Kit didn't want to burden him with trivia. Jim's injury was explained away as a simple blowback caused by an excess of mud in his weapon, and the whole exercise was deemed a complete success, thereby proving a point about small group infiltration. Kit had won round two.

As we showered and cleaned the thick mud from our bodies Nigel asked Kit about his recce on the tanks.

He smiled. 'How many tanks did you see?'

Nigel replied, 'About twenty, maybe twenty-five. Why?'

Kit's smile turned into a grin. 'There were twelve, some of them broken. The rest of what you saw were nothing more than full-sized wooden models.'

'Cheating bastards!'

'Come on, let's get our heads down.'

Commander Florez returned in the late afternoon. Fortunately we were awake by then, in time for him to hit us with yet another idea. His superiors had ordered an attack on Velika Pumpa, using the knowledge gained on last night's recce.

He explained that the pumping station and depot situated at the northern point of the zoo was a strategic target which, according to intelligence sources, was being used as the central ammunition and supplies point for the JNA. Self-propelled guns and tanks were hidden there. He also pointed out that the target was heavily defended by experienced soldiers.

He continued, 'This information would account for the extensively mined northern area of the zoo and the Serbians' aggressive retaliation on your abortive recce with the Yellow Submarines.' He gave Kit and the rest of the men a meaningful look.

'Before we consider a frontal assault, we must gain more information on the terrain and available armament. I suggest another recce. This time we bring back a prisoner for questioning. That is all, for the time being. We shall discuss it in detail later.'

Kit was the first to speak after Florez had left.

'It's no good looking at those fucking maps. They're crap! Let's go and have a poke around and see if there's something there. If there is, let's do it. We've got night optical gear and there's gonna be the lowest moon in six days. Just do your rain dance.'

Kit and Carl sat drinking at the kitchen table, discussing the probability of success should the attack take place. Carl, who disliked and distrusted Florez even more than Kit did, was unhappy about the whole thing. He stared morosely into space, concerned by the scale of the attack and the probable casualties.

'You've gotta watch him. He doesn't know what he's doing.'

Kit wasn't listening and turned to Carl. 'Who?'

'*El bandido* over there. Pancho Villa.' Carl continued, 'One thing we mustn't do. I'm not dragging any kids into it. I'm not having that on my conscience just so he can make himself famous.'

Kit nodded in agreement but said nothing. There had been a silent vote of no confidence in Florez from day one, when it was discovered that he'd had no military experience before being handed the position of commander on a plate. Further discussion with some of the original section leaders had led to the conclusion that it was his media connections that appealed to higher authorities, and with them the opportunity for excellent world-wide propaganda for the Croatian cause. His track record before our arrival had been abysmal, with many casualties being taken on unsuccessful missions.

A general depression deadened the atmosphere in the room as the men fidgeted and snapped at one another, staring vacantly at burning cigarette ends and empty cups. Waiting around for something to happen was no one's idea of fun.

'When's it likely to happen?' said Roy, looking nervously at Kit.

'I dunno. Florez didn't say when. He just said sometime soon.'

The gloom was broken by a request for interviews from the BBC producer. Roy, looking dispirited, followed the crew outside together with Dave, Andy and a few others, and when asked what he was doing in Croatia, replied, 'I don't really know. My mum thinks that I'm working at Euro-Disney.' He turned to the camera and waved, his chirpy young face grinning through thick camouflage paint. 'Hello, Mum.'

Andy told the BBC that he was AWOL from the British army, and said unconvincingly that he would probably choose to stay in Croatia permanently because he was having such a great time. A voice added quietly, 'In a body bag,' to dark laughter from the rest of the men.

Dave offered his philosophy with a smile. 'It's like Vietnam here. You get everything you want. You're the law and nobody messes with you!'

Kit and some of the others had joined us in an attempt to lift their spirits when the field telephone burbled in his pouch. The transmission was brief. 'That was a badly broken-up message from the patrol, sounds as if they're in a bit of trouble. So we're going out as a back-up.' The interview was called to a halt as the men ran back to the house, grabbed their weapons and jumped on the moving lorry, with the BBC crew included on this occasion.

When we arrived on the hilltop adjacent to the wood line, Kit tried to make contact again. 'Foxtrot. Foxtrot. This is the bear, over.' All he got was a crackle of frying bacon. 'These radios are shit. It's doing my head in . . .' He tried again. This time another broken message informed him that it had just been a little skirmish and our help was no longer needed. He stood up as artillery fire could be heard in the distance. 'So this is what they call a ceasefire. The bastards.'

No operations were called for that night, so we lazed around and let the sweat dry on our camo-tinted skin. The distant gunfire was temporarily forgotten as our heartbeats returned to normal. The radio played softly and cards were dealt, more by habit than with enthusiasm. Less than an hour passed before boredom set in and the lads dropped out of the game one by one. By now the air was thick with cigarette smoke and a lull fell over the banter as the men yawned, stretched and scratched their unwashed bodies.

'What about that time you were in Surinam, Carl?'

'Yeah, tell us about that!'

It was beer and bullshit time again – art forms at which all mercenaries excel. Topics ranged from heroic exploits with women and wars to football teams and pop music; lies were told with such conviction and so often that the storyteller now believes them, even if nobody else does. Who cares? It's all part of the game. Amongst the banter and the beer cans being crushed, someone will always ask the universal question, 'What's your favourite weapon?' This comes almost always from a young, inexperienced kid with a bandanna around his forehead and tattoos on his arms. The older merc will look at him with an expression bordering on contempt, replying cryptically, 'Whatever I've got in my hand, son.' But it doesn't end there. Someone else always picks up the question. It's what most of them want to talk about anyway, waiting for the opportunity, waiting for an opening . . . waiting.

Guns hold the greatest fascination. Even experienced soldiers worship their weapons. They clean them, oil them, polish them, cradle and caress them, talking to them in hushed whispers that no one else can hear.

After the inevitable debate on merit has reached its climax and all the alternatives have been torn to shreds, the Kalashnikov AK-47 remains supreme with the mercenaries. With its formidable fire power of thirty rounds of 7.62mm cartridges, each with a penetrating core of steel, the weapon will spit out a hundred rounds in less than a minute, travelling at 1,600 miles per hour – at close range literally cutting a man in half! Awesome, available, reliable, cheap and beautifully balanced . . . Poetry in motion.

You can bury them, dig them up and fire them. Neglect them, abuse them but still rely on them. African warriors sing freedom songs dedicated to the Kalashnikov. US troops in Vietnam often ditched their issued M-16s in favour of captured AK-47s. From the snowy wastes of Russia, through forests, deserts, towns and jungles, the 'Klash Klack' may well be the last sound you ever hear.

Jason waxed lyrical about automatic weapons. 'I love them. The bright orange flame a yard long spitting from the barrel. The noise and the feeling that goes all through your body. It's a high . . . fantastic.'

Another young guy piped up. 'You gotta look mean! It doesn't matter how you do it, but you gotta look like you ain't gonna take no crap from nobody. Me, I always wear my ammo belts crossed over my shoulders like a Mexican bandit I saw in the films. It's bloody heavy, mind you, but with four or five days of stubble on my face and loads of grenades hanging on my belt, I look really hard. I never smile ... well, not often, anyway ...'

He dried up when he realised that his mouth was running away with him as Kit and the rest of the pros shook their heads in disbelief, sighing deeply.

'Shut up, you prat. Didn't you piss yourself when we went out last night?'

The kid died a little under the scorn of his superiors, knowing that he should have kept his outburst for the younger lads. Slowly he moved from his exposed position to join his peers in the corner of the room where they were reverently displaying their fighting knives to one another.

Their voices were hushed, not wishing to draw attention to themselves. 'Look at this one, it's a Buck, US army issue. Fucking great, innit? Feel that blade ...'

The men showed little interest in these toys; their knives were battered and tortured old friends, used for opening cans, digging holes, cutting wood for fires – if necessary for killing the enemy, but only as a last resort.

'They don't understand,' whispered Kit, overhearing the muffled conversation. 'It takes a lot of bottle to kill a man with a knife. It's messy and they never die straight away. They cough and struggle and you've got to pull it out and try again somewhere else. Sometimes the knife gets stuck and won't come out – then you're in trouble.'

Men who live and die by the gun have a love affair with the tools of the trade, and the subject is inexhaustible. They continued to swap opinions until the early hours as one by one they dropped off into a fitful sleep, dreaming of the ultimate weapon ...

Carl was absent from breakfast the next morning. This had happened before after one of his drinking bouts. As the day progressed, Kit's concern at Carl's absence escalated. He wandered about asking, without success, if anyone had seen him. It was suggested that Carl and two other instructors had decided to leave, but as their bergans were still by their beds the theory was discounted. Several hours and many questions later the truth was revealed. Apparently Carl – pissed out of his skull with Terry and Richie – had publicly mocked Commander Eduardo Florez, threatening to leave in the morning. Instead, Florez had ordered that they should be arrested in their beds by the military police and thrown into jail.

Kit thought that this might be a test to see if he would attempt to get them out. But he was resigned to their fate, saying in a matter-of-fact tone, 'Army regulations are army regulations. I can follow that. I know where I am. It's the civilian law I have trouble with. Anyway, they had too much knowledge of our activities over the next two weeks, so they had to be put somewhere out of the way.' He paused for a moment, finally saying, 'We're just guests in this country, a lot of people forget that!'

Florez was none too happy about the whole thing, making his feelings clear to the BBC interviewer later in the morning. 'I hate more and more the so-called professional soldier. Some of them are animals. They do not have any respect for the human person. They simply come here because they want to kill. This is not my way.'

Florez would no longer accept Carl in his group after the public embarrassment, and upon his release from jail he was forced to return to the UK.

The morning briefing, from a tight-lipped Florez, once again dwelt upon the proposed raid on Velika Pumpa. Croat intelligence had concluded from its information from our recce groups and other ground forces that the build-up of the JNA was for the specific purpose of an intended major offensive upon Osijek in the very near future, in a stroke gaining yet more territory. The UN were proposing to visit Eastern Croatia shortly and would have no choice but to accept Osijek as a Serbian-held sector when proclaiming borders. A previous infiltration by our recce team had shown that a frontal assault by Croat forces would be impossible, due to large earth deposits designed originally to stop water rising from the river when in flood. An alternative method of attack was needed and Kit had been given the task of finding it.

However, Velika Pumpa was not the immediate problem. The current ceasefire – yet another – was enabling the Serbs to continue their build-up without harassment. This was not acceptable to the concerned powers at military headquarters who, desperate for a solution, thought up a devious and illegal plan of action and offered it to Commander Florez.

When the good people of Osijek were fast asleep in their beds, four of the lads drove into town intent upon an errand of utmost secrecy, their mission – should they choose to accept it – being to kick-start the war again as quickly as possible. Kit, who had worked out the details of the strategy, led them to playing fields, churches, schools and already shelled houses, where they dug shallow holes and laid anti-tank mines, placed upside down and covered with sacks of sand. These were detonated with one-minute fuses, exploding all over the city, much to the merriment of the 'terrorist' force. The UN observers who were monitoring the Serbian ceasefire, assuming the explosions to be artillery or mortar shells coming in from the JNA, blamed them once again for breaking the agreement and gave permission for the Croatian army to retaliate against this act of aggression. We were back in business. The news broadcast of the following morning confirmed the official view: 'There was yet another ceasefire violation last night when the eastern town of Osijek came under heavy shell fire . . .'

The whole thing was supposed to be hush-hush and would probably have remained so had the *Inside Story* team not reported our involvement in it when *Dogs of War* was transmitted in the UK some months and ten ceasefire violations later. Like the volunteer badges said, 'Freedom Fighters for Croatia'. What the hell, we were only doing our jobs . . .

Our two main tasks for the foreseeable future were clear: to harass the enemy; and to check out his defences and deployment. We were going to be busy, busy, busy over the next few weeks, planning and popping across the Drava for a look-see.

A familiar sight met us as we returned from one occasional visit to the underground bar at the Osijek Hotel. Lying sprawled out on the settee in spotlessly clean camos were the welcome figures of Pop and Sprog. At last they had made it.

'About fucking time,' Kit said gruffly. 'Where the fuck have you been?'

'Missed us, did you? You Geordie sod. Leaving us behind to pay the hotel bill.' Pop looked at him, eyes twinkling.

Nigel came in, seeming pleased to see them, and shook Pop's hand. 'It's great to see you again, you old bastard.'

'Well, what have you been doing here while we've been living it up in Split? Where's Ivan, Jim and Pete?'

Kit told them how we had lost Ivan on the trip, and how Jim had been injured in the grenade blowback. He filled them in too on the Osijek gig, explaining quickly the impending attack from the JNA.

'Looks like we came at the wrong time,' Sprog muttered. 'More fucking aggro.'

'What happened at the hotel after we left?' Kit smiled in anticipation.

'You bastards! We had to do some fast talking at the nick when they arrested us, but in the end we convinced them that we were just employees of yours and not responsible for your actions, so they let us go. The big problem was that some prat nicked a painting from the hallway. Worth a bit it was, too! But as we didn't have it on us they couldn't prove anything. Which one of you took the bloody thing?'

We looked at Nigel. 'I told you it was valuable,' he said defensively, turning to Pop. 'It's a Renoir, you know.'

'No it fucking isn't! The bloody thing is just a copy by a local artist who is doing two years in the slammer for fraud. It's only worth a bit since he got caught and put away. Apparently he's sold Picassos and Van Goghs all over the world and become famous for his forgeries.'

Nigel sighed. 'Ah well, life's a bitch.'

'Then you die,' Pop added flatly.

We hung around for a while waiting for Steve to return from patrol and go through the same procedure of hand-shaking and insults. It was good to have Pop and Sprog back with us; none of the new lads here was quite 'family' in the same way.

A tour of the town seemed appropriate, so we climbed into the Lada and took off for a drive, first taking them over the bridge to see the front line and chat to some of the English-speaking Croat soldiers. Time had become an important commodity since the last briefing, and we didn't hang around for too long, dodging here and there as we explained the layout of the city and its defences, finishing up at a local bar to celebrate their arrival. As they were not yet established as members of the Croatian force in Osijek or under any commitment, we left them to wander around for a while, alone, whilst we returned to headquarters and the job in hand. We had started to drive out of town on our way back when Kit skidded to a halt, staring at a British-plated Range Rover parked outside a restaurant.

'Either that's the SAS or it's somebody trying to flog some-thing,' he said with a knowing look.

We pulled over, parked, and Kit disappeared through the

restaurant doors and down the stairs. He was gone for about a half an hour, reappearing with a face lit up like a Christmas tree.

'It's Mike Stanton munching away in there! He's come over to flog some gear. I've told him he can stay with us and save some money on hotel bills.' Mike was an old buddy of Kit's from way back, now involved in the enterprising world of arms and equipment supply to whoever had the crinkly green stuff. Mike had told Kit that Dave Tomkins, another much-admired old friend and colleague, was intending to make the trip to Bosnia in the near future, selling amongst other things a new American Armbrust anti-tank weapon; lacking backblast, these are ideal for urban combat in the confined space of buildings or vehicles. Dave, a well-known and respected character in the mercenary world for the past twenty years, was a civilian entrepreneur without formal military training, but none the less competent and courageous under fire; proven by some hair-raising exploits in Angola and Colombia over the past few years. Kit was delighted at the news, bubbling over with enthusiasm as he described him in great detail as lean, tanned and elegantly dressed, with a tendency to wear expensive jewellery. He continued rambling on with stories of past adventures as we drove back to base. There an impatient Florez was waiting with the news that forty or more volunteers were expected within the next few days. Kit took this opportunity of telling him about Pop and Sprog, and he asked to meet them as soon as they returned from town.

The influx, although welcome, would cause problems with billeting the men all in one place. Kit put forward the idea of moving out of the already cramped house into something larger and more suitable. Various alternatives were discussed and abandoned; it was essential that we were away from the town and close to the front line. Finally, the now disused school was suggested. It would give us all the space required, plus outbuildings which could be used for storage and a playground outside for much-needed drill instruction.

Life was upbeat for a while as the lads divided into two groups: the 'locusts', whose job it was to obtain new gear; and the 'vultures', who toured the area appropriating reusable equipment. Both parties descended on the town and outlying areas in the dead of night, borrowing, stealing and liberating essential items of bedding, cutlery and cooking utensils. Lorries went missing from neighbouring farms as the transportation of equipment took precedence over everything. A dozen microwave ovens appeared one morning, donated by a kindly shop owner – or so we were told by a furtive-looking Nigel. Florez never asked how the transformation of the school had taken place but he seemed happy that for a while, at least, the men were behaving like a military unit with a common cause.

Chapter Seven

These, in the day when heaven was falling, The hour
when earth's foundations fled, Followed their mercenary calling And took their wages and are dead . . .

Epitaph on an Army of Mercenaries: A. E. Housman

Beli Manastir is a cute little place, a place where you could spend a
nice quiet holiday away from it all. It least it was, before the JNA
turned it into a garrison town and armament stronghold. About
twenty kilometres north of Osijek, and close to the Hungarian
border, it was an ideal stop-off point for transporting weapons
from outside the country.

Convoys of lorries heading towards Beli Manastir from somewhere inside Hungary had been detected for many weeks,
convincing our intelligence that their final destination was the
Serbian front line just across the river from us. The big push was
coming and something had to be done to slow it down, fast. A
serious attack on the arms movement was not feasible at this time,
due to our distinct lack of suitable equipment and trained men,
but hit-and-run tactics were.

'Love it, love it, love it.' Kit Freeman was in his element,
surrounded by friends, old and new, and with sneaky beaky
operations coming out of his ears.

The relocation from the domestic bliss of the house into the
school was now complete. Windows had been sandbagged
against flying glass, bunks appropriated from various sources
and the gymnasium at the far end of the building turned into a
very efficient armoury, with its roof and walls sandbagged
against shelling and mortar attack. The whole process had been
undertaken with lively enthusiasm by the lads as the building
took on an appearance of military efficiency. They even had their
flag flying over the parade ground – a red and white chequered
shield, crossed with a lightning bolt and sword, bearing the
legends '3FC HV' and 'Freedom Fighters for Croatia'. A lot of the
men actually began to smarten themselves up; some even washed
and shaved!

Covert operations, now called 'keeni-meeni' by the ex-SAS men in the group – a Swahili term for the movement of a snake in the grass – were almost a continuous activity, being undertaken throughout the day and night as information on enemy movements was collated and returned to army headquarters in Osijek for assessment. Kit, in a moment of madness, did a skinny-dip night-time swim across the Drava, returning with a detailed layout of the Serbian-placed mines. Although we all knew they existed, their number and exact positions on the far bank were unknown and had been a constant worry since our arrival in Osijek. Kit couldn't rest until he had checked them out and indicated them on our maps. Later, though, he regretted his expedition, as he tried in vain to remove the camo cream from his huge body.

Most of the new consignment of men had now arrived; from France, America, Spain, Germany and the UK and of course various parts of Yugoslavia. Many, far too many, were inexperienced. Some were simply adventurers out for a fast but risky buck. A few were useless, condemned forever to the kitchen and a long way from anything that went bang or fired a projectile.

The BBC crew continued to float about the place, finally deciding after about a month that there was enough in the can. The finished product – shown on television in 1992 – was an ambiguous overview of a bunch of vagabonds, outlaws and Walter Mittys . . . frighteningly close to the truth.

Payment for performing in this epic was by way of a candlelit dinner for fifteen men in Osijek, names being drawn democratically from a helmet. It was a pleasant evening, only slightly marred by the whistle of Serbian artillery shells passing overhead as we reached the second course of *lignji* (squid) or *govedina* (beef). Most of the lads were sorry to see the BBC go. The crew and directors had done their job well and should be congratulated for their unobtrusive handling of the occasional tense moment, and their subtle conclusion.

The lads were more relaxed after the BBC had gone. Conversation and action with cameras and microphones around the place is never natural. Most of the time they were talking for the crew while pretending that a cameraman wasn't lying on the floor as they put their boots on. It had become almost a ritual, giving the Beeb what they wanted, acting out the role of 'dogs of war'.

Florez wanted a prisoner for questioning. 'Now. Tonight!' he said. It was already ten p.m. A 'snatch' group volunteered and four men grabbed their weapons and jammed themselves into the recently liberated and now camo-resprayed VW Golf GTi. The little overladen car hurtled away, its back wheels spitting mud and stones as it screamed off into the falling snow.

'This sneaky stuff is OK if you're out there doing it, but waiting around ain't my idea of fun,' said a jumpy Pete to no one in particular.

An hour passed. The dull thump of mortars continued, together with occasional small-arms fire; the sounds had become so much a part of life that you really had to concentrate to even hear them.

'Something's going on over there.' Roy was starting to pace up and down.

'Something's always going on over there. Sit down. You're making me nervous now.'

Someone switched the television on, and Pete jumped up and turned the sound down. 'Can't hear anything with that noise,' he said, glaring at the culprit.

'It's getting cold in here since it started to snow, innit?'

'Roy, why don't you shut up?' said Pop. 'The lads are out there in the middle of it and all you can do is rabbit on about the fucking weather.'

The room fell into an expectant silence, remaining so for the next twenty minutes until the sound of the returning car made us all jump up from our chairs and rush outside to meet it. The recce group, all in one piece, fell out of the car with a very frightened and bleeding prisoner – who had 'slipped on the stairs, your honour', judging from the fast-appearing bruises on his face. The man wasn't wearing a regular JNA army uniform, just bits and pieces of uncoordinated camouflage, leather pouches and a necklace of dried and blackened ears. He was a big, mean-looking bastard with manic staring eyes which flashed briefly as he was pushed unceremoniously into the building; suddenly he lost his cool and cowered as he blubbered away in Serbo-Croat, saliva running down his chin.

'Radio Florez and tell him we've got him a present,' Kit told Steve, as he dragged the man to his feet and sat him in an upright chair.

They stared at one another, eyeball to eyeball, for a full minute, as if attempting to psych one another out and gain the mental upper hand. The captor and the captured. The big Chetnik sneered, contempt spreading across his scarred face. He was making his second mistake; the first had been getting caught.

Kit walked away, trying to get a grip on his rising anger, then turned and yelled, '*Da li govorite engleski?*' as the recce team clicked off their safety catches, pointing their weapons into the mouth of the now shivering prisoner.

The man didn't reply and clutched at his throat as if choking.

'OK. One more time. *Da li govorite* fucking *engleski?*'

The man looked up. '*Da* fucking?' he questioned.

'So you understand "fucking", do you, my son, but do you understand English?'

'*Mogu li dobiti . . . vodu?*' Can I have water?

'No, you can't have any water, you Chetnik bastard!' Steve replied impatiently, kicking the chair away and watching the prisoner curl up protectively on the floor.

'Hang on a minute, Steve. Put him back in the chair,' Kit said. 'Let's abide by the Geneva Convention. Get me a flannel and a bucket of water,' he instructed Roy, who did as he was told, returning with the question, 'What's the Geneva Convention, Kit?'

'I'll tell you later. Give it to me!'

Kit dipped the flannel deep into the water, holding it as it dripped on the Chetnik's face. The man's tongue darted through his cracked lips, searching for the moisture as it ran past his open mouth. The big ugly bastard didn't look so tough now, as his eyes rolled and his body sagged to the floor. He looked up at Kit, suspecting that all was not well, and curled in a ball, sobbing with terror.

'Haul him up on the chair again,' Kit told Steve and Pop. Then to the Chetnik, 'Last time, sunshine. Do you speak English?'

The man cringed away but said nothing. Kit waited for a full minute, then rammed the soaking-wet flannel over the man's mouth and nose, holding it until he struggled free. He waited and repeated the process, this time not allowing the Serb to move his head away until he started to splutter and choke.

'If you don't talk to me, I will drown you. Understand?' Kit was getting pissy now.

The prisoner gurgled as once again Kit thrust the wet flannel over his face, holding it tightly and making it impossible for the Serb to breathe. He counted slowly out loud . . . eighty-five . . .

eighty-six . . . The man fell limply to the floor, his chest heaving, just as Florez entered the room, looking anxiously at Kit.

'Is he all right? You haven't killed him, have you?'

'He's fine. We were just having a little chat when he came over all faint, so I got him a cold flannel for his forehead.'

'OK. I take him now. You have other things to do. I have planned an ambush for tomorrow night and I shall be coming with you. Don't make any other arrangements.' Florez started to leave with two military policemen holding the prisoner upright. Reaching the door he stared back, accusation written across his face as he said quietly, 'I don't know if you men are the solution . . . or the problem!'

The room was silent as we looked at one another, digesting his words of condemnation. Everyone knew in their heart of hearts that there was some truth in what he had said, although no one would admit it. These men were the warriors of the storm and could not afford the luxury of guilt, shame or regret.

'I'd like to see how he makes out without us, the plonker,' Pete said tetchily.

'What's the Geneva Convention, Kit?' Roy wasn't going to give up easily.

Kit took a deep breath. 'Well, in a nutshell, the Geneva Convention is a set of rules which govern the way prisoners are treated.'

'Oh . . . so you were joking about drowning him, then.'

'Roy, my son. These bastard Chetniks are the scum of the earth. They rape, torture and destroy . . . just for the fun of it. When you've been here for a while you'll see what I mean. If they ever capture you, which God forbid, they'll burn your eyes out then cut your fucking head off and stick it on a pole, just to show people that they've caught a mercenary. Nobody is going to stop me from giving the fuckers a hard time . . Nobody!'

The whole group nodded their heads in total agreement. Many of them had witnessed, first hand, the results of Chetnik savagery and none felt any sympathy for the prisoner as we all trotted off to bed.

Early-morning drill had become an integral part of the day at our new headquarters. Up at six and out on the parade ground for an hour's square-bashing. Lots of 'get your hair cut, you 'orrible little man' stuff – all taken with humour and a pinch of salt. A military sergeant major would have had a fit with this squad of oddballs wearing low-slung six-shooters, cowboy hats, long hair and earrings. It wasn't easy for the group leaders to knock these mongrels into shape – most of them had left the army because they didn't like, or couldn't take, enforced discipline, and had no inclination to continue it with the volunteer force. After parade we went to the firing range for some much-needed weapons practice – cutting up targets with a warm AK-47 is much more fun!

Then came SOPG – standard operating procedure, grenades. We started with a lecture on theory, with dry runs for those without any experience of the beasts. Kit laid a few stories of grenade fumbling on the new men, just to frighten them into taking care. Tales of a 'green' squaddie who had dropped a grenade after removing the pin and releasing the lever, injuring twenty men around him and mercifully killing himslf – who would have forgiven him? Grenade pins being pulled out by foliage in woods and jungles, short detonation times, duds and liberated grenades, doctored by the enemy. A tricky business is grenade warfare, it seems.

A short period of hand-to-hand combat came next, with a few bloody noses substituting for battle scars, followed by a fast run around the playground. So ended the morning training period for another day. An hour lounging in front of the television set rounded off an active morning.

The daily patrols had received their orders from Kit and left to infiltrate the enemy lines once again, while Florez filled Kit in on the details of the proposed ambush. For some time now, snipers had been picking off men on the Croatian front line. Although the number of deaths and injuries was low, the soldiers had become nervous at being subjected to indiscriminate attack, and morale was suffering as a result. The snipers always seemed to strike as the light was fading in the afternoon and the ambush planned to hit them as they were moving into position.

Kit's old friend Mike Stanton had arrived to take up the offer of accommodation, and we were introduced to this fresh-faced, moustached man of forty or so, wearing jeans, checked shirt and desert boots. He stayed for the briefing, becoming more interested as the story unfolded, finally asking if he could take part. At first Florez was sceptical, but with assurances from Kit on Mike's competence, he finally agreed.

'We have less than an hour to prepare and cross into Serb lines,'

Florez pointed out as he applied camo cream and checked his AKMS and bipod. 'You had better borrow some gear from one of the men,' he said to Mike. 'We cannot wait for you if you're not ready.'

Kit helped him scrounge the necessary, saying, 'You've got an itchy finger, haven't you, Mike?' Mike just giggled away like a kid going to the seaside.

'Ready?' Florez stood by the door, anxious to get away.

'Yo!' Mike replied, now fully kitted out with other people's gear and ready to go.

'He's a fucking nutter, mind you, so watch out,' Kit whispered as we climbed into the truck.

For a tactical infiltration, the whole thing was a disaster. Kit and Mike just couldn't take it seriously. They pissed about, laughing and joking all the way to our lines, becoming silent for only a few moments as we ventured into the woods. Florez installed the ambush across the path, suspected to be the route taken by the snipers, and he and Kit set up their AKMS on bipods, ready. The others were positioned by Florez in such a way that had the enemy approached, our men would have been cut down by their fire. He wouldn't listen when Kit tried to explain the positional error, insisting that his was the correct decision.

We waited ... and waited. Three hours passed ... four hours passed in silence before a buzzing sound captured our attention. Nobody moved as we tried to locate the source. It was close, very close. Florez was looking around nervously. It was getting louder, rising and falling in waves. As the sound reached a climax, it suddenly dawned: some bastard had fallen asleep and was snoring!

I looked up cautiously, only to see Kit and Mike pissing themselves with laughter as they threw stones in the direction of the noise in an unsuccessful attempt to waken the guilty party from his slumber.

As darkness filtered through the dense trees it became obvious that the Serb snipers had taken the day off, and stiff as boards from the long wait, the ambush was aborted. There was nothing left but to pack our gear and move out, making our way back to the friendly lines after phoning ahead to ensure a friendly welcome from the Croatian front-line troops.

Things were tense between Kit and the Commander after the ambush incident. It wasn't anyone's fault that it hadn't come off as planned. Perhaps it was just as well. Had there been an attack, wiping our own men out with his haphazard deployment could well had ended Florez's career.

Over the next few days, the snipers returned with a vengeance, killing eight men and injuring twelve others. Not only were they popping away at the front-line soldiers, but our patrols were being ambushed as they went about their routine business. Some of the Serb marksmen were deadly. Some, you never saw, never heard, never sensed. A whip-like crack and a body was lying at your feet with a look of surprise on its face and a neat bloodless hole terminating its existence. Then silence as the birds stopped singing and your neck hairs prickled with sweat, waiting for the bullet that you would never hear.

It couldn't go on. The woods were fast becoming a no man's land as men developed mild illnesses, preventing them from going on patrols into enemy-held territory.

'Something's got to be done about these bloody snipers,' Kit said to no one in particular. 'They're doing my head in.'

Pop, Steve, Nigel, Roy and a dozen others nodded blankly.

'Well,' said Kit. 'I'm open to suggestions.'

'What about . . . No, it wouldn't work.'

'What if . . .'

'How about mining the place?' Roy offered.

'How can we mine a place with them shooting at us?' Steve replied with more than a trace of sarcasm.

'Got it!' Kit jumped up and peered at the map. 'The zoo, that's the answer. We'll create a diversion, that'll fuck 'em up.'

'The zoo,' said Nigel flatly. 'What are we going to do? Let the animals out?'

'Yeah! You've got it in one. Gather round, children, and make yourselves comfortable. Uncle Kit's gonna tell you a story. This is going to be a bit of a laugh if we can pull it off.'

The map was taken from its place on the wall and spread on the table for all to see. Beer cans were zipped open, cigarettes were lit. It was down to business. The Bear had a plan.

'We've got to draw attention away from the zoo. That's the first priority. The Serbs know we're after something, that's why they're bringing in the snipers, so we've got to create a diversion for a few nights and make them think we've lost interest.' Kit looked around at the men, who were attentive and excited.

'We'll change our tactics. Tonight, six of us will head towards

Beli Manastir and bivvy down through the following day. Tomorrow we'll hit anything that moves – or doesn't, for that matter. Now, the guys that come have got to be good and willing, so let's see some volunteers.'

Twenty hands shot up.

'Can't take you all. Only five. Pop. You sure you wanna come?' Kit looked at his old friend. 'It could be fucking dodgy.'

'Perhaps you're right, Kit. The old legs ain't what they used to be. I might slow you down.' He withdrew his hand with a sigh of regret.

'OK, I'll make the decision. Steve, Pete, Nigel, Roy ... no ... Damiar. We'll need someone who speaks Serbian.' He looked around the room at eager faces and pointing in my direction – the only non-eager one – 'And you as a spare. You're definitely a spare something.'

He pursed his lips at the crestfallen looks from the lads. 'Don't worry. Some of you can come on the zoo breakout when we get back. Anyway, this is gonna be a shitty one.'

Over the bridge again. This time keeping well to the east of the zoo, we clambered through our muddy trenches, smiling and saying, '*Dovidjenja*' – see you later – to the tired and scared Croatian soldiers, who gave us that look which clearly said 'madmen' or 'prats' – it's difficult to interpret Croatian looks. We were loaded like packhorses with L2 grenades, AK-47s, FNs, 66mm M72s, claymores and of course our secret weapon, canisters of brightly coloured party string.

It was going to be a long haul through this enemy-infested twenty kilometres of countryside. We were all afflicted with the condition known as fighter-pilot twitch, our heads twisting and turning at the slightest sound. We managed to skirt the Kopacki Rit swamp without losing anything or anybody in its oozing mire, and headed due north, finding every little bit of cover mother nature had provided. A Serbian helicopter worked the tree line, dipping and hovering as its spotter/gunner peered through his dirty plexiglass door-screen. For a heart-stopping moment we thought he had seen us as he suddenly veered in our direction, swooping low over the swamp before climbing with a roar and heading back northwards.

We slogged on through the desolate open country for the rest of the day – most of which was spent face down in the mud. The odd Serb patrol passed, often a little too close for our well-being. The main road connecting Osijek with Mohacs, to the north of Beli Manastir, created a wall of uncertainty as we lay on our bellies counting passing military vehicles carrying clean and efficient-looking soldiers and supplies southwards from Hungary. An ambush was tempting but foolish. Compromising our position at this stage would jeopardise the entire operation; this was a job for our return trip.

Steve was sent up the road for a few hundred metres and Pete down, giving us a signal. As the road became clear we scuttled across like rabbits and dropped into the brush, just in time, as another APC blasted past. The bloody thing looked brand new. Where did they get them?

We skirted Bilje, the only village on the route, and headed out into the hilly area and a little more cover. With Steve upfront as scout we made better time, and within an hour were over halfway to our destination.

'We'll find somewhere safe and bivvy soon,' Kit said. 'We've got to flank Beli Manastir in the darkness, so it's only going to be a short kip.'

A small hollow was found and we settled down to some cold grub – C rations and water; we couldn't afford the luxury of drawing attention to ourselves with smoke or smells from food cooking. The lying-up point was well concealed and its position so easy to protect that only one man was needed for stag. The short straw was duly elected, changing every hour. By the time you had managed to shut off and get to sleep it was time to get up again!

With brains only half in gear – due to lack of sleep – we started out again, rubbing our eyes, with dense expressions on our sagging faces.

'How long is it gonna take, Kit?' Pete sounded knackered.

'Depends,' was his disgruntled reply.

'Bollocks then!'

We ambled sleepily onward, through the damp morning darkness, tripping over stones and quietly cursing. Soon lighted buildings began to appear to our left.

'Beli Manastir,' whispered Kit.

The place was larger than I had imagined, with gentle traditional buildings and cobbled streets now illuminated by arc lights, enabling maintenance work on vehicles to continue throughout the night. Through the darkness, and outside the town, it was just possible to make out the monastery itself – after which the town had been named – now shared by Serbian soldiers and monks in an uncomfortable alliance.

We had been lucky so far. The twenty-kilometre trip had taken less than five hours, right through the centre of enemy lines with no real confrontation.

Kit held his arm up and we dropped like puppets with our strings cut. Singing . . . we could hear singing, right behind us as we melted into the ground. Three soldiers appeared, arm in arm, swaying as they staggered in the direction of town. There was no way they were going to miss us. We were lying across their path. 'Damiar, do something,' Kit breathed. 'Now!'

Damiar looked over at Kit, shrugging his shoulders with a 'like what?' gesture. Kit replied with an 'anything' expression. It was like watching a silent movie, only not so funny. One of the Serbs stumbled over Nigel's prone body. '*Izvinite*' – Excuse me – he slurred, not even looking down.

Damiar climbed to his feet, dropping his helmet in the grass, as inspiration spread across his cherubic face. He swayed forward, taking a bottle from the Serb's hand, pouring the liquid down his throat in one deft movement. '*Specijalno pivo, da?*' Strong beer, yes? The Serb looked at him with unfocused eyes and held his hand out for the now empty bottle.

Damiar fumbled in his smock, withdrawing his cigarettes and offering them in return.

'*Izvolite cigaretu?*'

The soldier continued trying to focus as he answered, '*Ne pusim . . . Prestao sam da pusim.*' I don't smoke . . . I've given it up.

We could all hear and understand the dialogue so far and it wasn't going too well. This sort of thing always worked in the movies, but we had to get a soldier who had quit smoking!

Damiar was beginning to panic as he offered his cigarettes to the others. Both refused. The four of them stood there swaying and looking blankly at one another.

Finally Damiar spoke. '*Da li bih vam mogao doneti neko pice?*' Can I get you a drink?

He had struck the right chord. They turned to one another and smiled, clasping Damiar around the shoulders as they all staggered back the way they had come.

'Fuck it. Now what?' Kit climbed to his feet as the three Serbs and Damiar disappeared into the darkness to sounds of tuneless singing.

This was a problem of major proportions. In the darkness the drunken Serbs had been unable to distinguish Damiar's different uniform and shoulder patch, but in the light of a bar he was going to be in dead trouble, and so were we.

'We can't hang around,' Kit whispered. 'It'll start getting light in a few hours and we've gotta be long gone by then.'

'We can't leave him. Shall I follow and do them?' Steve suggested.

'No, you can't do that. Someone will know they're missing at roll call in the morning.' Kit scratched his shaven head and stared at the stars in desperation. 'Shit, this could be funny if it wasn't so tragic. Let me think.'

We sat there on the cold ground as our brains went into overdrive, watching Kit fiddle with his radio.

'It's no good, we've got to move out. If we wait, the delay will jeopardise the whole caper.'

We gathered our gear together, this time having to cope with Damiar's as well, and loaded ourselves up, ready for the off. We looked back in the forlorn hope that Damiar would appear, but no such luck.

'OK, let's go,' Kit said in a resigned tone, leading us on our anti-clockwise loop around the town. We tried to keep our failing wits about us. There was a lot of noise coming from the square as lorries were loaded for a pre-dawn run southwards, reminding us that we were here to stop this sort of thing.

For some reason Pete had finished up getting lumbered with most of Damiar's gear, and his progress was suffering as a consequence. He stumbled and muttered curses, dragging behind us as we tried to make up some lost time. It wasn't going to work. His extra load was simply too much, so we stopped and waited for him to catch us up for a redistribution of his pack.

'I'm knackered, Kit. Can't we stop for a bit?' His face was white with effort as he panted up to us.

'Five minutes only. No talking.'

We took some of the gear from Pete, who visibly straightened before our eyes before lying back for a blissful few minutes' break. A sharp crack of breaking twigs and the rustle of bushes put a stop to that. Kit and Nigel grabbed their AKs and rolled to the side of the clearing, safety catches coming off as they went. Steve, Pete and I froze. Only our eyes moved. Something was out there. Kit and Nigel slid away to flank the intruders, leaving the three of us to play targets, pretending to hear nothing as we busied ourselves with the gear.

Crack! In the darkness it sounded like a pistol shot, and we instinctively ducked. 'Sod this!' Pete grabbed for his weapon and clicked off the safety, aiming directly at the sound of the noise.

'It's me . . . It's me . . . Damiar. Don't shoot . . .'

By that time Kit and Nigel were behind him as he walked out of the brush, hands in the air.

'You were fucking lucky there, my son,' Pete said. 'I was just about to let one go.'

'Yeah, it's been a lucky night all round,' Damiar replied. 'Two of the bloody Serbs passed out before we got to the bar and I left the other one with them. I'm supposed to be going back to sign them all in, but I don't think I'll bother.'

'Great to see you back,' Kit said hurriedly. 'Now let's move!'

Daybreak was cutting through the dense clouds as we skirted the sleeping village of Popovac, keeping far to the west out of harm's way. Our attempt at silent approach was almost ruined by a dog barking at us from the nearby farmhouse as we stole some eggs, causing some consternation but stopping before any damage was done. We scurried away like poachers in the night, heading for our first target, the main E73, the route through the Hungarian border taken by supply trucks into Beli Manastir.

It was time to find a suitable spot for a lying-up point. We all needed a good rest and daylight made travelling a hazardous occupation this far into Serbian-held territory.

'This'll do.' Kit threw down his pack. We had come upon a small copse a long way from any buildings, with a clear view on all sides. It was a good spot in which to kip unseen, unless we had to defend it. In which case it was bloody terrible.

Without any further discussion we all got our heads down, leaving Nigel on first stag with Pete to follow two hours later. We slept like babies, until woken by the 'cook' shoving fresh free-range eggs at us. We munched away slowly as Kit gave us a quick recap on the mission and its objectives.

'Now you all know why we're here?'

We nodded in unison.

'Just in case you've forgotten, I'll remind you.' This time we shook our heads, but he carried on regardless. 'We are here to harass the enemy and draw his attention away from our main target, which is the zoo. We are not here for a full-scale battle. We are not here for a face-to-face punch-up. We are not here for a fight of any kind . . . understand?'

'Yes, Kit,' we chorused.

'It's shoot and scoot. Blow and go. OK?'

'What are we going to blow first?' Steve asked.

'I'm glad you asked that, Steve, it shows initiative. I dunno.'

He had all day to think about it as we listened to trucks passing no more than a hundred metres away from us as they trundled their way south. In the late afternoon Pete covered himself with branches and crawled slowly to the edge of the road, reporting back that two tank transporters had gone past with T-72s on board. Pity we missed that one.

Typically, it had started to drizzle. A fine mist filled the air and darkened the sky, uncomfortable to work in but useful cover for our purpose. The question was, should we attack a convoy with RPG-7 rocket launchers or blow the road with anti-tank mines? One way we were sure of a worthwhile target, but with problems getting out. The other was hit and miss but we could be miles away before the big bang. A show of hands was called for. Democracy rules, OK?

'What if we attack and another convoy is following close behind? I don't fancy being caught out this far from home. We'd never get away with legging it.' Nigel voiced everyone's thoughts.

'That's no problem. One of us could go up the road and another down, signalling when there was nothing in view.' Pete added his opinion.

Kit was silent for a moment. 'If we had more time we could work out the schedule. These Serbs are methodical bastards. I'll bet the convoys run like clockwork.'

'Yeah, but we haven't got more time,' Pete replied, unnecessarily.

'We'll blow the road.' Kit's voice was matter of fact. 'If we set it up at night we can get back to Beli Manastir and cause some havoc there before making our way back to Osijek.'

Decision made, we sorted through our claymores, trip wire, timers and plastic-bodied Yugoslavian TMA-2 anti-tank mines.

'Are we gonna use timers, "clackers" or trips?' Damiar asked.

'It's gotta be trips. We don't know when a convoy is coming and we don't want to be around when it does. Do we?'

The gear was now sorted, laid out and checked. At last light we were ready to go, as the Serb chopper droned over our heads, following the road south toward Osijek – searching for terrorists, maybe?

In the gloom of drizzling rain we crawled across the open ground and up to the road. Nothing had passed for an hour or more, signalling, we hoped, the end of transportation for the day.

We dug like beavers for well over an hour, burrowing under the road as far as possible with our limited digging equipment. Trip wires were attached and positioned across the road, right side only. We weren't interested in empty trucks going back northwards. Claymores came next: some positioned each side of the road and facing inwards on a time delay to get men running from lorries, others facing outwards to pepper them as they ran away. The claymore anti-personnel mine is a vicious beast, spreading an arc of steel balls over sixty degrees wide and two metres high – like a static shotgun.

We completed the task before nightfall, returning quickly to collect our gear before beating a hasty retreat. Just in case we'd got it wrong and other traffic used the road before the daybreak convoy run.

'Check and clear everything. Everything! Bag up your shit and stow it in your bergans. We don't want anyone to know we were here. If it all goes wrong they could follow our tracks and ambush us further down the line.'

Kit did the final check, as always, before we moved out of our hole and retraced our entry route back towards Beli Manastir.

With the lightened packs we were able to maintain a good pace over the smooth ground, arriving at the town ahead of schedule. Men were moving around loading and unloading as we found a hollow and crawled into it for a kefuddle.

'Two of us will go in,' Kit said before we'd even had a chance to settle. 'The rest of you keep a good lookout. I don't want any surprises. Steve, you come with me.'

They kitted themselves out with grenades and explosives, checking their pistol and AK-47 magazines before reapplying camo cream to their faces and hands.

'You ready?' Kit said.

Steve nodded.

'Let's do it!'

They moved slowly towards the back of a storehouse until they were hidden from the street ahead, then, jumping to their feet, they ran like whippets, pressing themselves against the wall before inching forward to look around the corner of the building. All clear. They looked back at us, waved, and were gone.

There was a lot of noise coming from the town centre. Guttural engine clatter and exhaust fumes filled the air and drifted in our direction.

'That's a fucking tank,' Pete said in an authoritative tone.

'Reckon?' Damiar whispered.

'Too bloody right,' Pete confirmed.

'We'll soon know, when the lads come back.'

All I ever seemed to do was wait. I remembered the quote, but not the source: 'They also serve who only stand and wait . . .' Still, it was a whole lot better than running around getting shot at for a living, like these guys.

Nigel looked at his watch for the fourth time. 'They've been gone for half an hour,' he said. 'It's getting cold sat here.'

'Go and have a look if you're bored,' Pete told him with a smile. 'I'm sure they could do with some help.'

'Bollocks!' was Nigel's traditional response.

The engine noise died down and was replaced by loud, urgent voices.

'What are they saying, Damiar?'

'Can't hear . . . Something about a crane . . . lifting . . . dunno.'

A clanking, grinding sound took over, drowning out the raised voices. It was driving us mad. Like when the screen goes blank on a television and they continue in sound only, and you sit there trying to imagine what the characters are doing.

'Go and have a peep,' said Pete. 'I won't tell.'

'You go, if you're so curious.'

Pete shut up and sat picking mud off his smock, flicking it in the air.

'Look! They're coming back.'

The shadowy but unmistakable figure of Kit could be seen lurking by the corner of the outbuilding as he waited for Steve to join him. He gave a thumbs-up; everything was OK.

They dropped to their bellies and snaked across to our position in the hollow, arriving breathless but high on adrenaline.

'Did you get on all right?' asked Damiar quickly.

124

'Did we get on all right? You'd better believe it. Let's get the fuck outta here. This is no place to be right now.'

'Are we going straight back?' Damiar panted as we tried to put as much space as possible between us and the town.

'No,' replied Kit. 'We've got to make sure all of the roads into Osijek are fucked up. Hang on, let's have a quick shufty.'

He rummaged in his smock and withdrew a crumpled De rouck cartography map of Yugoslavia, bought in a Zagreb bookshop. Not very tactical, but easy to read, with all the trig points clearly indicated.

'Look, there's Osijek. We've still gotta do the 17-1, before or after that little village . . . Lug, isn't it?' A crease on the map made the name difficult to read. He continued, 'We've set the timers in Beli Manastir for one hour. That means,' he looked at his watch, 'we've got forty-five minutes before it blows. Bags of time.'

Off we went again, circling east towards our third objective. All at once Kit held up his hand, stopping us dead in our tracks.

'This is stupid. We don't need six of us to blow a poxy little road.' He pointed at Nigel. 'You can handle that, can't you? Take Pete and Damiar, some timers, mines and a few claymores. Don't bother about trips – just blow a few fucking great holes in the road.' He added a warning: 'And be careful about patrols. We've been lucky so far but they're out here. Move a little, stop, wait and listen. If everything's quiet, move on. You know the drill.'

He looked at Nigel, who was busily sorting through the gear, and added quietly, 'And look after yourself. We'll meet you back here in thirty minutes.'

They scuttled off, leaving us to embark upon our final mission; the railway linking Osijek with the north. Time was foremost in our minds as we headed westwards to pick up our final objective. This one should be easy; we could blow the rails at almost any point we chose. There was no tactical advantage in selecting a specific position – with the exception of a bend in the tracks, perhaps.

'There it is!' The dull moonlight etched the burnished curves of the track a few hundred metres before us. 'It's bloody exposed,' Steve murmured.

Kit was scanning the open area with his night-vision binos. He pursed his lips in doubt.

'Yeah, let's move up a bit. We can crawl down that depression over there.' He pointed to our right, where there was some marshy ground and a slight dip leading to it. 'Come on, we're behind schedule.'

The point at which we arrived at the track had been levelled with gravel chippings, making the planting of explosives and timers a simple task. The whole process took less than ten minutes of feverish activity. We were sweating like pigs as we slithered up the depression and, crouching low, ran back to our bergans, strapping them on as we made our way back to the rendezvous position.

Nigel and the lads were already there, faces beaming with satisfaction. 'All done, boss,' he said. 'Ready to go when you are.'

'No trouble with patrols?' Kit asked him.

'Nothing. It was a doddle. We did a line along the centre of the road. It's going to make a hell of a mess when it blows.'

'*If* it blows,' Pete whispered.

Kit checked the time, staring in the direction of Beli Manastir in the failing light. 'I'd love to be around when it all goes up. Oh, and I forgot to mention . . . Those tank transporters we saw on the road are there. Two lovely T-72s aren't going to be much use to the Serbs after all the stuff we shoved in them detonates.'

He looked again at the town and with a final disappointed shrug waved us on.

It didn't sound like an explosion at first – more like distant rolling thunder. In the dense night air, filled with rain and damp mist, the noise had become distorted and muffled. We stopped and turned, seeing the night sky take on an orange glow as repeated blasts melted into one gigantic roar, subsiding briefly before starting again on a lesser scale, much closer and to our left.

'That's the railway,' said Kit, as another series of explosions to our right joined in. 'Two, three, four . . . five.'

'And that's the road,' Nigel added. 'They all worked!' He was elated at his first solo success in demolition, insisting upon explaining in detail to a bored Steve how and where he had placed the mines.

Apart from the glow in the sky there was little else to see. We made our way back to Osijek and through the jubilant lines of soldiers, who had also seen and heard the results of our night's work.

By the time we arrived at the school, Florez was waiting by the entrance, having driven out from headquarters to meet us with the news that intelligence reports had confirmed all of the missions as successful. A convoy travelling down the main E73 from Hungary had lost four trucks carrying men and machinery. The arms and ammunition buildings at Beli Manastir had been partially destroyed, with two tanks reduced to scrap metal, and the railway and road had been badly damaged but with no casualties. Repairs to both could be completed within a week, we were told. It didn't matter; we had achieved our objective, and the diversional breathing space required, without loss or injury. Florez was a very happy man – which pleased Kit not a bit.

'That bastard's going to take all the credit for this and it had nothing to do with him,' he fumed as he angrily scrubbed camo cream from his face. 'But what can you do?' He shrugged. 'That's the army.'

We wearily dropped our gear where we stood as some of the lads came over to congratulate us, shaking our hands and pouring much-appreciated drinks for our parched throats. Nigel went straight into his demolition story, explaining in great detail how he had worked out the correct positioning of the mines. The kids listened. The vets didn't. Nigel enjoyed reliving it, though, and it was harmless fun for a change. All was well in our camp of vagabonds and gypsies, for the time being at least. The next heavy op was going to be the zoo. But not before a warm bath and a long, long kip.

The following day drifted past in a blur of semi-consciousness as we tossed and turned, trying to avoid fragments of conversation from the lads as they went about their patrols and other duties. The occasional loud voice filtering through a dense wall of sleep and the odd shriek from a passing shell interrupted our slumber. Nothing mattered much. The whole operation had been outrageous, and we deserved the rest.

'Jumping Jack Flash' finally did the job. Waking with a start, we were faced with a grinning Pop – who took his collection of Stones tapes everywhere.

'Great operation, Kit, bloody magic! Now get up, you lazy sod, there's trouble at mill.'

Kit sat bolt upright, staring straight ahead, his hand moving rapidly toward the AK-47 propped by the side of his bed. 'Whassamatter. Oh . . . Pop. What did you say?'

'We got a problem. Dave's knifed a German journalist in a brawl.'

Kit was fully awake now. 'There's nothing I can do about it, Pop. Has he been arrested yet?'

'Yeah. They came and got him straight away.'

'Well. That's the end of it then.' Kit sighed. 'Something like this was always on the cards for Dave anyway. You only had to listen to him to see that he'd go off the rails and do somebody one day.'

The room was full of chatter. The incident had caused quite a stir in the town last night, but no one knew any details, apart from the fact that a fight had started in a bar and a journalist had been stabbed. No doubt Florez would enjoy filling us in later with a lecture on the unacceptable behaviour of the mercenaries under his command.

We had slept the day away and felt better for it. As evening set in, Steve, Pete, Nigel and Sprog were playing cards, loudly arguing when Sprog kept winning. Kit and I were going over my notes, and the rest of the lads were sprawling around the place, doing nothing but with a lot of style.

What sounded like a heavy table being dragged across the floor in the next room grabbed our attention. Then the noise changed into the distinct clatter of continuous fire from a weapon on full auto.

'Fucking hell, we're under attack,' Pete screamed as he dived for the floor, followed by most of the others.

The noise stopped abruptly, at about the same time as we realised that we had taken no hits. But before we could move from our prone positions the door to the next room opened and a blood-covered Australian stumbled in, collapsing on the floor. Kit and Steve were the first ones up, dashing into the room to find an equally bloody Damiar and another guy holding his punctured arm.

'What the hell's going on?' was the immediate question. Unnecessary; the picture was clear. Damiar, looking white and sheepish, held a Zaggi in his limp hand, its magazine now empty and on the floor by his side. The walls around him were peppered with a neat row of holes from floor to ceiling.

'The fucking thing just went off,' he said mournfully. 'There was nothing I could do to stop it.' The gun dropped from his hand as he passed out.

The 9mm Zaggi is a very bad Croatian copy of the SMG, its major fault being a continuous discharge of the magazine as the trigger is pulled, with no way to halt it. Damiar had been cleaning the gun, tripped the trigger by accident and sprayed the room, shooting himself and two others as he tried, unsuccessfully, to withdraw the magazine. It must have been a terrible experience for those men, trapped in that room with an uncontrolled automatic weapon spitting at them, and with nowhere to run or hide. Everyone's nightmare.

Fortunately, although the men required hospitalisation, none of the injuries was fatal; thanks to Kit, who injected morphine into Damiar and saved his life with an insane, horn-blaring drive to Osijek Hospital where the doctors took over, pumping blood into his leaking body. He smiled up at us as we started to leave, murmuring 'Sorry . . . so sorry,' as he drifted in and out of consciousness. There was nothing more we could do for him, so we collected the two walking wounded from the casualty wing and returned to base, just a little depressed at the stupidity of the whole thing.

'Let's get the show on the road.' Last night's episode forgotten, Kit was planning the zoo caper. 'This time we'll take a team of ten. We need to be in and out fast. Once we've opened the cages we'll have more than the Serbs to contend with.'

A large-scale map of the zoo had been acquired, by kind permission of somebody who knew somebody who used to work there. We were all staring at it, trying to get our bearings.

'Everybody got it sorted then?' Kit started drawing impressive-looking lines on the map. 'This is the perimeter fence and here are the Serbian lines, through the north of the zoo. First of all we'll cut the perimeter wire in twenty places, just to make it easy for the animals to find exits. Make sure you've all got wire-cutters.'

'When are we going?' asked Roy.

'Tonight,' replied Kit.

'Tonight?' repeated Roy, his voice rising an octave.

'Tonight.' Kit smiled. Roy's face was a picture of dismay at the immediacy of the mission. 'Are you sure you wanna come, Roy?' he enquired.

'Oh yeah, 'course I do. Just asking, that's all.'

We were leaving at dusk, this time travelling light, with just wire-cutters and personal weapons, plus a few grenades, maybe a claymore or two . . . You never can tell how it's going to turn out. Can you?

Chapter Eight

Those who kill for pleasure are sadists, Those who
kill for money are professionals, Those who kill for
both are MERCENARIES. . . . that's what it said on
the T-shirt.

Operation Zoo Quest was finally adopted as a suitable title for our mission of liberation after many silly alternatives were tossed around and rejected. The name, chosen by a nostalgic Nigel who recalled watching the programme on television as a kid, was appropriate for the task, or so he assured us as we plotted and planned throughout the entire day, trying to predict the problems that would arise from releasing dozens of wild animals into the open countryside. Would they run? Would they attack us? Would they stay put? We decided that the probable answer was all three. It didn't help.

'We'll operate in three groups, each with a radio and call sign. I'll stick with the Bear. You, Steve, can lead one of the other teams. What call sign do you want?' Kit was cooking with excitement.

Steve thought for a moment. 'I think Snake would be an appropriate name for us . . . we'll be slithering in and out.'

'Fine, you plonker. Take Sprog and . . .' He looked around the eager faces, his gaze settling on a new American volunteer, an ex-CIA guy – or so he told everyone. 'Do you wanna go, Spooky?'

'Uh . . . Uh . . . yeah. But I ain't killing no animals, mind you.'

'Nobody's killing any animals, Spooky. That's not the objective. Will you fucking listen?'

He turned to Steve. 'OK. That's you, Sprog and Spooky in group two. Now, how about you, Pop? Do you want to lead a group? You've been a lazy old sod since you got here.'

'Yeah, OK, I'll give it a go.'

'Right. What about a call sign?'

'How about Hippopotamus?'

'Are you taking the piss? You can't have that!'

'Why not?'

'It's too fucking long to start with! Think of something shorter like . . . Frog or Pig. Something like that.'

'Sod off! Why should I have a crappy call sign when you're having the poncey ones. We'll have Hippo, OK?'

'Yeah, OK. You take Roy and Tommy in group three and I'll have Pete and Franz.' The latter was a German ex-GSG-9 lad, hard as nails, twice as ugly and known to all as Kraut.

I was given the option of accompanying the group of my choice, so I went for Kit's. Better the devil you know, as my old grandpappy used to tell me.

Kit called a halt to our planning brief as he went to the telephone. *'Gde ima doktor koji govori engleski?'* Where's there a doctor who speaks English? His Serbo-Croat wasn't perfect, but the hospital receptionist got the message, leaving Kit to wait, drumming his fingers impatiently, staring at the ceiling.

'Doctor? The patient brought in last night. Damiar . . . I don't know his other name. How is he?'

After a few minutes of one-sided conversation he returned to the table and our questioning eyes.

'He's had a bad night but is showing some improvement. The doctor said that an early diagnosis indicates that he could lose the use of his left arm where it was hit at the elbow. They won't know for sure until later in the week.' He sighed. 'Gutsy little bastard he was, too.'

There was a short silence as we all tried to think of something to say. Nothing came, and a cup of coffee seemed as good a solution as any to break the spell of descending gloom.

'He'll be all right,' said Pete. 'He uses his right arm anyway.'

'What for?' Roy asked.

We all looked at one another, smiling, then laughing at his naivety. The melancholy mood lifted and we returned to work on our 'Save the Animals' mission of mercy.

'Better check the radios,' Kit suggested. 'The bloody things are crap. What we don't need is to lose contact with one another out there.'

We checked, finding that only four out of a possible twelve actually worked – and those squawked and burped at us. Batteries were flat, water had shorted connections out, others were fit only for the knacker's yard. In fact, most of the gear supplied to us by the Croats was old, battered and in many cases bloody dangerous, requiring an almost constant programme of maintenance. Many of the weapons in use by the Croatian army were of World War II vintage, rusty and worthless, due to the arms embargo inflicted on them by the more powerful countries of America, Britain and others. We could never fully understand why the Serbians weren't penalised in the same way. 'Fucking politics,' was Pop's profound explanation.

Commander Florez suddenly appeared at the door without warning and Kit took the opportunity of asking him if any information had been obtained from the recently captured Chetnik. Florez was evasive and kept changing the subject, getting snappy as Kit prodded for an answer. His whole attitude made us suspicious. We even wondered if the man had escaped whilst in his custody and he was trying to hush the whole thing up.

'How are your plans coming along?' Florez asked, looking over our shoulders at the map of the zoo. 'Do you want some of my Yellow Submarines to help you?'

Kit struggled for a while before answering. 'Everything's coming along fine, sir, but thanks for the offer. We've got it sorted now. Anyway, I expect there are more important things for your men to do than mess around letting animals out.'

'Yes, you're right.' Florez nodded gravely, completely missing the irony in Kit's comment. 'When are you going?'

'Tonight. At dusk.'

'Good luck. Report to me when you get back.' Florez turned abruptly and left, bad vibes hanging in the air like the smell of dog shit.

We spent another two hours going through the motions of planning and trying to make some sense of the old zoo map, with its creases and tea stains obliterating much of the important detail. We discussed escape and evasion tactics should the whole thing go belly up, and made final adjustments to our gear and equipment. Now there was nothing left to do, apart from getting our heads down for a few hours before the sun set and it was time to do the business.

Clattering noises from the kitchen woke us one at a time. Pop, always the first one up, was making some scrambled eggs for us. We rose slowly, stumbling bleary-eyed to join him at the table, and ate in silence as the daylight slowly faded.

'It's time to go, lads.' Kit's voice had a finality about it that was disturbing.

We picked up our meagre equipment, trooping slowly out to the now open-top DAF truck. It had been modified a few days earlier by Kit, who complained that the low roof 'does my head in'. His alteration, though extreme, did allow us a clear view of the sky, and we registered immediately that the weather was far from ideal for a trip of this nature. It was a clear evening, with a full moon lingering behind dark clouds, constantly threatening us with its silvery light. It was a moon for werewolves to howl at, lovers to gaze at, astronomers to contemplate through telescopes. What it wasn't was a moon for wandering around enemy-infested countryside. We all knew it, felt it deep in our gut, but nobody said a damn thing as we turned left and started to drive over the Drava bridge for what felt like the hundredth occasion. Only this time it was different.

Franz saw it first, pointing down into the thick, mud-coloured water as it swirled through the weeds below the bridge. We stared, but could see nothing. 'There. Over there!' He moved his arm as the current swept piles of debris downriver. 'Look! On the opposite bank.' It was difficult to make out the shape for a while until our eyes had become accustomed to the gloom. 'Can you see?' Kit stopped the truck as the moon broke from behind a cloud, illuminating the surface in its eerie light. Yes, we could see. A body. No, two . . . three bodies; floating face down in the river, their white, bloated flesh shining in the moonlight. We watched as two broke away from the bank and drifted under the bridge. The third, a naked woman, was caught in the reeds by her tangled, shoulder-length hair which gently waved in the heavy swell. She was young, maybe only sixteen. We could see her face now as the movement of the water turned her body in our direction. She had been pretty, before her eyes had been burned out with hot pokers.

'What shall we do?' Sprog broke the silence.

Kit looked at his watch, suddenly making a decision. 'We can't leave them floating downriver like that. We'll get them on the bank and radio back for help. Come on, otherwise the current will drag them too far down.'

The first two bodies had now drifted under the bridge, coming to rest on our side of the river. The torrent – caused by heavy and continual rain – buffeted, lifted and sucked them back as we tried to grip their slippery flesh.

'For Christ's sake, get a grip on them!' Kit swore at the sky.

We grabbed at ankles, arms, anything, in an attempt to speed the process up, bile rising in our throats as we saw that one body, that of an old woman, had been slashed at the chest and its heart torn out through smashed ribs.

'Fucking Chetniks!' Pop spat, turning to Sprog who was now vomiting in the bushes. 'Bastards . . . bastards . . . bastards!'

None of us were feeling good, swallowing back the nausea, feeling our stomachs churn as we lifted her out of the river, watching water drip like a curtain on to the muddy bank at our feet.

The other body, an old man, was easier to lift. His arms and legs had been hacked off. All that was left was a torso. His toothless mouth was still open, showing blackened gums from wrenched-out teeth.

We gave the bodies one last glance before covering them with a poncho. A prayer seemed appropriate but nobody knew the words.

'What about the girl?' Steve asked.

'It ain't gonna be easy,' Kit replied. 'The far side of the bank is mined.'

'Yeah, I know. But we can't leave her.'

We crossed the bridge on foot and stood on the bank looking down. She was caught firmly by her tangled hair as the reeds wrapped themselves around her naked body like protective serpents.

'Get me a torch, rope and some party string,' Kit ordered Tommy. 'And tell Sprog to stop bringing his boots up and radio in and get someone out here to collect the bodies.'

Pete drove the lorry over the bridge, turning it to face the river and switched on the headlamps. The oblique beam picked out the silver lines of tripwires, criss-crossing the bank.

'Good idea, Pete. That'll help a lot. I won't need the party string now.'

Kit, Steve and Franz slid down the steep bank, stopping short of the first line of wires as Kit moved forward to cut them, indicating the position of the mines as he did so. Progress was slow and dangerous, taking a good twenty minutes before they reached the river edge. They looked at one another but didn't speak.

'Gimme the rope. I'll go in,' Franz said quickly, wading out chest high into the reeds and unsteadily tying it around the floating corpse. He paused as the lapping water twisted her body, pushing it against him. Her tortured face was next to his for a moment before he turned to the bank, the beam from the lorry headlamps etching deep lines around his tightened mouth as his Adam's apple jerked convulsively.

'Pull . . .' He guided her in gently, until she was at the bank side, her hair still caught in the reeds.

'Steve, give me a knife,' Kit asked quietly.

'You're not gonna cut her hair are you?' Franz pleaded. 'She wouldn't want it cut.' His voice was unsteady.

Kit ignored him and chopped away at the reeds until the body was floating freely. Then he threw the rope up to the rest of us on the bank above.

'We'll guide. You pull.'

We looked at the mud covered body, slim, youthful. In her early teens, as we had guessed. There was nothing to say as we carried her to rest with the other two bodies – her parents in all probability.

We wondered in which riverside village they had lived. Were they farmers? Perhaps in Nard, only a few kilometres away, or Belisce maybe . . . We would never know. There was some slight consolation, however, slender but worth hanging on to. One day the men responsible for this act could be the men in our sights. Revenge is sweet, sometimes more so than financial gain. Right now there wasn't a mercenary here who wouldn't have hunted them down for the sheer pleasure of seeing them die in agony.

We climbed aboard the truck as some medics arrived to collect the bodies, waving at them as we pulled away. The delay had lopped an hour off our schedule and dusk had turned into darkness before we crawled over the trench line, once again into no man's land.

'Shine on, shine on, harvest moon, up in the sky . . . Fuck this for a game of soldiers. When I was in 'Nam,' Spooky started, but never finished.

'Jesus! Don't you give us that Vietnam crap. We heard it from bleedin' Fontain all the way from Zagreb.' Kit glared at him. 'Now forget it, or we'll all start on our war stories.'

'Just tryin' to be friendly, brother. Don't mean no harm.'

He was really just trying to get the picture of those bodies out of his mind in the only way he knew how. Soldiers have a habit of using humour to disguise their fears and frustrations.

We kept in single file, nervous and twitchy. This was sniper country and we made beautiful targets in the moonlight. Kit held up his hand and we froze, then he waved us forward into a huddled group.

'The perimeter's ahead. We'll all go through at one spot, then split up. Steve, you can do the difficult bit and go through Serb lines into the northern enclosure. You can do the east side, Pop, and make sure you cut at least twenty gaps in the fence. Big ones, mind you. We'll do the west side. Our entry will be the RV. Got it?'

He looked to see if there were any questions. There weren't.

'If any group runs into trouble from man or beast then get out. The rest will have to take care of themselves. Finally, if you've got to blow any cage doors, do it last, with thirty-minute timers. See you back here in one hour.'

Osijek Zoo was built in the traditional style, with narrow overgrown hedges lining the visitor walkways. The wilder species were caged in rows and the less dangerous kept in walled compounds. Parts of the zoo had been fenced off in an attempt to provide certain animals with the opportunity of roaming freely in something close to their natural habitat. Bears were kept in deep pits; monkeys, chimpanzees and gorillas in large wire-mesh buildings. The whole place had a run-down look about it – and why not? It was right in the middle of a war zone.

We could hear the methodical 'snip, snip' of Pop's team cutting way at the perimeter fence as we crept away, heading into the centre of the zoo. To our left we could make out the tigers and panthers as they stalked us, thankfully on their side of the bars. 'Soon, my darlings,' said Franz, as he stopped and looked at a beautiful lioness. 'You can go out on the tiles soon.'

There was a bit of a commotion coming from the monkey house to our right, and we assumed this to be the arrival of Steve's team on their way through to the Serb lines in the north. The screaming and chattering could attract the attention of guards and cause a problem for Steve, but we consoled ourselves with the thought that the Serbs would probably attach little importance to the noise, being used to it by now.

Kit pointed at the reptile house but walked on. Nobody felt like having snakes or alligators crawling around the place.

We arrived at the far western point of the zoo and stopped to check the map just as the moon disappeared behind a nice large, dense cloud. It was time to start springing the animals.

'Where do we start?' Franz whispered.

'I don't fucking know!' Kit replied. 'The more I think about it, the more I realise what a stupid idea it was.' He had a ponder. 'We'll cut through the fences of the open area first; that'll free the wild deer, zebra, water buffalo and whatever else they've got in there. Then we'll move back the way we came, levering the padlocks off the rhino and hippopotamus enclosures. After that we'll do the cats, then we'll get the fuck out.'

The first part was easy, snipping away at the fencing until our hands were raw and the cutters refused to bite. The next bit wasn't too bad either. It was the third that was difficult. Every time we approached the doors of the lion or tiger cages the creatures wandered over and looked at us, standing there with their eyes flickering in the moonlight, a look of curiosity on their faces as they swung their tails and licked their lips. We all took it in turns. As one of us walked away from the door the animal did the same, settling itself down for a sleep at the back of the cage. We would wait for a while and try again. Each time the cat would uncurl itself, get up and nonchalantly pad back to stare at us.

'Let's give up, Kit. This could go on all night.'

'No! There's got to be a way. Let's find some food.'

Kit took off in the direction of a large building at the back of the cages, returning with a huge sack of raw meat.

'Go and get some more. There's loads of it.'

Four trips later we had bags of bones and meat piled at regular intervals outside the cat houses.

'We've gotta do this quick. Get the food as far back as you can keep chucking it in faster than they can eat it. As soon as they're gobbling, break the padlock but leave the door shut. It'll take them a while before they realise they can get out. By then we'll be long gone.'

The idea worked. The animals leapt on the food, tearing it to pieces and ignoring us completely as we set upon the padlocks with our bolt-cutters. The only one to give us trouble was the lioness Franz had spoken to on the way in – I think she had taken a fancy to him and wanted to be taken for a walk. She succumbed in the end though, growling and purring at the same time as she tore the food to shreds.

'Let's go!' Kit was already on his toes and heading for the RV when the sound of automatic fire broke the enforced silence.

'Double fuck!' Franz yelled. 'That'll make the animals panic. They'll be out of those doors in seconds and after us. Don't forget we're covered in blood from the food we slung in.'

The auto fire increased, followed by mortars. Somebody had been rumbled. We reached the perimeter at the same time as Pop and his lads, and scrambled through breathlessly. Obviously Steve's group were attracting the attention of the Serbian gunfire.

'We'd better go and support them,' Kit said, climbing back through the fence and into the compound.

We all followed him as he legged it in the direction of the gunfire, cutting back out of the zoo and into the woods to flank any attackers from the right. Suddenly it was bedlam, with mortars landing around us and kicking up the soft mud in our faces. We could hear running feet, and Steve appeared, followed by Roy a few metres behind.

'Where's Tommy?' Kit screamed above the roar of mortars.

Steve pointed back into the woods.

'Is he hit?' Kit asked.

Steve shook his head. 'No, I don't think so.'

'Let's go and get him then.'

We were getting mortars, auto fire and rifle grenades now as we picked our way through the mined woodland. This was not the way it was supposed to happen. It should have been a laugh, and for a while it was. But not any longer.

The shape of a charging figure appeared ahead, arms flailing as he tried to keep his balance, hurtling through the dark, wooded night, bumping into trees, branches tearing at his face and hands, everything a blur of green. The stuff was catching him up . . . passing him . . . coming back. Wood chips splintered from tree trunks as the impact of bullets sent them flying through the air like needles, puncturing his skin. He tripped, staggered for a second and fell, rolling into a ball as he smashed into a tree and lay still.

We stared at the inert body for a second as the firing continued, getting closer and closer and accompanied by the sound of thudding boots. Steve ran forward before Kit could stop him.

'You'll never make it!' he shouted after the running figure.

Tommy had fallen about three hundred metres away. The Serbs were almost on him now, intent on catching the intruders. Their bullets zipped through the foliage above our prone bodies.

Steve reached Tommy as he started to rise, shaking his head, finally clambering to his feet. They both took a deep breath and started their dash back to safety as we stood, giving them covering fire above their heads.

Steve stumbled and lost his balance, and Tommy tripped over

him, still running. He should have stopped, but didn't. He'd regret it later, but now was all that mattered. Run, Tommy run . . .

We could hear the Serbs crashing through the undergrowth. Steve rolled behind a tree. He knew he wasn't going to make it. You can't outrun a bullet travelling at sixteen hundred miles an hour.

Tommy had reached us by this time, trembling uncontrollably as he jabbered away with his excuses for not waiting for Steve, but nobody wanted to listen.

'I wish we'd brought mortars,' said Kit as he directed Pop, Roy and Franz to the left of the oncoming Serbs, who we could hear but still not see. 'Flank them,' he ordered, as the rest moved to the right. 'Chop them up and let's get out of here.'

The firefight was brief. A dozen M-26 grenades lobbed into the undergrowth with rapid bursts of AK fire did the trick. The Serbs – suddenly aware that they were facing stiffer opposition than anticipated – skidded to a halt as they saw us crouched in a gully, then turned to run back the way they had come with a hail of bullets surrounding their fleeing figures and cutting the foliage to ribbons.

Steve walked slowly from behind his tree, looking suddenly old and tired, his face white with a mixture of fear and fury. He tried the nonchalant technique for effect.

'This has turned into a right pantomime, Kit. Anyone got a fag?' Pete passed him one and lit it with shaky hands.

Tommy walked over to him, about to speak. 'Don't say a word, you gutless bastard,' Steve snarled. His tone made the unspoken threat as he turned away, paused, then faced him again. His eyes narrowed as he looked into the face of the man who had left him to die.

'Take care of it later, Steve, we've got to get back. The fucking animals will be on the loose after all that noise. Come on, leave it for now.' Pop picked up Steve's gun and handed it to him. 'It'll keep until we get back.'

Pop was right. There were a lot of strange noises coming from the compound now. We could sense rather than see movement as we picked our way, more carefully this time, out of the wood into the open country, gratefully reaching the mound of earth which preceded our lines.

It was a tense ride back, with few words spoken by anyone. Tommy sat in sullen, gloomy silence, his eyes avoiding contact with his comrades as he stared at the floor of the truck. It was going to be difficult, if not impossible, to live this one down – and he knew it.

Even crossing the bridge had lost its coming-home-safe feeling. Our eyes were drawn to the swirling water as once again we pictured those lifeless, bloated bodies.

The post-op brief with Florez was cut short by news from intelligence sources that our Zoo Quest liberation effort was causing the kind of disruption we had dreamed of. Most of the animals had managed to find their way out of confinement through our holes in the perimeter fence and into the woods. Although the information was sparse at this early juncture, reports had been received that a rhino had charged a group of Serbians engaged on a pursuit patrol after our engagement, killing one and injuring two others. Monkeys swinging through trees were causing chaos among itchy-fingered guards, and best of all, a lion had burst through the tent of the JNA field commander, attacking his aide and destroying operational maps and paperwork in the process. By mutual agreement the whole thing had been a good crack, if tainted by the Tommy and Steve incident.

The following days were filled with rumour. Croatians on the front line reported many incidents of deer and antelope grazing in the fields opposite. Hippos were seen blowing water spouts as they wallowed in the river, and one report swore that a chimpanzee was spotted dragging a grenade launcher through the woods. A sad occurrence was the death of a water buffalo, killed stepping on a mine as it made its way down the river bank. The stories went on and on, each providing fuel for the next person with a fertile imagination. One fact beyond dispute was the story of a Croatian corporal who took a baby monkey home for his kids to have as a pet!

Three days after the event Florez arrived clutching a communication from headquarters and handed it to Kit with a half-smile. 'Read this,' he instructed, and turned away, looking through the window to hide his amusement.

Kit scanned the document quickly before bursting into laughter. He turned to us. 'You have all been bad boys. This is a copy of a letter from Greenpeace, who have written to the UN complaining of your actions in letting wild animals loose to fend for themselves in the countryside. They say that it was an irresponsible act and one that should be punished. They also condemn the wilful destruction of trees and shrubbery.'

He turned to Florez. 'Are they serious?' he questioned.

'I'm afraid so,' Florez replied.

'You can't fucking win, can you?'

There was a lot of shit flying around the place over the next week as teams of investigators sought to trace the persons responsible for the release of the animals. Florez wisely kept his head down, denying any involvement and suggesting that the JNA were probably responsible. Without proof the matter gradually diminished in importance as many of the animals were recaptured and returned uninjured to the zoo. Some, however, made their escape from the area and remain free to this day, presumably still roaming the battle-scarred countryside of Croatia, wondering what the hell all the noise is about.

The battle at Velika Pumpa was looming, getting closer by the hour, minute, second . . . Many of the lads were nervous at the thought of a full-scale attack on a well-equipped and trained enemy. They muttered in dark corners, shaking their heads. Fragments of conversation were overheard, punctuated with the odd word: 'money . . . not getting enough . . . our weapons are crap . . .'

Bunks were often empty in the morning as their occupants disappeared in the night, heading for a less dangerous part of the country. Kit was philosophical about the whole thing, pointing out that as volunteers they were free to stay or go as they pleased. That was what he said anyway.

One last recce was called for, this time to determine finally the extent of heavy weapons available to the JNA at Velika Pumpa – not that the result would make any difference. The Croats had no choice but to attack, unless they were prepared to surrender or pack their bags and walk away.

Members of the recce team were selected by the democratic short-straw method. Kit would lead a team of three men, chosen by fate: Billy, a Canadian of Croat descent; John, a Scouser; and Jezz, from deep in the Welsh valleys. The CTR – close target recce – was planned for last light, taking in a fast observation of Beli Manastir on an anti-clockwise loop back to Velika Pumpa and home. They were going to travel light this time; belt order, weapons and a few grenades. Speed was of the essence.

The little Golf GTi was used for this recce, speeding off in a cloud of exhaust with the lads waving through the mud-spattered windows with apprehensive smiles. Nobody likes going on the last trip, the last patrol, the last anything, especially if you're combat superstitious – and everybody is. Just check out the St Christophers, crosses, medallions and lucky pieces worn or carried by the lads. Listen to the tales of bullets ricocheting off Zippo lighters, belt buckles, even wristwatches. They figure that it can't do any harm, and you never know for sure . . . do you?

We knew something had gone wrong when Steve woke us at four a.m., having got up for a piss to find the lads had not returned. Their beds were empty and the car wasn't parked outside. The operation should have taken no more than five hours, six at the most. They should have been back by three at the latest. Steve looked out of the window at the sky now streaked with cold, orange light as the morning sun cut through the dense clouds. Without turning he murmured, 'They've been snaffled. I can feel it.'

'No way!' Pete replied. 'Maybe they're back and just chatting to the guys at the front.'

We made some coffee, sipping it moodily amongst cigarette smoke and nervous chatter as another hour passed.

'They'll be all right. It's no big deal. Just a little hike,' Pop tried to console us. 'The whole thing is a piece of piss for Kit.'

'We can't just sit here. Let's take the lorry down to the front and find out.' Steve was already heading for the door.

'OK. But you'll see. They'll be down there having a cup of tea and a good laugh when we arrive.' Pop didn't sound convinced as he threw his coat on and joined us at the lorry.

For the next hour we drove up and down the line asking if anyone had seen the men return. A sergeant at the western point had been on duty when they left and pointed out the Golf, still parked a few hundred metres away, confirming our worst fears.

'Let's go in and find them,' Pete suggested without enthusiasm.

'Where do we look?' Steve replied.

'We'll head towards Velika Pumpa and circle around to Beli Manastir. They may be trapped and need back-up.'

Steve asked the sergeant if he had heard any sounds of small-arms fire in the night. He thought for a moment and spoke to one of his men, returning with the information that sporadic gunfire had been heard from the direction of the pumping station at about

1200 hours. The sounds had lasted for less than five minutes, after which all was quiet.

It was going from bad to worse. We sat, bleary-eyed, looking over the lines into the woods without the slightest idea of our next move.

'We'd better report this to Florez and let him make the decision. That's what he's paid for,' said Nigel, suddenly coming awake and taking control. 'Come on!' He climbed into the driving seat and started the engine, while the rest of us wearily stepped up into the back.

A loud yell from the wood line stopped us in our tracks. The Croats trained their weapons on movement from the trees. We looked in the direction of the sound, straining our eyes in the early-morning gloom. The yelling continued, and another voice joined in ... then another. The words were indistinct, barely audible above the chatter of gunfire in the distance. Then the bushes parted slowly, revealing four white figures with their hands high in the air, shouting at the top of their lungs: 'PRIJATELJA! PRIJATELJA!' Friend! Friend! We were too far away to be sure of their identities but knew instinctively who they were, and ran to the trenches to watch the disgusting sight of an almost bollock-naked Kit, Billy, John and Jezz hobbling barefooted into focus; hopping the last few metres to safety pursued by a dozen Serbs, who did a quick about-turn and disappeared back into the wood, away from the line of highly amused Croat soldiers.

They arrived shivering at our side, bruised, bloodstained and filthy. 'Good morning,' said Nigel. 'This jogging will be the death of you, Kit.'

'Get me some clothes. I'm fucking freezing.' His teeth were chattering as he jumped up and down to keep warm.

'We haven't got any spare clothes. Get in the car and I'll drive you back.' Steve climbed into the driving seat of the Golf and waited for them.

Ten minutes later we were back at base. Spooky took photographs of the four pathetic figures for his collection of memorabilia, as an angrily embarrassed Kit covered himself with a blanket. 'Get some coffee, somebody,' he demanded gruffly, still shivering in the warm room.

As they gulped at their warm drinks we waited patiently for an explanation, until we could stand it no longer.

'So what happened?' Roy asked, with the courage and stupidity of youth.

'Give us a minute!' John replied tersely. 'We're escaped prisoners of war, you know. We need time to readjust.'

'Yeah,' Jezz broke in. 'I might write a book on it when I get back home: *My Six Hours of Captivity and Terror at the Hands of the Serbian Army*. It could make me a fortune like those Gulf War blokes.'

'The title's a bit long and the porridge a bit short, don't you think?' Nigel said cynically.

It was obvious we would get no sense from them until they had settled in. The hysterical humour resulted from relief at their escape, and who could blame them? Being a prisoner of an unpredictable enemy is every soldier's worst nightmare.

Kit finally broke the silence on his third cup of coffee.

'Let's get this over with,' he said in a resigned tone. 'We'd done the recce on Beli Manastir and everything was going great. Then on the way back through the woods we lay up for a bit because there were a lot of patrols about – it was like Piccadilly Circus out there. We were in a hollow, curled up like babies, when a twelve-man section of JNA soldiers literally stumbled over us. They froze as we pretended to be invisible, but they weren't having any and stuck their guns up in a aggressive manner. With all that fire power pointing in our direction there was nothing else to do but put our hands up. They herded us together and I let Billy do the talking because they might have shot us if we spoke in English . . .'

Billy broke in. 'They just asked me who we were and what we were doing. So I told them that I couldn't say and gave them the big four – name, rank, serial number and date of birth – but they weren't very interested.'

Kit continued. 'The section leader seemed to be a new boy and didn't really know what to do with us, so they all had a little chat before prodding us in the direction we were going anyway. When they got us to the pumping station they slung us in an outbuilding and left us for about ten minutes before coming back and making us strip off. Then they did us over with their fists.' He pointed at the bruises on their bodies. 'I think they did it just for a bit of fun. None of them asked any questions, just battered away as we did our "ouch, ooh, agh" routine for about five minutes, then they got bored and left us alone.

'We had a chat about what to do and figured that tomorrow

could be a bad day for us if we stayed. The Serbs would have to do something, and we reckoned it was either a trip into Beli Manastir for interrogation, which was a no-no, or they would top us, which was an even bigger no-no. We all agreed on that . . . even Billy. We had a look around the building and found a few rotted wooden slats at the back covered by piles of sacks. Jezz took a cautious peep through the slit window at the front and told us the soldiers were about twenty metres away having some grub and making a bit of noise in the process. So we pulled away a few more strips of wood and with nothing to lose, moved the sacks and had it away on our toes.'

He pointed at their torn and bloody feet. 'Fucking painful running through the woods it was too. Look! I've broken my toenail.'

They all looked a hell of a lot more damaged than they were. Most of the cuts were superficial, caused by bumping into trees and branches as they ran through the darkness. Even the bruises were mild; they would have been a lot worse had the Serbs used gun butts instead of fists. They did look a sorry sight though, almost naked but for the blankets covering their scratched, slimy, mud-and-dried-blood-covered bodies; with Kit nursing a swollen left testicle which he refused to reveal for inspection.

Were we sympathetic? Were we commiserating? We were not. Getting caught . . . the plonkers!

Although the recce hadn't quite turned out as intended, the group had managed to check out some areas of Velika Pumpa as they were being herded away into the shed, enabling them to confirm the presence of self-propelling guns and rather more tanks than Florez had led us to suppose.

The result of the recce was phoned through to army headquarters and a briefing – which included all of the remaining volunteers – was called for 1800 hours that evening. Its objective was to devise and finalise attack plans for proposed implementation within the next few days.

Florez arrived early, loaded down with maps, compasses and weather reports as if preparing for a re-enactment of the D-Day landings. He scurried about the place like Action Man, with deep furrows creasing his brow but not quite managing to conceal indecisive eyes or the nervous tic that seemed to have developed over the past few weeks.

When unsure of himself, he had the habit of pressing his tongue against the inside of his cheek, creating a large lump which moved up and down as he studiously avoided eye contact. All the signs of a last stand were mirrored in his face as he called Kit over with the rest of the section leaders and poured himself a drink, lighting a cigarette from his previous one. It was obvious to us that this man didn't know his ass from his elbow, or, more relevantly, his butt from his barrel. Regrettable as it was, he was in charge of the operation. The men weren't too happy about going along with the game, hoping that Kit and the rest of the experienced officers would be able to convince him to follow their line of reason.

Fear hung like sweat in the air as the lads trooped into the briefing room. You could smell it on their breath, see it in their eyes, even feel the vibrations in their speech as they chattered inanely, voices rising and falling as the hubbub increased to deafening proportions. Battles are different from firefights, patrols and recces. Battles are places where people get killed in bulk – like discount warehouses. Piled high and sold cheap!

Commander Florez called for silence and blew a stream of smoke through his nose which briefly hid his face from the group. 'Your attention, please. Attention!' It wasn't going to work. They were here to talk, not listen.

Kit stood up, bellowing, 'Will you lot shut the fuck up for a minute?'

The roar of voices slowly subsided to a mumbling drone as most of the men looked in the direction of the officers and saw the impatient figure of Kit Freeman glowering at them. They shuffled their feet as they sat down in preparation for the bad news.

'You all know why we're here.' Florez spoke quietly.

Somebody belched loudly, causing a ripple of amusement to create once again a barrier between the officers and the men.

'I will repeat . . . as you did.' He looked at the offender, and a smile flitted across his face at the joke. 'You know why we're here.'

He pointed to a map behind him and turned to Kit, whispering something inaudible. Kit stood and moved to the map.

'Right, I'll make it brief. Most of you are aware that the JNA are poised to take Osijek. The build-up has been going on for quite some time now, and many of you have been on recces for the specific purpose of collating information on their supplies and weapons. Those that haven't can talk to those that have. The latest reports from Croatian intelligence have confirmed the intention of the JNA to attack and capture the town within the next few days. I'll say it again . . . within the next few days. So, lads, we gotta do it to them before they do it to us.'

The room was now silent as Florez poked his tongue in his cheek again, looking around the room with hooded eyes. He rose to his feet, attempting to take control, clearing his throat loudly.

'I'm sure that I can rely upon you to do your duty and drive the Serbs back . . . and demolish their armament . . . and soldiers.' He floundered, his voice wavering as the well-prepared pep talk ground to a halt under the suspicious gaze of the men lounging expectantly before him.

There were isolated catcalls from the back of the room.

'You gonna lead us in, Florez?' an anonymous voice enquired.

'From the rear!' Hysterical laughter greeted the one-liner, rolling around the room and coming to an abrupt halt as Kit jumped to his feet in an attempt to save the situation.

For a few moments he stood, saying nothing, and the room became silent under his accusing stare.

'OK. That's enough! Shut up and listen. What you hear may save your life . . . or mine.'

Florez tried again, but his mojo wasn't working. The delivery was mechanical, without passion or fervour – both essential ingredients for any speech inciting men to violent action. He'd picked the wrong bunch at the wrong time. Dying for a cause wasn't in the contract; they'd checked the small print.

A chair scraped and crashed to the ground as three men climbed noisily to their feet, walking out without comment – apart from a single finger in the air. The door slammed with a finality that cut like a knife through the remaining men. The whole thing was turning into a fiasco.

Kit stood his ground. 'Any of the rest of you wanna leave?'

They shuffled and mumbled, but remained seated, feeling vulnerable under his cold stare.

'What did you come here for? You're soldiers . . . mercenaries. You're paid to fight other people's battles. That's what you do!' His voice was rising with emotion. 'Christ Almighty, we're not talking about a major offensive here. The Serbs are crap, you've all said it. So what's the problem?'

He'd grabbed them by the short and curlies and now waited patiently for a reaction.

A lone voice piped up. 'He's right. A bloody good punch-up

will do us all good. We've been getting lethargic with all this fucking patrol crap.'

That voice in the wilderness did the trick. In a moment the room buzzed, as opinions flew thick and fast and everyone took on the vacant role of commander of operations, offering tactical advice over the babble.

Kit allowed them to continue, knowing that the battle of hearts and minds was won, for the time being at least.

'Let's get it in perspective.' Kit raised his voice over the fading roar. 'Let's understand the objective clearly. We're not taking on the JNA. We're not out for a confrontational battle. What we're going to do is simple. We are going to destroy their armaments, their fuel and supplies, their ability to strike at this town. In other words we're gonna cut off their balls.'

'How we gonna do that then, Batman?' The tone was more sarcastic than questioning.

Florez had been sitting quietly, listening to the wave of revolt subside, his tongue tracing the inside of his cheek. He climbed to his feet and moved hesitantly to the map.

'The sole purpose of the operation is strategic. To blow ammunition and fuel dumps, destroy tanks and remove the threat of invasion. We want to make the JNA move on to another town and leave this one alone until the UN arrive and accept it as part of Croatian territory. That's the objective. I'll leave the tactics to those more qualified.' He finished abruptly and returned to his seat, duty completed.

'Time is of the essence, lads, we've only got hours now and there's a lot of organising to be completed. The group leaders will tell you what to do. So get stuck in and let's do the work we're being paid for.'

Those last words should have stuck in Kit's throat. These volunteer soldiers were being paid a pitiful basic wage plus an occasional bonus – often late and without guarantee. They had every justification for walking out. Only Kit and a few other officers were receiving salaries commensurate with the risk; sums in the region of two thousand Deutschmarks per week, plus a further ten thousand DM bonus for the Velica Pumpa offensive.

Florez looked relieved as the room emptied, leaving the officers to undertake the task of organising the offensive. He stayed for only a short while before making his excuses and returning to headquarters in the town.

The battle planning continued: crayons drew brisk lines across maps, notes were shoved into the hands of runners to deliver to respective group leaders. Nobody noticed the day fade and darkness take over. By tomorrow's light we would be ready . . . there was little choice.

Kit glanced at his watch for the first time. 'Bloody hell, it's twelve o'clock. I'm knackered. Let's get our heads down,' and as an afterthought, 'It's done anyway.'

I looked at the pile of mugs, cigarette ends, bottles and cans. The table looked like a battle zone with a great many casualties waiting to be dumped in a suitable container and dispatched to God knows where.

Although tired, we couldn't sleep, tossing and turning as yet another shadowy figure crept across the room on his way to the kitchen for coffee, hushed conversation or to check his weapon for the hundredth time. Even Kit was unable to settle, grunting and twisting in a mild nightmare. Come the morning some of the men would have gone, their courage failing in the lonely small hours when no one was watching.

'The most recent ceasefire seems to be holding as the eastern town of Osijek returns to normal after many weeks of bombardment from Serbian artillery,' the BBC World Service announcer droned in an authoritative tone as we sat eating breakfast. 'But not for long,' Spooky added absently, buttering his fourth piece of toast before stealing a sausage from Roy's unprotected plate. 'This one will give them something to talk about,' he continued, still muttering to himself.

There was a lot of it about this morning, a strange isolation from reality, as if they were all pretending that this was just another day instead of the one they had dreaded for the past few weeks.

Kit leaned over, grabbing Roy's remaining sausage. 'You don't want that, do you?' An irrelevant question; he'd eaten it before Roy could answer.

'After you've finished breakfast, report to your section leaders for work detail. Final briefing at midday. Don't be late.' He looked around the room meaningfully before leaving for another meeting with the brass at brigade headquarters in Osijek.

A huge photograph of Velika Pumpa dominated the entire east wall of the briefing room, an impressive panoramic view, accomplished by taking dozens of colour stills from the top of the thirty-storey Osijek Hotel and joining them together to form a massive mural of infinite detail. This was more like it.

For this final briefing, Kit was alone, pacing to and fro, obviously anxious to start the proceedings. He moved to the blackboard before the lads were seated.

'Right! Let's get on with it,' he said impatiently. 'Malaria, you're in charge of the sixty-mil mortar to be sited a kilometre behind us.' He pointed first to a position on the map and then to the photograph. 'Your team is here. To the right will be a four-man group protecting your flank, with claymores about a hundred and fifty metres to your left.'

The positions of the mortar team, flank protection, and claymores were indicated on the blackboard. 'You got that?' Nodding confirmed understanding – just as well because Kit wasn't hanging around for slow responses.

'My group will move forward, placing claymores to defend our left flank, with four men to our right. The flanking guard will be equipped with night vision to enable them to follow the operation and identify the attack team on its return.'

Kit paused for a moment to let the information sink in as he pointed to the positions. 'Has everyone got that?'

'What about communication?' Steve enquired.

'I was coming to that,' Kit replied gruffly. 'No talking . . . none. All signals will be by way of radio clicks until after the operation has been completed. The only one you need to be concerned about is three clicks. That's when I initiate the attack with a RPG-7, which, with a bit of luck, will take out the ammo dump. I'll be backed up by two lads with 66s who will open up immediately as I reload before sending in two more rockets.'

He called to Malaria, who was busy doodling on his pad: 'Are you listening?'

Malaria looked up and nodded, his thumb extended in the universal signal of agreement.

'Your first round will be smoke; this will enable me to direct all further mortars on target. You will then expend all ammunition, doing as much damage as possible. Remember, you'll be firing over our heads, so make sure you get it right first time!'

'What's the weather forecast?' Nigel asked.

'Wet! Drizzle with a westerly light wind,' Kit replied.

He continued drawing on the blackboard before turning to the lads once again. 'After the briefing I want all of the leaders to come up and familiarise themselves with the terrain shown on the photographs. It's gonna be dark and the area after the track is mined, so you had better be sure of every blade of grass, in case we've got to go in . . . which is unlikely.'

'What sort of opposition are we likely to meet?' asked Pop, always the cautious one.

'I'm glad you asked me that, Pop, 'cause I don't know,' Kit replied calmly. 'Florez has told me that there are about two hundred Serbs in Velika Pumpa at the moment but not all of them are combat-trained soldiers. Some are simply civilian workers employed to do menial tasks. Trouble is, they'll be wearing uniforms as well, so we don't know who is or who ain't. Don't worry, though, we can kill 'em all and let someone else sort 'em out later.'

'Jesus Christ, Kit! There's less than thirty of us. Fucking outnumbered or what!' Pete exploded.

'We've got the tactical element of surprise. Anyway, you've already been told that we're not there to fight them. Just kick shite out of the place, not engage in a fucking firefight!' He gave Pete a withering stare.

'Yeah, let's kick some ass,' Spooky added enthusiastically, jumping to his feet.

'Bollocks!' Nigel spat. 'You fucking Americans and your gung-ho crap.'

'Right. If there are no more questions, be ready for the off at 0400 hours. We'll be travelling down to the bridge by coach so don't forget your bucket and spade.' Kit finalised the proceedings and started to pack away his maps, while the team leaders gathered around him for that last-minute answer to that last-minute doubt.

The rest of the lads dispersed rapidly, heading back to their rooms; to write letters, talk to their weapons or just get their heads down for a few hours of fitful sleep. As the day drew to a close, none would rest as adrenaline pumped and anxious stomachs churned, making it impossible to relax as they watched the big hands of the school clock march incessantly towards dawn.

Chapter Nine

We don't make good civilians. It's a well known fact.
So what's left? Just the 'buzz' it seems. Doing what
they do best.

Bleary-eyed and sleepy, they stood in wavering, ragged columns, staring straight ahead with ashen faces, limp and vacant. Headaches, backaches, colds, and other mysterious pains had plagued them this damp morning, refusing to go away. Had this been a conventional army they would all have been on sick parade, carrying notes back to irritable sergeants requesting to be excused duty.

It was not to be. Mercenary forces rarely, if ever, have qualified medics on the payroll. If you can't shoot, you can't earn.

The weather was lousy, an unremitting, drizzling rain that ran down your neck and gnawed into your bones, making them feel like lead. Last night's met report hadn't mentioned the bitter cold. Like grasping fingers it clawed at minds and extremities as they stood in shivering lines, wishing that they were anywhere but here.

'Morning lads,' a chirpy Kit Freeman greeted them. 'First we'll all jump up and down – one at a time. I want to hear if you rattle.'

He moved in front of each man as one by one they jumped in the air, and pointed to pouches or weapons creating sounds that would betray their presence to the enemy. The MG-42s – German World War II machine guns – were causing the biggest problem. With sheet steel construction and badly fitting feed plates, they rattled and clanked at the slightest movement. 'Tie that down. Tape that up,' was the curt order.

A small rattletrap coach with 'Yugo Excursions' emblazoned in bright orange along its side had arrived a few minutes earlier, causing chuckles of mirthless amusement.

'Going on a sightseeing tour are we, Kit?' Big John, one of the new recruits from Bolton, asked with dry sarcasm in his deep, husky voice.

'Told you to bring your bucket and spade, didn't I?' Kit replied, passing radios with ear pieces to section leaders and confirming their call signs for the umpteenth time.

He shouldered his RPG-7, grabbing six rockets in a single, practised movement.

'The coach is only taking us over the bridge this time, lads; we're walking through the cornfield from there. We want to avoid Serb observers detecting anything that might be construed as an offensive. So we'll split up after we disembark and regroup at the RV.'

Moodily we climbed into the brightly decorated coach, its interior adorned with coloured pictures of inviting mountains, villages and seascapes. 'Osijek, the garden city, gateway to Hungary,' they proclaimed without conviction.

'Gateway to hell,' Steve muttered, as he curled up for a ten-minute doze before we hit the white-painted, graffiti-covered Drava bridge and showtime.

Squelchy mud sucked at our boots as we stepped wearily from the coach into thick, ground-hugging mist. We watched it roll across the chopped cornfield in waves of ethereal surf, right up to the river bank and beyond. Gloomy and dank-smelling, it muffled all sounds as we moved in silent, preoccupied groups towards the mound separating us from enemy territory. One by one we slipped through a previously made tunnel in the earth – avoiding a skyline silhouette – to make our solo twenty-five-metre dash across the open area of no man's land and into the safety of the woods.

'It's like those old war films you see on the telly, ain't it? Like when they're escaping from Stalag something,' whispered Sprog, counting the men arriving breathlessly by our side.

Kit turned up last, looking exhausted and a bit pissed off. 'Who dug that fucking tunnel?' He glared at Pete and Steve, who apparently hadn't made allowances for the size of the Bear in their calculations and would pay dearly in the bar on our return.

The mist had crawled its way across the fields, over the dyke mound, settling eerily throughout the wood. Bushes became figures as the swirling white smoke twisted around the undergrowth, hiding our boots, hiding our comrades, hiding the enemy. We plodded on, ears tuned to the slightest sound, trigger fingers poised in readiness for a solid figure to rise from the cotton-wool earth and fill the air with the crackle of gunfire.

Nigel – at the sharp end – stopped abruptly, beckoning Kit

forward as he pointed to a telltale wire glistening in the dew. We watched as he traced it gingerly with his finger across our intended path and into the undergrowth; knowing that if the wood was mined we were in the shit, with this enveloping mist hiding everything at ground level.

We stood immobilised with fear as Kit disappeared to do his thing. Nobody moved, breathed, blinked . . . just in case.

Thirty-five seconds later – exactly – he returned, grinning broadly, with the news that it was merely a disconnected wire, left from a previous sweep a few nights before.

'The whole area should be clear. Me and Spooky did it on Tuesday night when you were all kipping,' he offered by way of consolation. 'But you can never be too careful,' he added whimsically.

Bent double like burdened animals, we continued our nervous trek through the wood, our darting eyes never still for a second until we arrived at Malaria's designated mortar position without further incident. The chilly, drizzling rain, combined with slow progress, had taken its toll. Without body heat to combat the cold, our fingers were rigid and our clothes and bergans soaking wet and cumbersome.

Kit put his hand in the air, rotating a single finger to signal stop. With gratitude for his kindness flooding through us, we rapidly unloaded thirty HE mortar bombs, red smoke phosphorus bombs, ammunition and claymores in readiness for the lads to set up in their respective positions. Malaria and his mortar team immediately darted about, trying to locate suitable firm ground on which to site their L-16A2 on its K-mount base plate, as the flanking team equipped with a MG-42 moved to their position on the right.

With no time for idle chitchat, and a further kilometre to travel, Kit beckoned the rest of us onward over the first track, slowly through the long grass and up to the second. We had a nasty moment as Pete waved us down, pointing to a figure on the dyke mound. We froze – which was easy in this temperature – and clicked off safety catches before he signalled us forward again. It had been a sack or something. Definitely non-hostile. 'Useless sod,' Nigel breathed as we staggered on.

By the time we arrived at our attack position some three hundred metres from the target, our throats were dry and swallowing required some effort. We unloaded grenades, rockets, launchers and spare magazines for the AK-47s, handing them out to the lads as Kit peered through the long yellow grass at Velika Pumpa, vaporising between the ground mist and the slowly lifting darkness. He checked his watch again, muttered something about being late and ordered the six men in Spooky's flanking team, armed with two German MG-42s, to move to our right for support and protection. Pete and Nigel went off to set up claymores on our left. In less than five minutes they were back, preparing their 66s and grenade launchers in readiness for the imminent onslaught.

Kit slowly eased the radio from his pouch and with a deep sigh pressed the signal button three times before bringing his RPG-7 slowly to his right shoulder, nestling it lovingly into the base of his neck. 'Here we go, here we go, here we go,' he sang softly, aiming through the leaf sights at the unfenced ammo dump. His index finger curled gently around the trigger.

There was a pregnant pause as he took a deep breath, exhaling slightly before the final pressure. Steady . . . steady . . . we willed him as his finger tightened.

The release of the missile startled us for a moment. We watched it spit from the end of the tube with a thunderous hiss, flattening the long grass in its wake as the warhead sped towards the target in a graceful arc. For a moment it faltered in its path as a brisk wind tore at the tail fins, threatening to blow it off course. We held our breath as Kit – never one to wait and see – stuffed another up the tube in readiness. We shouldn't have worried. The rocket curved slightly, but as the wind dropped, resumed its course and buried itself dead centre in the ammunition hut.

There was a millisecond's pause before the sky erupted with bright orange flame, spitting overheated rounds in the air and making us duck as they zipped across the open field. A second explosion followed as Steve, John and Nigel opened up with their 66s, hitting ammunition cases piled up by a waiting lorry.

Kit was on the radio, yelling into the mouthpiece above the roar of outgoing 66s, 'Smoke, you bastard . . . smoke!' Malaria must have got the message, a 'whumph,' followed by billowing red clouds, landed thirty metres to the right of the operations hut, making the occupants run in terror straight into the next barrage. Pete and Nigel whooped like gleeful children as they opened up with grenade launchers at the Serbs, who were now running around like headless chickens.

Kit grabbed the radio again, cradling it in his shoulder while he tried, with difficulty, to reload the RPG-7. 'Left thirty, over . . .' His conversation was aborted as we heard the rhythmic beat of the MG-42 from our right. There were no signs of earth being kicked up in the Serb compound, meaning only one thing. Our flanking team was under attack.

'Shit! I didn't expect them to counter so soon,' Kit yelled, sending another rocket into a group of three dug-in T-55 tanks. He missed them by inches. Roy came running back from the flanking team with the bad news that a dozen JNA were attacking them from the woods.

'Sorry, Roy, I'm a bit busy at the moment. Can you pop back later?' Kit screamed sarcastically over the noise.

Roy looked at him as if he had lost his mind. 'The fucking flank is under attack, Kit!' His eyes were wide with fear. 'Do something about it.'

'You've got the MG-42s. You do something about it!'

With that, he loaded his RPG again, then turned back to the frightened lad, calmly saying, 'Tell Spooky he's got to take care of the problem. We're gonna storm the place any time now. He's got to hold them. Remember . . . got to!'

Christ! Doesn't time fly when you're having fun? I looked at my watch. So far we were only four minutes into the assault. Just enough time to boil an egg.

Roy took one more pitiful glance at Kit's preoccupied figure before turning and sprinting back to the flank team, soon disappearing in the slowly evaporating mist.

Kit's radio burbled, the earpiece no longer required. 'Keep it coming for two minutes exactly. Then cease fire,' he told Malaria. 'We'll be going in then.'

The ammo dump was now history, blazing away vigorously, spurting out clouds of acrid smoke which blew occasionally in our direction with the ever-changing wind. There was still a lot more to accomplish before we had achieved our objective, as Kit pointed out, aiming at one of the T-55s he had missed earlier.

'How did they do that?' he spluttered, as the tank's bow machine gun opened up and the 100mm turret gun sluggishly tracked in our direction.

'Down!' he yelled. The whistling shell tore over our heads,

sucking the air from above us and exploding harmlessly into the dyke.

'Did you see anyone get into the tank?' he asked helplessly.

We hadn't. Not that it mattered. This was no time for debate. The gun dropped slightly, then re-elevated for another salvo, the 7.62 machine gun maintaining its rhythm, ensuring that we kept our heads low.

'I'm gonna have to get it this time or we're in real trouble.' Kit lay on his back, cradling the RPG. 'Lay down some grenades to give me cover,' he instructed Pete. 'I've got to stand up to use this thing and there's no way that fucking machine gun won't get me first.'

The biting hiss of bullets continued in sporadic bursts as Pete loaded his trombone – grenade launcher – and pulled himself up into a kneeling position. A tight smile tugged at his face as he peered through the grass, rounds zipping past his head. He squeezed and dived to the ground as the charge whipped through air. There was a dull explosion. He'd missed.

'Prat!' Kit hollered, his face contorted with fury. The big gun had stopped moving and was now aiming straight at our position. What were they waiting for?

'Oooh ... fuck ... it!' The drawn-out oath preceded Kit's movement by seconds. He leapt to his feet, levelling the RPG and pulling the trigger in one movement. The warhead covered the distance to the tank before he had time to dive for cover, exploding in a flash of brilliant white light as it impacted on the supplementary fuel tanks. The machine gun was silent. We poked our heads cautiously above the grass and saw a burning mass of twisted metal lying on its side in the ditch, a single scorched body lying a few metres away.

'Fucking brilliant!' John pounded Kit's back. 'What a star.'

'It's not over yet. We've still gotta get the fuel dump. Malaria can't seem to hit it, so it's down to us.' Kit still wasn't pleased with progress so far, it seemed. The whole thing was taking far too long, giving the Serbs time to reorganise. Any time now we were due for a counterattack.

Machine-gun fire from our right reminded us that Spooky was going through a hard time as well. The burst of MG-42 mixed with AKM, RPK and grenades indicated that far more than a dozen Serbs were now attacking our flank. If they got past Spooky and the lads the game was over.

With the only active tank disabled and the others hopefully unmanned, it was time for a final offensive on the remaining targets before the JNA got their act together and retaliated in force. Seven T-55s and one T-72 had been reported by Croat intelligence, plus static and mobile artillery. Trouble was, we couldn't see the bloody things through the smoke.

'We're gonna have to go down there and look,' Kit suggested with as little enthusiasm as the rest. 'Otherwise the job's gonna be unfinished and the Serbs can still do Osijek.'

'We can't just walk around looking for bleedin' artillery, Kit. The JNA will see us. There's nowhere to hide. The area's too open,' Pete pleaded.

After a thirty-second communication with his grey cells, Kit agreed. 'Tell you what. We'll take out the fuel dump first. Then we'll move to a different position away from the smoke and see if we can locate the rest of the equipment. OK?'

'Yeah. Anything you say, Kit, as long as we don't do it right now.'

The fuel dump was sited at the extreme left of the camp, well away from the tents and what was left of the operations hut. Kit loaded the RPG with his penultimate rocket, planting a loving kiss on its nose as the others levelled their 66s. They knelt in line, sighting through the haze, and fired as one. The rocket led the way, twisting and buffeting through the dense rain. The rifle grenades brought up the rear, but they weren't needed. The hollow-charge warhead did its job without assistance, splitting the air with a scream of pleasure as it slid gracefully into the fuel dump and exploded in a fury of ignited gas. The air reverberated as a muffled howl rapidly changed into a roar. Debris hurtled skywards like fragments of shrapnel – and almost as deadly.

'What the hell did they have in there?' Pete yelled wildly.

'God knows. But it ain't there now,' replied Kit laconically.

Impenetrable oily smoke spiralled upwards in waves, corkscrewing to thirty metres or more before bursting wildly into clouds of black, flaming tar, falling like napalm on the panic-filled Serbs who ran screaming from this nightmare. Their clothes, skin and hair were burning wildly, and the viscous substance clung like glue, refusing to extinguish as they rolled on the ground, beating one another feverishly.

We gazed in awe at the impact of our rocket attack. The whole area was ablaze; the heat-dried long grass surrounding Velika

Pumpa became a brush fire, a brisk wind fanning the flames and sweeping them across the field in jagged lines toward the JNA perimeter trenches some eighty metres away.

'Bet that'll piss them off,' Steve muttered absently, slinging his AK-47 over his shoulder.

How right he was. A dull thud, a puff of smoke and flying earth made us aware that somebody had decided enough was enough. It was payback time.

'Christ, they're accurate,' Steve said, as another mortar burst less than five metres away from the group on our right.

'They've got range cards out. Look!' Kit was right. Small white rectangles were scattered about the edge of the field, enabling the Serb mortarmen to zero in with almost absolute accuracy on any position.

'Let's move. Now!' It seemed one of Kit's better ideas as another mortar landed, its blast causing Pop to stagger and fall backwards in a heap.

'Are you all right?' Steve dragged him to his feet, shaken but unharmed.

'Course I'm all right! It's not the first time I've been knocked over by a mortar blast.' Ever conscious of his age, Pop pulled himself erect, away from Steve's grip, and snatched up his fallen gear roughly.

'Let's go, comrades.'

The monotonous drum of the MG-42 had started up again. We headed away from its throbbing beat across the track between us and Velika Pumpa, into a wilderness of sound and fury. It seemed the whole world was in flames.

'Jeeesuuus! Look at that! Will you look at that?' Pete had stopped for a moment to adjust his bergan straps, his normally pale face glowing in excitement at the sight before him. The reflection of the flames flickered in his bloodshot eyes as he licked his dry lips like an animal savouring his prey.

Kit snarled at him. 'Move, you dozy bastard. We haven't got time to admire the fucking view.'

Bent low, we shook ourselves into a line and followed the edge of the dyke for another hundred metres towards the Serb camp, firing sporadic bursts at a wall of shimmering heat. There was no one there – we knew it. But it felt better than just walking blindly into nothingness. A hedgerow twenty metres behind us shook as if struck by a heavy wind, flying apart as another mortar missed us by too small a margin.

'Good, aren't they?' Admiration from the normally silent Benny.

'Too fucking good,' replied Steve, opening up into the void with another worthless burst of AK fire.

'Cease fire. You're just wasting ammo,' Kit told him impatiently. 'You may need it later.'

A clear area ahead made us drop to our bellies, sliding through charred, acrid-smelling grass. The stubble tore at our hands and we gagged, wiping tears from our running eyes. A thin film of oil impregnated the earth and caused the irritation and a strong desire to cough was suppressed in anticipation of attracting interest from the enemy.

With heads and stomachs pressed tightly to the earth, we could see clearly under the hovering blanket of smoke as we inched forward in a straggling line. Kit paused, looking over his shoulder towards us, as a vague shape loomed fifteen metres to our right, and we followed his boots as they changed direction towards it. Bingo! Kit made no sound, but his lips formed the words. Straight ahead were a matching pair of SPGs - self-propelled guns. Behind them, and about five metres further on, we could just make out the distinct shape of a T-72 tank turret, with three dug-in T55s close by. Not quite a full house but their destruction would certainly complete our mission to everyone's satisfaction.

For a moment we stared in the direction of the tanks, absorbed in thought and forgetting our exposed position in the middle of an open field, surrounded by a rapidly reorganising Serbian army intent upon punishing the perpetrators of this carnage.

Still on our bellies, we could see their legs beneath the mist and smoke. The sound of voices heading in our direction jolted us back to reality. The Serbs were hunting in packs, systematically prowling the field but as yet unable to see us beneath the obscuring cloud which threatened to expose us within minutes – seconds if the wind picked up again.

Kit cursed under his breath. Our options were limited. We could put our hands up and rely upon their kind hearts to send us home after a good telling-off, or leap to our feet and be cut down in a hail of bullets. The final, and most appealing, choice was to crawl as quickly as possible towards the tanks and hide until someone thought of something better.

Telepathy is a wondrous form of communication. When practised in tight situations, it rarely fails. With a nod from Kit we wriggled in unison towards the tanks, any second expecting a shout to be followed by a stream of bullets pumping into our rear ends. But we made it – just – the cloud of smoky mist finally thinning out and drifting upwards as a breeze blew across the open space. We were safe for a moment in the tank ditch, until daylight arrived in time to bring more trouble.

'Innit time for a cuppa?' Pete muttered as he dived in on top of us.

'Yeah, I was just thinking that myself. Where's the canteen?' Pop replied, his voice muffled under a pile of bodies trying to sort themselves out.

'You've just blown the fucking thing up.' Kit quietened them down before it got out of hand.

We untangled ourselves, finally working out which boot belonged to which foot, and lay gasping for breath against the side of the T-55 after the exertion of the belly sprint.

'What have we got left?' Kit looked around at the sparse armoury, seeing one RPG rocket, three 66s, a few grenades and some plastic explosives. He nodded. 'That's enough to make a decent stew, I reckon.'

He rummaged in his bergan, bringing out a length of detonation cord and several detonators. 'Remember Mostar?' he whispered. Those present at that attack nodded; the others guessed.

'What's the date?' Kit asked unexpectedly, looking at Pop as he unpacked the explosives.

'I dunno. Uuh . . . March the . . . I can't remember.'

'It's March the twenty-first,' Nigel responded. 'Why?'

'It's my thirtieth birthday tomorrow,' replied Kit thoughtfully. 'Wonder if I'll make it.'

There wasn't time to speculate; a Serb rifleman poked his head over the edge of the ditch, his mouth open in a scream that would never come.

Steve saw him first and yanked him forward on to the bayonet he was using to cut the detonation cord. It sank in his soft flesh up to the hilt, and we watched him quiver and twitch, his eyes widening as the knife twisted into his stomach, withdrew and slit his throat. Blood pumped from the pulsating arterial wound, spraying Sprog's face and chest. He jumped to his feet, frantically wiping at the warm liquid as it ran into his eyes, down his cheeks and into his open mouth. Repulsed by his first sight of and proximity to violent death, he shuddered and sank to his knees, his face the colour of putty, blood soaking into his para smock.

The waxen face stared up at him accusingly, head askew, eyes gazing vacantly at the unseen sky.

'Don't you dare vomit,' Kit told Sprog sternly.

'Don't worry, I won't.' He gulped, looking at the body of a very young man lying dead before him. 'He's just a kid,' he sighed. 'Christ, he's younger than me.'

We could easily work out what was going through his mind as he stared at the corpse.

Kit dragged everyone back to the present problem. 'Shove him over there. We'd better get on with it. Someone's gonna come looking for him soon and we don't want to be around when they do.' The kid was dragged away and stuffed out of sight under the tracks of a tank.

We no longer knew what was going on above the surface of our hole in the ground. The mortars had fallen silent as visibility returned and the Serbs found no target to fire at. We were sure, however, that their hunt for us was continuing.

'Pop, you and Steve cover the rim but keep your heads down until I tell you. I'll set up some timed charges on the tanks. Then we'll do the clever bit.' Kit moved quickly to the bow of the nearest T-55.

'What's the clever bit?' John enquired.

Kit hesitated. 'Getting out before the fucking things blow.'

'How the hell are we going to do that? It's at least a hundred-metre run before we hit the perimeter. I'll never make it,' Pop pointed out.

'You'll make it, Pop. A spoonful of fear and a couple of bullets make a wonderful stimulant. Better than any of those vitamins you take.'

Kit and Nigel ignored his moaning and set about attaching explosives to the tanks. Sprog was still in shock but no longer pale as he moved to help them, his trembling hands holding the plastic in position as Nigel taped it to the most vulnerable parts of the armour plating and pushed in detonators, Kit bringing up the rear with detonation cord and timers.

'That's it! I've set them for fifteen minutes. That'll give us plenty of time to get out.' He tugged at Pop's arm. 'Stick your head up and see if it's clear.'

Pop looked at him as if he had gone mad. 'You stick your bloody head up!'

'Quiet!' Kit spat, pulling Pop down.

The sound of advancing boots and muffled voices came closer, stopping momentarily above the rim. We held our breath, looking at the timer as it ticked its way backwards to zero. The voices drifted away, finally silent as they moved out of earshot.

'That's two minutes gone. Now for fuck's sake look over the top!' Kit ordered.

Pop didn't argue on this occasion, realising that time was running out, and with the support of our hands moved gingerly to the rim of the ditch. 'It's clear to the right,' he reported, 'but they're still poking around for us. Most of them are in a huddle and the others are trying to put out the flames around the ammo dump and operations room.' With that he slid back down.

'OK. That's it then. Up and over. Run like hell to the right. Steve, you and me will bring up the rear. When we get past their trench positions we'll send in our last rockets on the SPGs. Before we go I'll just give Malaria a quick buzz and get him to send in some mortars to distract them and give us cover.'

He grabbed the radio, looking at the ticking timer as he hit the call button. There was no response. He hit it again. It crackled and Malaria's too-loud voice came over the hissing air waves. Kit gave his call sign, immediately instructing him to expend ammunition at a point twenty metres right of his original smoke position. Button off.

'Just hope he remembers it,' were his last words before the sizzling sound of incoming shells burst in exactly the right position.

'Let's go! And don't forget it's my birthday tomorrow.'

Kit was first over, rolling then twisting as he leapt to his feet, the rest of us so close behind that we kept tripping on his flying legs.

Bent double with our faces downward, all we could see was smouldering ash and charred tree trunks as we hurtled towards the safety of the wood, now only fifty metres away. We could hear the dull 'crump, crump' of mortars landing somewhere to our rear. Malaria was doing a grand job distracting the Serbs; so far none had fired at us. The whole escape was going well.

The empty Serb trenches and sanctuary were now only a matter of a few metres in front of us when the chatter of auto fire sounded off to the left and the ground started sprouting around our feet as bullets walked toward us, cutting a line across our path. We spread out instinctively as they were joined by the sound of incoming mortar fire whooping over our heads. In less than a moment we had turned from joyous victors into frightened rabbits. The noise was deafening and the terror absolute as bullets snapped around us, trying to damage our fleeing boots. Pete went down, a groan of agony escaping from his lips as he rolled into a ball. Kit grabbed him, dragging his limp body into the trench ahead. We were lost in a delirium of violence as we tumbled in behind, grateful to be alive if only for a moment.

Malaria had exhausted his supply of ammo and stopped firing. We were on our own.

'Nigel, look after Pete,' Kit instructed, loading the RPG with his final rocket. 'Pop and Steve, grab the 66s. We've got one last shot, so make it count. Target the SPGs, I'll go for the T-72.'

By now the isolated Serb mortar attack from our left had been joined by another from a sandbagged position close to the western perimeter, turning the sporadic bombardment into a continuous barrage. Like sharks smelling blood, they were determined that we would not get out alive and were pounding our position with more enthusiasm than accuracy. The trees behind us were being flattened as we crouched low, just waiting for our final rocket attack before we could get the hell out of here.

'Pete's all right,' Nigel said. 'It's just a flesh wound.'

'Can he use a gun?' Kit responded automatically, then looked at his watch and muttered, 'Shit, we've been here twenty minutes, the whole thing's taking too long.'

'Yeah, I can use a gun,' Pete replied before Kit had finished grumbling. He hoisted his AK from his shoulder sling.

'Good,' Kit replied in a flat, calm voice. 'If you look over there by the mound of earth you'll see four Serbs with autos coming at us. Take them out!'

Four JNA soldiers with little regard for personal safety were charging through their own mortar fire in our direction, bobbing, weaving and screaming like madmen, a continuous spray of bullets from their blazing Kalashnikovs preceding them.

Pete and John looked at one another, nodded and stood upright, spewing rounds in the direction of the advancing Serbs, who, taken aback by this display of stupidity, broke ranks and released their triggers for a split second. That was all the lads needed. The first man hit the ground as ten rounds slammed into him, dropping to his knees for a second before crumpling in a heap on the still smouldering grass only about three metres from where Pete stood. Another stumbled, falling on a spot milliseconds before it erupted as a mortar shell landed, blowing him into the air like a rag doll. The other two, gathering their wits, opened up again, only to be cut down by Pete's fireburst as they charged forward, almost reaching our position.

Meanwhile, Kit had screwed the rocket propellant cylinder into the warhead and loaded it into the muzzle of his RPG-7. He pulled the safety pin, nodding to Pop and Steve to take aim at the SPGs with their 66mm M-72s, and lay against the wall of the trench with his back to the target. 'Ready . . . fire!' He turned quickly, sighting at the tank some ninety metres away through the falling mortars, and squeezed the trigger savagely as Pop and Steve did likewise. The rocket ejected with a whoosh of escaping propellant, the backblast flattening the bushes behind as it screamed away at 120 metres a second. It remained true to its course, never wavering a centimetre as it homed in on the T-72 low in its bunker. A metallic crack followed as it dived through the open turret door and exploded inside the tank, igniting diesel fuel auxiliary containers in the process. Much to our disappointment, little visible damage seemed to have occurred – even with this direct hit – the advanced armour-plating absorbing the PG-7 HEAT warhead. We knew, however, that the inside of the tank had been totalled and was now inoperable.

The 66s arrived on target milliseconds later, pounding into the self-propelled guns with enthusiastic zeal, blowing their tracks high into the air as they teetered for a moment, failed to regain balance and rolled over on to their sides.

'Bit fucking lucky with that shot, weren't you, Kit?' Pop jibed.

'Lucky! What do you mean, lucky! I was aiming for the turret opening.'

'Balls!'

The bantering was temporarily aborted as the explosives attached to the three T-55s detonated in unison, leaving a junk heap of twisted, smoking metal. The air was once again filled with the dense odour of cordite, oil and flame.

'The job's finished,' Kit commented in a matter-of-fact tone. 'Let's get out!'

It was easier said than done. With renewed vigour the JNA were increasing their mortar attack, focusing a deliberate and continuous barrage on our vulnerable position on the eastern perimeter. Machine-gun fire kicked into gear on our right flank, supporting a fast-moving twenty-strong infantry platoon coming at us with vengeful expressions on their blackened faces.

'I don't like the look of this. We're pinned down here,' Peter murmured ominously.

'Oh really?' Nigel replied in his best Guards officer put-down voice. 'That's a very astute observation, old boy. Have you anything constructive to add?'

'Yeah. Let's get the fuck out of here!'

'Stop nattering, you two, and lay down some covering fire. We'll make a run for it into the trees and cover you.'

With no further discussion, Pop lobbed two M-18 smoke grenades in the direction of the advancing Serb platoon and scrambled out of the trench, leaving us momentarily stunned at his immediate reaction to Kit's order. With a quick adrenaline burst the rest of us followed close behind, as clustered mortars dropped like hailstones, bursting around our darting figures.

'They're trying to fucking kill us!' Steve yelled. He sprinted past, his long legs blurred as he leapt over mortar holes appearing from puffs of smoke everywhere we looked.

Benny suddenly took off, flying through the air with his arms waving like a demented swan, before hitting John in mid-flight, bringing him crashing to the ground in front of Sprog, who tripped over them both. They landed in a heap, lying dazed for a moment before continuing their dash to the safety of the wood, now only a few metres away.

'Everybody here?' Kit enquired, gasping for breath. 'Everybody OK?'

Benny didn't look too good. He had taken some shrapnel in his side and the gaping wound had opened up with his final sprint. He was sweating and gritting his teeth with pain. Kit looked at the injury, peeling back his smock for a closer inspection. Benny started to gasp. It was a nasty one. Not life-threatening under normal circumstances, but these weren't normal circumstances.

'Stand still and let me have a look!' Kit prodded the bleeding cavity. 'Mmmmm. Yes,' he murmured in a practised medical tone before fumbling in his first-aid pouch and sticking a morphine needle into Benny's exposed shoulder. 'That'll make you feel better.'

The renewed chatter of small-arms fire focused our attention back to the trench, where Pete and Nigel were doing their best to slow down the advancing Serbs, without much success. Heavy machine-gun fire from a foxhole on the far side of the camp was now elevated above their heads, aiming for the tree line and our position just inside it, cutting large chunks of bark from the trees and spraying them around us like jagged pointed arrows. Mortars continued to fall in waves, unseen until they were caught by branches in their orbit and exploded over our heads. Fragments of shrapnel fell like burning metallic leaves, scorching our clothes and singeing our hair.

John had started to panic, and Kit dragged him back from the edge with a brusque order to cover the lads in the trench. After a feverish hunt through his bergan for grenades, he knelt to support Pop as he opened up with automatic fire, cutting through the first line of Serbs about to overrun a desperate Pete and Nigel. A second line stepped over their comrades without a backward look, firing in staccato bursts at the tree line and the trench. The onslaught had reached the peak of its fury, every training manual forgotten as the air was filled with the most frightening sounds and smells imaginable: screams, shrieks, roars, deafening blasts. Almost continuous explosions converged with rapidly concentrated focus on seven men – all scared shitless.

'We've got to get them out. Now!' yelled Kit, as Pete looked pitifully back at us for a second before lobbing a grenade high in the air, more in hope than accuracy.

Four AK-47s burned their barrels red in a five-second blast of consolidated fire power as Nigel and Pete – knowing that this was their last chance – leapt over the edge of the trench and came tearing towards us, weaving and bobbing, jumping and crouching. The Serbs, momentarily surprised by the audacious move, kept firing at the trench. By the time they had worked it out, the lads were safe.

The AKs kept up a steady rhythm, spent shells flicking through the air and piling up around our feet. The situation was getting desperate. Our ammunition was dangerously low and we had a casualty to carry out. But as often happens in such circumstances, fate took a hand. The infantry attack slowed as casualties increased, finally petering out before pulling back in disarray. The mortars and machine guns ceased firing as if a tap had been turned off.

The silence felt so sweet you could roll it around your mouth and taste it. For the first time we were able to assess through the mantle of smoke, crimson flame and intermittently exploding ammunition the considerable damage we had caused.

'Let's go,' Kit said quietly, looking at the childlike bundle of Benny lying on the charred bracken. 'Carry the poor sod,' he sighed, tucking his RPG away for another day.

We straggled aimlessly back through the woodland, battle sounds still echoing in our deafened ears. Splintered tree stumps smouldered with wispy, bitter-smelling smoke that burned our nostrils before curling upwards through skeletal branches. The lifeless, mangled bodies of small furry creatures lay burning at our feet as we trudged wearily towards the flanking position, held – we hoped – by Spooky and the lads.

The MG-42 had long since ceased its distinctive drumming, and we speculated on what we might find, fearing the worst. There was no sound from the clearing as we approached, circling cautiously, weapons cocked and ready for almost anything. Steve, at 'point', waved us on and we reached the clearing with some trepidation.

Dozens of dead and dying Serbian soldiers lay around the perimeter line. Spent shell cases littered the ground. Spooky, leaning against the machine gun, looked beaten. The others were spead unevenly around the clearing in exhausted piles.

'You OK, Spook?' Kit mumbled wearily, walking over to the slumped American.

'The Alamo or what?' Spooky replied, looking at the bodies strewn around the field.

'Oh. So you're Jim Bowie now, are you?'

'No, Kit. He got killed.'

'Many casualties?'

'Some. Four injured. Not serious. None of our lot killed.'

'That's something.'

'You?' he asked Kit.

'About the same.'

Kit collapsed at his side on the grass. 'I could do with a fag,' he sighed.

'You don't smoke,' Spooky pointed out.

'I know. But it's times like this I wish I did.'

'Yeah. I know what you mean.'

I think they would have stayed there all day if it were possible,

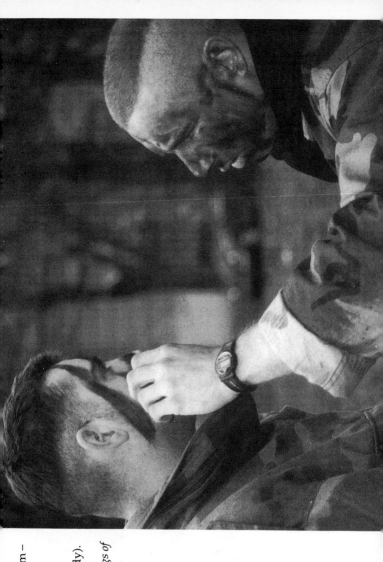

Buddy system – camo applications (Dave face painting Andy). © Stephen Lambert, *Dogs of War*

Left: Ex-Portuguese commando and part of the volunteer force in Osijek. © Stephen Lambert, *Dogs of War*

Below: A quick break before patrol near Osijek

Right: Taken in Duvno (now Tomislavgrad) – Ivan with cousin

Below right: Hertz VW Golf – in its DPM livery used for fast movement around Osijek

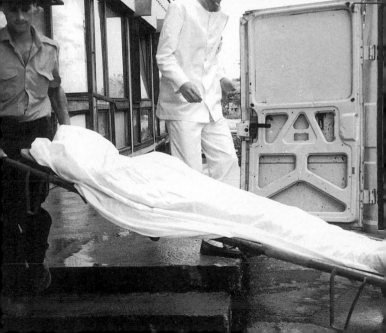

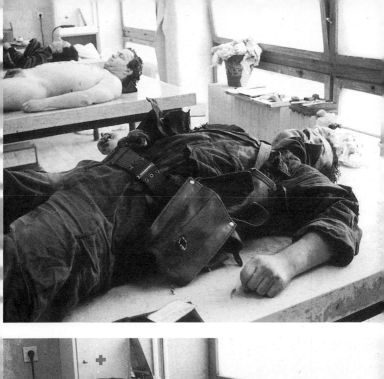

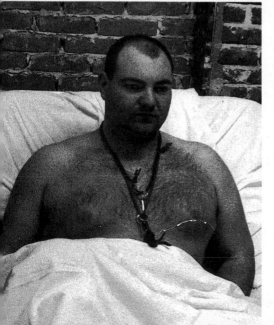

Above: Kit – day before Velika Pumpa battle

Left: Kit – day after Velika Pumpa – (Happy Birthday!)

Top right: Block of flats after direct hit by MiG 21s

Right: Boys relax with AK-47s in quarry

Ammunition

7.62	x AK47.	200 Box's	(2000 Per Box)	20.000 DM
7.62	x NATO.	100 Box's	(2000 Per Box)	10.000 DM
7.62	x BELT.	100 CASE'S	(1000 Per Case)	10.000 DM
7.9		5 Box's	(2000 Per Box)	500 DM
9m	PARA.	1 BOX	(1000 Per Box)	1 000 DM
120mm	H.E.S.H.	600 RNDS		24 000 DM
R P G	ROCKET S.	40 Box's	(9 Per Box)	8 000 DM
64mm	ROCKETS.	600		30000 DM
RIFEL	GRANADES	A/P	10 Box's	1 000 DM
RIFEL	GRANADES	A/T	20 Box'	1000 DM
CLAYMORE MINES		40 Box's	(12 Per Box)	6000 Dm
ANTI TANK MINES		50 CRATES	(4 Per Crate)	2000 DM
HAND GRANADES		100 Box's	(50 Per Box)	10.000 DM
PLASTIC EXPLOSIVE.		60 Box's	(40Kg Per Box)	3000 DM
TROTEAL BLOCKS		300 KG.		500 DM
DETONATOR CORD		40 ROLLS	⎫	
FUSE CORD		60 ROLLS	⎬	4000 DM
FUSE CAPS.		20 Box's		
ELECTRIC DETS		3 Box's	⎭	

x152.000

156.200

Above: An order from the Muslims written by Kit Freeman – July 1993

STOP GENOCIDE... ARM BOSNIA

HUMAN RIGHTS COMMITTEE OF THE MUSLIM PARLIAMENT

Tel: 071 388 2581 Fax: 071 383 5006

uttering the odd word from time to time between slow swigs of ice-cold beer – if we'd had any.

'Shall I check the bodies?' Pop asked.

'Yeah. You look at the Serbs and tell Nigel to patch up our guys. We'd better not hang around,' Kit answered, slowly rising to his feet.

Pop wandered around the inert bodies with Sprog in tow, still looking as if he were in shock from the incident in the tank ditch. They poked the bodies, turning them over, removing anything of interest. The Serbs' weapons were piled up for disposal or liberation, depending upon condition or value.

'Nice knife.' Pop, holding a Russian bayonet in his hand, turned to Sprog. 'Want it?'

The kid looked at him in disbelief, walking away without a word as Pop stuck it in his belt to sell or swap at a later date.

He continued checking alone as Sprog sat against a tree, staring into space at a hazy picture still haunting his mind.

'What we gonna do with the injured Serbs?' Steve asked cautiously.

'How many are there?' Kit enquired.

'Three. All badly hurt.'

Kit thought for a moment as Steve looked at him with an 'I'm not doing it' expression.

'What do you think, Spooky? Kill them or leave them?'

'Dunno, Kit. It's your decision. But if you . . .'

The quivering whistle of an incoming mortar brought the conversation to an abrupt halt. We all looked at one another in astonished disbelief.

'The bastards. Don't they know we've had enough for one day?' Spooky groaned, leaping to his feet, weariness forgotten.

The first mortar shell was followed closely by another, only seconds behind, shattering trees a good twenty metres ahead. Fortunately the Serb calculation was a little overcompensated – they assumed we had been moving faster and had covered a greater distance. The inspiring chat between Kit and Spooky had delayed our departure and might well have saved lives.

In seconds the pile of listless forms sprang into agitated life, clutching weapons in preparation for whatever came next. Apprehensive faces turned skywards, watching the barrage increase in ferocity as further mortars were brought into action, their shells spiralling overhead from a mauled but not yet defeated JNA force impatient for blood.

If that wasn't enough, the distinct sound of pounding boots grabbed our diverted attention and focused it towards the wood. A small group of bandanna-wearing Serbian irregulars burst crazily through the undergrowth, furiously spraying the clearing as they ran towards us, screaming at the top of their Chetnik lungs and taking us completely by surprise. Not for one moment had we expected this spirited retaliation after giving them such a severe pounding only minutes before at Velika Pumpa.

Bewildered and in disarray, we had little time to organise ourselves, managing more by luck than judgement to return fire with equal ferocity, piling rounds into the enemy as we hastily withdrew into the battered woodland and straight into the ceaseless incoming mortar barrage.

A sheer wall of almost continuous fire from Spooky and his flanking team forced the Serb attack to falter, while a few hand-thrown grenades from Steve drove them back for cover beyond the clearing, where they sniped away in isolated bursts at our retreating figures backing up to the tree line with mortars coming in behind us. Now with a hidden Serb patrol ahead, mortars landing behind us and five injured men, we were in a spot of bother.

Kit yelled over to John a few metres away and still running, 'Sort them out. Send in some grenades!'

John nodded to confirm the instruction and courageously knelt in the open to take aim. It was then that he repeated Jim's earlier almost fatal error. His adapted Yugoslavian Zastava required the recycling of gas in its chamber to provide propulsion for the grenade. In the chaos surrounding him he forgot this simple rule, recocking the weapon and putting a live round in the chamber. When he pulled the trigger the round, finding its exit blocked, blew the weapon apart in his hands.

For some of us it was *déjà vu* of the worst kind. Small pieces of razor-sharp metal zipped through the air, cutting everything in their path. For the briefest of moments, time froze. Then Kit rushed back into the open and grabbed John by the arm, dragging him into the trees. John's face was a bloody mess of hanging flesh and exposed bone. Metal had penetrated his shoulder, eye and mouth. Teeth were hanging from his torn gums, swinging loosely as Kit dumped him on the ground in whimpering shock.

'You four . . . get them back.' He pointed at the flanking team, who hurriedly lifted Benny and John to their unsteady feet.

'Wait!' Kit looked at John's mouth and with a quick tug removed three teeth from his gums. 'He might swallow them. Now go!'

'Orhin, orhin . . .' John tried to mumble through uncontrollable lips.

'No morphine,' Kit replied. 'Sorry, John, you aren't going to be able to run if you're spaced out. You'll have to put up with it until they get you back.' With that they were off, veering to the right and away from the incoming mortar fire, dragging both the injured men limply between them.

'Right, lads, we need to do something about those Serbs. This mortar fire and them shooting at us is doing my head in. Pop, Nigel, you flank them clockwise. Steve, Sprog, you go the other way. We'll count to twenty and open up to grab their attention as you circle around. Don't be long. I wanna get out of here.'

'. . . eighteen, nineteen, twenty. Fire!' The bursts were short. It was pointless wasting ammunition on a target we couldn't see. Seconds later AK fire opened up from our right. Steve and Sprog were doing the business, with Pop and Nigel joining in moments later.

They returned, panting breathlessly. 'We got two of the bleeders. Didn't want to waste time chasing the others so we came back.' Pop was holding his chest, breathing hard in hesitant gasps. 'Is that all right?'

'Yeah, that's fine,' Kit replied. Fatigue was flattening his voice to an almost inaudible whisper. 'Now it's our turn to go home.'

He looked at the sullen morning sky, now streaked with orange daybreak. His lips moved silently; he was calculating the spaces between mortar shells and relying upon his sixth sense to judge the period between barrages. For a full three minutes he counted as they fell, exploding around us in bursts of bone-destroying smoke. Finally he uttered an urgent, 'Ready? The next break and we're off!' before kneeling in a sprint position. We followed his example, poised for a signal and a crouching, zigzag dash for deliverance from this misery.

A shell burst behind us, followed by another – closer this time. The Serbs had re-elevated, their aim now getting dangerously focused.

Kit tensed, his face a mask of concentration as he leapt to his feet like a pursued antelope, starting to lean into a turn.

The shell burst came as a shock to us all. Without warning, it exploded less than a metre behind his poised, unbalanced body, its discharge throwing him forward head first into a tree trunk before twisting him around with its uncontained force and lifting his body off the ground, dumping him in a heap. He tried his best to rise, staggering momentarily, grabbing at air before looking at us through helpless, this-is-it-I'm-dying eyes. then he slumped to the ground.

We couldn't believe, wouldn't believe it! Kit killed by a rogue mortar – never! Steve dived across to the prone figure, shaking him wildly, but he didn't stir.

'Try his pulse!' yelled Pop, running forward to help. 'Kick him. Do something . . . anything. But get him up!' Steve felt his pulse. It was slow but steady, his breathing shallow.

'Lazy bastard. Get up!' Sprog screamed. 'Kit, Kit . . .' His voice trailed away, tears in his child's eyes.

Oblivious to the continuing attack, we crowded around the unconscious figure, suggestions coming from all directions. Mouth-to-mouth, face-slapping, body-shaking . . . everything was tried unsuccessfully before we resorted to the advanced cold-water technique. It did the trick. As liquid from four canteens spread over Kit's face he opened his eyes as if trying to work out where he was and struggled to his feet, leaning groggily against a tree, looking as if he were returning from a good night out.

'You all right, Kit?' No response. 'Kit, can you hear me?' His eyes flickered, stayed open and he dropped like a stone.

The Serbian irregulars had returned with JNA replacements, sniping across the clearing at us, more irritating than accurate. Ricocheting rounds spun through the undergrowth, adding yet another dimension to our increasing panic.

'Kit . . . Kit . . . can you hear me?' Nigel had joined Steve to help prop Kit up. No reaction. His eyes moved skywards, his head slumped. He was out again.

'We gotta go. With or without him.' Spooky interrupted our paramedic demonstration with an urgent reality.

'Yeah, you're right,' replied Steve, taking charge of the situation without consultation and ordering two of the biggest lads to drag the bulky Kit, as once again we prepared to evacuate the position, fighting a rearguard action against the Serb platoon now gaining confidence at our lack of retaliation.

'Around to the right,' screamed Steve, his nerve ends displayed for all to see. 'Follow the line taken by Benny and John . . . Now!'

With a last blast of covering fire from Spooky raking the Serb position, we jumped to our feet. As if possessed by demons we dived headlong into the bushes, waiting for the next mortar blast to take at least one of us out in a puff of smoke.

We ran blindly, stupidly, frantically along tracks that could be mined, leaping over smouldering tree trunks and pushing aside branches that barred our way. We laughed hysterically at frightened animals crossing our path and threw jokes into the faces of panting comrades as our panic subsided with the knowledge that we were safe out of mortar range.

Malaria's position appeared a few metres ahead, now empty apart from his booby-trapped mortar and piles of cigarette butts. We didn't pause, veering to the right and struggling through the long yellow grass. Kit kept coming and going as we ran, occasionally muttering rubbish about his thirtieth birthday, which event seemed to be playing on his concussed mind.

The dyke embankment welcomed us like a castle fortification as we jostled for position and dived head first through the inviting gap, cursing Pete and Steve for not making the hole larger as we struggled through the narrow tunnel and safety.

Steve slipped the radio from Kit's pouch, punching buttons in a haphazard fashion before getting a receive signal. His message was brief. 'This is the Bear. This is the Bear.' He used Kit's call sign to avoid confusion. 'Request ambulance and medics at the bridge for injured men. Over.' The line crackled and a voice replied, '*Da. Koliko?*' – Yes, how many? Steve scratched his head before answering, '*Tri!*' a smug smile of satisfaction breaking out on his face at the correct translation.

Benny and John, with Spooky's team, were crumpled in a heap some two hundred metres ahead, anxiously waiting for our arrival. We dragged ourselves on, crawling most of the way to join them as soldiers from the Croatian line ran to help us.

Both John and Benny were in a hell of a state, barely conscious; hunched up and moaning in agony as we approached. Benny's gaping wound, now covered in pulsating blood, oozing encrusted mud.

'Christ . . .' Sprog turned away. 'Will he be alright?'

Pop shrugged, but said loudly for Benny to hear, 'Course he'll be alright. A few days in hospital and he'll be back on the job.'

John's facial injury had also turned nasty. His eye was a pulpy mess of flesh, his battered mouth a yawning cavity of congealed blood. The mad scramble through tearing branches had added to both their injuries.

With help from the Croatian soldiers we hoisted the casualties into a covered truck, driving slowly to the bridge and waiting medics who immediately injected John and Benny with a blissful sleep called morphine. Kit woke for the briefest of moments, but unable to register any interest in the proceedings, slumped back again. We lifted the three of them on stretchers into the ambulance, which sped off on a siren-wailing trip to Osijek hospital.

Chapter Ten

'Listen,' said Spooky. 'We're not here for the killing or
the money. It's the comradeship and excitement that
most of us want. If there's a price to pay, so be it . . .'

It was a subdued bunch of twenty-five men who slumped by the
Drava bridge, gazing blankly into the muddy river as it swirled
beneath them. A few threw stones, watching them plop in the
water as they waited patiently for transport back to base.
Memories flickered like death's-head moths trapped in a jar.

One of the guys in Spooky's team kept dry-firing his shotgun,
click, click, click, beginning to get on everyone's nerves. Steve
grabbed the Remington from his hand, hurling it spinning
through the air. The owner stared at him for an instant, shrugged
his shoulders and lit a cigarette, too bushed to care. Pop started to
hum a tune which sounded familiar. Something that might have
been classical but wasn't . . . just the theme from *M A S H*.

I waited for a medevac chopper to swoop over the skyline and
whisk us away. It didn't. The mind wanders when exhausted.

Nigel took some folded sheets of paper from his wallet,
scanning the first page before tearing them into pieces and
throwing them away. The top section, caught by corn stubble,
read: 'Dear Mum and Dad, I don't want to alarm you but things
are getting a bit nasty here now, and I don't know if I'll be coming
back from the next job. Give my love to Jean . . .'

The pages blew lightly across the field. He should have kept the
letter, saving himself the trouble of rewriting it another time.

Steve jabbed absent-mindedly at the earth with his bayonet –
that bayonet. Sprog watched him clean the dried blood of the
Serbian boy soldier from the blade.

Pete nursed his arm, complaining that he should have gone to
hospital with the others.

'Do you think they'll be all right? Kit looked real bad,' Sprog
said distantly, still staring at the bayonet and looking like a lost
kid a long way from home, but no longer scared.

'Sure they'll be all right,' Pop and Steve replied in unison.

'John's injury looked nasty,' Spooky added unnecessarily, to nods from some of the others.

'What about my fucking injury!' Pete winced in apparent pain as he moved position to face the others.

'Bollocks! It's a flesh wound. If you were in Spooky's army you'd get a purple heart and be sent on R&R to Saigon or somewhere.' Nigel shut him up with a contemptuous glance.

'Stupid of John forgetting he had a round up the spout, wasn't it?' Pete threw in quickly, before realising he had overstepped the mark and dropping into brooding silence.

There was a long pause as we listened to the distant sound of gunfire coming from the Croatian line. 'I'm going home,' Sprog whispered, more to himself than anyone in particular.

'We're all going home as soon as the bloody coach comes,' snapped Steve.

'No. I mean *home*! Back to England. I'm gonna get a proper job. I'm pissed off with people I don't know trying to kill me.'

They all fell silent, considering his remark and realising that at this moment few would remain if given an opportunity to do otherwise.

'You'll feel different tomorrow,' Nigel said softly. 'Especially when we get our bonus for this job.'

'No. Not this time. I'm too young to die in some crappy foreign country.' He turned to his mates, adding with a smile, 'Specially with a bunch of psychos like you lot.'

Pop chucked a grenade at him and he caught it high in the air.

'You forgot to take the pin out, Pop.'

'Sod it! Throw it back and I'll try again.'

'Here's the coach,' murmured Steve, not moving from his spot as the vehicle slowly turned on to the bridge, pulling up in a cloud of smoke a few metres away.

'Look at it! "Yugo Excursions". It's the last time I'll book with them. Fucking sightseeing tour, my ass.' Spooky climbed to his feet, throwing his bergan on the coach before him. 'Still, the job proved one thing. You don't have to live a long life to feel old!'

We climbed aboard without a further word being spoken and settled into contemplative silence. The coach shuddered, crunching its gears before taking us across the bridge for what was to be the very last time.

Commander Florez was waiting, impatient and apprehensive. He had heard of the injuries by radio and was especially concerned by the fact that Kit would not be available to provide a detailed account of the operation for his superiors at brigade headquarters.

'How is he? Can he talk?' were his first words as we tumbled out of the coach.

'We don't know how he is,' replied Pop. 'Anyway, when we left him twenty minutes ago he was unconscious . . . like Benny and John.' Pop was reminding Florez that not only Kit had been injured.

'Oh, yes, of course.' Florez realised his apparent lack of concern for the others. 'And how are they?'

'Fucking awful!' Steve growled impatiently. 'How would you feel with lumps of shrapnel in your face and body?'

Florez could tell he wasn't getting anywhere and tried a different approach.

'I'm sending out a scouting party of Yellow Submarines, although I've been told by soldiers on the front that the whole operation was a great success.'

'Yeah. We can see the smoke,' Steve said flatly, turning to look at the distant skyline and the black clouds still hovering over Velika Pumpa.

'I'll leave you to sort yourselves out and come back later.' Florez edged away, unsure of how to continue his debriefing, and disappeared into an outbuilding.

We straggled across the compound through schoolhouse corridors to our rooms, dropping bergans, weapons and ammunition pouches in our wake. Nothing on earth had such appeal as sleep, long, blissful, free-from-noise-and-smoke sleep. The last thing I remembered was Nigel's voice muttering 'Bollocks!' as the world turned a soft grey, then black.

Without Kit to wake us, we slept the rest of the day and the following night, waking at about eight a.m. to the sound of Pop at the stove cooking an immense pile of scrambled eggs. We hadn't eaten for more than thirty hours. 'Yugo Excursions' didn't provide food and we'd missed breakfast at Café Velika Pumpa.

'You know what day it is, don't you?' Sprog mumbled through a mouthful of yellow mush.

'Yeah, it's Sunday,' replied Nigel.

'Not just any Sunday. It's March the twenty-second.'

'So?' Nigel queried.

'It's Kit's birthday, for fuck's sake. Don't tell me you forgot, after he kept reminding us all the way back?'

'No, course I didn't forget!'

We continued chomping like cows in a field, intent upon clearing the grass back to its roots.

'Better phone the hospital,' Steve said suddenly, climbing to his feet and moving to the phone. 'See how the old bastard is.'

'Sod the phone! Let's jump in the Lada and go down there. Pete ought to have his arm looked at anyway, and the other lads could do with some professional treatment.' Spooky kicked his chair back and still chewing, gulped a mouthful of coffee before heading for the door. 'Anyone coming?' We trooped behind him, standing outside for a moment as we discussed the improbability of getting twelve people into a five-seater car, and opting instead for the chopped-roof DAF truck.

The countryside this bright morning was strangely quiet without the occasional shell passing overhead or the dull crunch of mortars. The sky was clear with a hint of blue, and it felt good to be alive. Birds chirped and twittered, and it wasn't raining – for a change.

Benny was in the operating theatre when we arrived. His condition was unknown by the receptionist, and all other staff members quoted the same mechanical stuff about him being 'as well as can be expected' without knowing the cause or extent of his injuries.

John was lying flat in bed, his head, neck and shoulders completely covered in bandages, with only a small hole where his nose should have been. A sign in Serbo-Croat, English and French stated, 'Nil by mouth.' Unnecessary; he didn't have one.

Kit lay in the next bed, white and bloodless, looking like Frankenstein's monster in its late stages of development. Multi-coloured tubes ran from just about every orifice, with wires attached to his chest leading to a machine with a limited musical range. He shifted his eyes as we entered, without moving his head – just in case it came off.

What do you say to a monster with a huge hairy chest? Nothing; you just wait until he's finished filling the bottle by the side of his bed and pretend you haven't noticed. Then you say something original like 'How do you feel?' and hope that he doesn't tear your throat out.

A doctor and two nurses probably saved us by appearing at his side, examining with great interest the chart at his feet. Steve waited for a moment as they rambled away in Croatian before asking about his condition in very bad Serbo-Croat. The doctor smiled at his attempt, instructing a nurse to take Kit's temperature before replying in perfect English, 'He is an extremely lucky fellow. Had he not been a large man he would have been killed by the blast. He is concussed. Three ribs are broken and he has suffered hyperextension-hyperflexion injury to his neck.' Our blank looks drew another smile. 'Sorry. The sudden thrusting forward and snapping back of his unsupported head has caused severe whiplash. Oh . . . and we found this embedded in his shin bone.' The doctor handed Steve a 7.62 round. 'It must have been a ricochet, otherwise the velocity of the bullet would have shattered the bone. Like I said, he's a very lucky man.'

Steve tried again. '*Hvala vam na pomoci, Doktor.*' Thanks for your help, Doctor. He'd got it dead right; we were impressed. The doctor ackowledged the gratitude, sweeping away with his entourage in tow.

Four of us stayed with Kit, listening to the steady 'beep, beep' of his cardiac machine and feeding him information about Florez, as Pete and the others with minor wounds joined a small queue in the out-patients' department, soon returning with bandages, antibiotics and tales of primitive torture.

It wasn't much fun trying to communicate with coloured tubes, beeping machines, voodoo eyes and an immobile neck. So with a chorus of farewells we were starting to leave when Spooky reminded us about Kit's birthday. Can you sing 'Happy Birthday' to someone in that state? It doesn't seem right somehow, but we tried. To be honest I think even Kit had lost interest in the celebration of his birth. Another time maybe. At least he had lived to see it.

The Mayor of Osijek greeted our return to the school; a nice man full of praise for our efforts in saving his town from the invaders. Commander Florez fussed around, beaming with pleasure at the lavish praise showering from on high. He explained in infinite detail his attack strategy and execution plan. Hands were shaken and minor injuries discussed. We were invited to the Mayor's home for a meal . . . one day soon.

'We should live so long,' muttered Pop through immobile lips, smiling graciously at the invitation.

Photographs were taken for the local newspaper, with Florez

shaking hands for the camera as the mercenaries all looked on with suitably grim 'Soldier of Fortune' expressions. It was soon over and we drifted inside to lick our wounds, both mental and physical.

There was little for us to do now that the threat of invasion had ceased. Patrols were no longer required but training continued as further mercenaries arrived seeking work in the region. On Tuesday morning Sprog did not appear at breakfast. We checked his bunk and locker to find that all of his belongings had disappeared. Further investigation solved the mystery. He had taken the early train south with two other mercs to a small town called Vinkovci. Out of the frying pan . . .

The next few days were spent in idle loafing, hospital visits being the high point. Kit continued to improve rapidly, his powerful body responding to treatment and enforced rest. Within days he was up, hobbling around on crutches, his damaged neck held firmly by a metal brace. Benny was also fortunate, the injury to his side showing remarkable recovery after surgery to remove several large lumps of shrapnel. John, however, wasn't doing quite so well. Fragments of metal, always the most difficult to locate and remove, were embedded in his eye, and the hospitals in Osijek and Zagreb didn't possess the essential equipment to remove them. His sight was in danger of being lost if specialist surgery wasn't available, and this problem gave Kit something to think about as he lay in the adjoining bed, watching nurses inject needles into John's eye, asking him if it hurt.

Florez did not visit. He even sent Slavko – the leader of the Yellow Submarines – to fill us in on the results of their Velika Pumpa verification patrol. Normally he appeared two or three times a day, giving orders, suggesting incursions.

'They are gone.' A man of few words, was Slavko.

'Could you perhaps elaborate?' Nigel enquired in his most pompous voice.

'*Da!* The JNA have left.'

'Oh. That's so much better,' said Nigel sarcastically. 'Any chance of some detailed info?'

Slavko looked at him perplexed. 'Info?'

'Information,' Steve cut in. '*Do you have any detailed information?*'

'*Da*, I have information.'

We waited impatiently as Slavko worked through his book of

two thousand useful English phrases. He smiled. A big, gap-toothed grin of accomplishment. 'The JNA have left Velika Pumpa with all equipment.' He flipped through a few more pages. 'They have pulled back to Beli Manastir and are moving out of the area.'

'You mean that they have withdrawn?'

'*Da*.' He delivered another enormous smile before giving Steve, the nearest body to him, a rib-crushing bear hug.

'*Hvala vam mnogo* . . . Sorry I forget. Thank you very much.'

'*Molim*,' replied Steve modestly. That's all right. He shook Slavko earnestly by the hand with the air of a conquering hero.

'We fucking did it then! Scared the bastards off. That'll please Kit and the lads.' Malaria punched Steve on the arm, dancing round the room in exhilarated relief at not having to repeat the process.

Complications had set in with Benny, slowing his recovery, and his reaction to the news of our success didn't induce the kind of enthusiasm expected. He tried, but you could see in his eyes that the pain was acute, taking precedence over just about everything. John showed some signs of pleasure by lifting his thumb upward. Kit, however, was ecstatic at the result, even moving his head slightly, if cautiously. He had been told that they were letting him out tomorrow – another cause for celebration.

He turned up late in the morning of the following day, hobbling on alloy crutches covered in camouflage tape – just to make him feel at home. He seemed to have developed a Florez fixation while in hospital. 'Do you know that bastard never came to see me. Not once,' were almost his first words.

When Kit and Florez finally came face to face they circled one another like suspicious dogs, both unsure of how to proceed. Many stories had circulated over the past few days suggesting that Florez had told his commanders that he should take credit for the raid. Like Chinese whispers, they grew and grew; in the end even those present began to doubt their memories. Kit bottled up his anger until it smouldered, burning anyone stupid enough to discuss Florez and Velika Pumpa in his presence. They stalked one another moodily, avoiding contact wherever possible. It wasn't going to work any longer, we could tell. The time had come to move on, leaving Florez to sort out his own salvation without the benefit of professionals to take care of the sticky bits. But not until Kit was fit and well again.

A sleek, heavily laden Range Rover pulled up by the school-house entrance, and its two occupants piled out, stretching arms and yelling loudly for Freeman. One was immediately recognised as Kit's old friend Mike Stanton; the other was a stranger. Dave Tomkins was in town on a mission of mercy – to sell arms to the Croatian army. He looked completely out of place in this world of cropped hair and unwashed camo clothing, being tall, sophisti-cated and casually dressed. His long grey hair framed an expensively tanned, just-back-from-the-Riviera face. Kit wel-comed the pair with a look of absolute joy. It was party time and everyone was invited.

I couldn't keep up with the animated chatter, and left them to their own devices for a few hours. Raucous bursts of laughter echoed throughout the building as they lied and bragged to one another, laughing at past experiences and those to come, before getting down to the serious business of moving the merchandise – in this instance weapons, ammunition and military clothing.

Kit phoned HQ at Dave's request and asked to speak to Commander Florez. The conversation was short and without any pleasantries. An appointment was made for Dave to present his samples to the brass for inspection the following day. That night Osijek was hit again, this time by three old comrades hell bent on recapturing the good old days.

Kit's only visible reminder of the battle was his inability to walk unaided; crutches not being part of the image a mercenary wishes to portray to his critical public. He was offered a parrot from Osijek Zoo to accompany him on his shoulder as he hobbled about the place, but he declined with threats so malevolent that the subject became taboo – to his face at least.

Unable to take part in training programmes, he kept himself busy trying to organise medical assistance for John, in the process learning about bureaucracy, Balkan style. They have a magic word in this country which is repeated by all, regardless of allegiance or ethnic group. The word, which solves all problems, is spoken sometimes with a smile, sometimes a frown. Either way the message is the same. *Sutra* – tomorrow, always tomorrow. never *danas* – today. After numerous telephone calls and *sutras* coming out of his ears, Kit was able to get John transferred to Osijek eye hospital where with equally limited resources the doctors tried their best, without success, to remove the metal fragments.

Running out of ideas by now, the next move came in a flash of inspiration. Kit had developed an affinity with Roger Courtiour, associate producer of the BBC *Inside Story* documentary, and had been given his home telephone number. He rang, explaining the problem in short, gasping sentences and requesting assistance from the BBC to bring John home to the UK. It was a long shot, born of desperation, but Roger Courtiour agreed after consultation with his colleagues. Arrangements were immediately made for John to be taken by train to meet a Yugoslavian lady representative of the BBC in Zagreb. Kit was jubilant, vowing never to watch ITV again, and leaving within hours to make the journey with a bandaged John by his side, on his way home at last to Britain and specialist NHS eye care.

Roger Courtiour made these comments to me when discussing the incident some time later:

'I recall that there was a distinct possibility that John might lose the sight in one eye, and obtaining suitable treatment for a British mercenary in Croatia at that time was a long way down in the pecking order of things. To some degree this was understandable. The Croatians had inadequate medical facilities for their own injured people, let alone a foreign mercenary. Kit contacted me, requesting assistance which we were only too pleased to provide – proving that BBC film-makers do have hearts.

'This was a side of Kit that I actually respected. He looked after the people under his assumed command and accepted responsibility for their welfare in times of misfortune – a quite genuine side to his nature.

'He knew about soldiering and tried to look after his men. It did seem entirely appropriate to help when he came through and said that they wouldn't give him any money to get John out, and would I please do something for him.'

With that problem solved, Kit returned to the barracks, only to find that Dave's sales pitch to the brass at brigade headquarters hadn't met with the desired enthusiasm. The Croatians argued that the asking price was far too high, and no amount of haggling made any difference. It was a bummer, Mike and Dave's dangerous trip a waste of time. Still, they were here now and there must be some kind of deal available for enterprising businessmen in a war zone.

'What about the armoury?' Kit suggested without explanation.

'What about the armoury?' Mike replied.

'I've got a friend in Zagreb who's interested in some weapons. I met him by chance when we were waiting for the BBC bird yesterday.'

'What's his name?' Dave pricked up his ears.

'Ivan Urirch – he's the chief of police.'

'The chief of police?' Dave repeated, curiosity making him lean forward in anticipation.

'Yeah. He wants some arms to send down to his police friends in Bosnia. The armoury here is full of gear . . . and I've got the key.'

In Kit's own words: 'I went and sucked up to Florez and said that as I couldn't do much at the moment, was it all right if I had a couple of days off in Zagreb.' Florez agreed – no doubt glad to be rid of him for a while. With the first part of the scheme resolved, final planning took place. Kit and his friends sneaked out in the dead of night, creeping through the shadows, and looted the armoury; Kalashnikovs, ammunition, Zolyas, grenades and side arms were taken and stowed away in the Range Rover. Mike paused as the tailgate was closed.

'What happens if we get stopped?'

'Don't worry,' Kit reassured him. 'I've got my ID card. It won't be a problem.'

The first part of the trip went without mishap but as darkness lifted an ominous shape appeared in the road before them, in the shape of two enormous sandbags, behind which were the unmistakable barrels of automatic weapons – an official check-point manned by the police.

Dave Tomkins turned to Kit. 'You'd better know what you're fucking doing!' he said. 'I'm trying to get used to five-star hotels. There's no way I'm spending another night in jail.'

The car slid to a halt, Kit and his ID clambering out from the back seat. 'Morning, Officer. Looks like a nice day. Can I help you?'

The policeman, gun cocked, indicated that he wanted to look inside the vehicle. Kit, playing for time, continued speaking in English, while the others simply sweated. The policeman was joined by another getting anxious at the delay. '*Nemojte se pokretati!*' – Don't move – he barked, thrusting the barrel of his gun in Kit's ribs and pushing him away as the first officer opened the rear door. There was a metallic clank as a Zolya rocket launcher rolled to the edge, dropping on to the road at his feet. That did it; with the threat of terrorism rife in the area these men were taking no chances, especially with a bunch of suspicious-looking foreigners. Kit waved his identification card, pointing at himself and the others as the police surrounded them. There was the sound of safety catches being released. 'Commandos! Commandos! Osijek . . . We are from Osijek,' Kit yelled, as the officer in charge looked at the ID card, examining the occupants of the vehicle suspiciously before walking back to his car and making a phone call.

'Who do you think he's phoning?' whispered Dave.

'I dunno. Hope it isn't Osijek brigade headquarters,' replied Kit through clamped teeth. 'We're in the shit if he does.'

'We're in the shit if he doesn't.'

The officer returned, still looking perplexed, but with little choice, allowed them to proceed through the checkpoint, taking note of the vehicle number as they passed with triumphant smiles.

'Fucking close that, wasn't it?' Mike muttered, exhausted by the tension. 'I thought they were gonna shoot us for a second.'

'*Nema problema*,' replied Kit, almost wetting himself with relieved laughter.

The weapons were received by a grateful police chief without question, and the sum of 3,000 Deutschmarks was paid for the haul – plenty enough for a gigantic piss-up in Zagreb, with a little bit left over for a rainy day.

Kit left his friends, who had further business in the area, and hitched a lift with an American mercenary, returning apprehensively to Osijek the next day. He need not have worried; so far the loss of the equipment had gone unnoticed, and as the days passed the likelihood faded that the mysterious disappearance of all that hardware would be attributed to him.

Kit finally ditched the crutches after about ten days and was left temporarily with a slight limp, his freedom from reliance upon them making him aware that the time had come to hit the road again. Florez no longer made any attempt to co-exist with the volunteers, making his feelings of contempt for them evident at every opportunity. But the simple fact was that Kit and the team had accomplished their task and were no longer required. They had trained an effective fighting unit, organised infiltration patrols and destroyed the JNA offensive which had threatened Osijek with Serbian domination – not a bad epitaph for a bunch of vagabonds and psychopaths!

It was time for pastures new. Posusje beckoned and a telephone call to Governor Drago confirmed that the offer made some months ago in Split still remained open for negotiation.

'How the fuck are we going to get there?' Pete groaned, memories of perpetual road blocks engulfing his mind. 'Posusje's right down by the coast, innit? Just past Split.'

'Stop whining, you miserable sod. There's a ceasefire on at the moment, so we shouldn't have problems like the last time,' Kit replied in his Don't-give-me-no-aggro tone.

'But, Kit . . .'

'Do you wanna come or not?' Flat, final, no room for discussion. Pete shut up and nursed his arm, a habit he had dropped into when feeling aggrieved.

'Right. Who wants to come then? Let's see a show of hands.'

Nigel, Pop, Steve and a hesitant Pete raised their arms. Spooky resisted for a moment before joining them. 'Is that it then?' Kit enquired. 'What about the rest of you?' Shrugging shoulders indicated indecision. Some would stay for a while, others would go home; wherever that might be.

'OK, so we've got six, including me.' Then, looking in my direction, 'Oh, mustn't forget him . . . seven.'

Transport; the perennial problem. Nick a lorry or a Land Rover and be arrested by police *en route*. Florez would love that. He'd be on the phone like a shot if any vehicles disappeared. Kit rang the Panorama Hotel in Zagreb, hoping to catch Mike Stanton.

'Mike, it's Kit.'

'Yeah. What are you after?' A nasty, suspicious mind has Mike.

'A lift to Posusje.' Kit was nice and casual. Get the fish on the hook before reeling him in.

'OK. Dave's finished his deal and gone home, so I can go that way. When do you wanna leave?'

'We'd like to go tomorrow, if possible.' That's it, sneak in the 'we' gently, so he doesn't notice.

'We . . ?' He does . . . sod it. Keep talking fast.

'Yeah, me and a few of the lads. We've been offered a little job by the Governor.' Play it pitiful. Appeal to Mike's better nature.

'OK, see you tomorrow. Halves on the petrol mind you. Bye.'

Gotcha!

We ate breakfast, and without bothering to wash our plates loaded the bergans to capacity with anything that wasn't nailed down. Kit rang Benny, still in Osijek Hospital, and told him about

186

John going home, wishing him a speedy recovery and offering him the opportunity of joining us in Posusje when fit again. Benny didn't even think about it before replying, 'Thanks, but no thanks.' Who could blame him?

Malaria drove slowly through the shell-battered town, allowing us our last look at its clanking trams, boarded-up shop windows and blank-faced inhabitants; none of whom gave a damn for the truckload of men passing by. We arrived at Osijek station feeling just a little bit unappreciated and bade farewell to a misty-eyed Malaria, who insisted on hugging us one by one before letting us go – just in time to watch the 0900 train to Zagreb pull out without us.

With an hour or more to kill before the next train, we were at a loose end, with little to do but guard our belongings and drink the bitter mud they call *kafu* – coffee. Pete started again about the journey. 'Why can't we fly down? Look at the map, there's an airfield at Pleso.'

Kit answered him in exasperated tone, as if talking to a child. 'There's a war on, dummy. If there are planes flying out of Pleso they'll be military, and if I'm wrong, the civilian ones won't be going south anyway. They'd get blown out of the sky by Serbian artillery. Now forget it. None of us wants to travel by road if there's a choice, but there isn't.'

Pete made a face and nursed his arm, wincing for effect rather than sympathy. He'd realised long ago that pity for his injury was in short supply.

Kit, never one to sit still for long, wandered off and engaged a pretty-looking girl in conversation, returning after ten minutes with her telephone number scribbled on a matchbox.

'Lot of good that's gonna do you,' Pop told him.

'You never know,' Kit replied. 'I might be back here one day on holiday when the war's over.'

A scuffle from the station entrance brought the ribbing to an abrupt halt. A station guard was wrestling with a young Croatian soldier who, holding a handgun aloft, was shouting drunkenly at the top of his voice. Kit tried his best to interpret. 'He's saying something about going home . . . can't understand it all.' The official was losing the battle. 'Suppose we'd better help,' muttered Kit, striding across to the fracas, with Steve close behind.

'*Zovite policiju!*' gasped the guard, holding on to the man's arm like grim death.

187

'We don't need the police,' Kit answered in English. 'Just let go of his arm and leave it to me.' The guard released the soldier's arm and sprang back out of the way. 'Naughty, naughty!' Kit waved his finger at the young man then hit him low, watching him double up before wrenching the pistol from his grasp. He quickly released the magazine and cocked the pistol; a round popped out. The Croat had been waving the gun with a round up the spout, just waiting for a gentle squeeze. This made matters worse. The arrogant stupidity of it offended Kit's military senses, and without pausing he hit him again, standing back as the young man gasped for breath on the platform.

'I've been fighting in the war,' the Croatian choked in perfect English, 'I'm going home.'

'You're walking around the place pissed out of your skull, with a loaded gun just waiting to go off. You could kill somebody just because you're incompetent. Now fuck off before I report you.' The soldier picked up his gun and slunk away, to disdainful looks from his countrymen.

'It's all good fun, isn't it?' Kit said, shaking hands with a grateful guard, who didn't understand a word that had been spoken.

Our tired old train finally puffed and clanked its way into the station, and we climbed aboard with our heavy bergans, thankful that our long journey was underway at last. After settling down, we plunged into silent contemplation, looking through dirty carriage windows at the once pretty villages of Koska and Jelisavac before the railway line crossed over the main road heading north-west towards Varazdin; the last stop before the southward run into Zagreb.

Steve broke the brooding silence, thinking aloud more than trying to start a conversation.

'Poor old Ivan, getting killed like that,' he whispered to himself. 'Damiar, Jim, Benny, John. They'll never be the same again. Remember old Johnny the Groundhog? Wonder where he is now. Back home in the good old US of A, I guess. Fucking glad that Tommy left; I'd have killed the bastard if he'd stayed on. Still, we had some good times, didn't we?'

He looked around for a response but Kit wasn't listening, lost in his own memories out there in the Yugoslavian countryside. Nigel nodded, saying nothing. Steve didn't pursue the question, sinking inside himself for the rest of the journey until with a shuddering halt we arrived in Zagreb, where Mike was waiting for us.

'You're late,' were his first words. Kit had phoned him with our arrival time. His second words were, 'How the fuck am I gonna get all these blokes and bergans in my Range Rover?'

'Don't worry, we'll manage,' replied Kit. 'Two in front, three in the rear seats and three in the back. The bergans can go on top.'

'OK! Let's load up and get on the road then. Oh, I've got some good news,' Mike added.

'What's that?' Kit asked quickly, suspecting a problem.

'The ferry has started operating again since the ceasefire came into force. So we've only got to get to Rijeka and it's a boat ride around the coast and straight into Split.'

Pete could have kissed him, his smile of gratitude lighting up the whole of Zagreb station.

It was straight down the E65 this time. Fifty kilometres of almost perfect road taken at speed. One road block interrupted our progress, but the police looked at Kit's almost worn-out ID, accepted two bottles of booze and waved us on – right into Karlovac and a lot of bad memories about rats and dead bodies. Steve, still in nostalgia mode, narrated the story to Mike, Pop and Spooky, who didn't seem to be that interested; you had to be there. The place had changed a bit since our last visit, and not for the better. Buildings which had stood undamaged before were now piles of rubble, people still wandered with vacant expressions, stray dogs continued to plunder suspicious bundles. But the shelling had been suspended . . . for a while at least. We didn't stop for a burger or a piss. With over a hundred klicks to travel and an absolute certainty that the ceasefire was just a temporary blip – enabling all sides to catch their breath – speed was of the essence, and we tore through the town a little higher than the designated speed limit.

The last twenty kilometres were the worst. Not because of military intervention or militiamen causing aggro . . . No, it was Spooky. You can't keep an American ex-something quiet. They've always got a tale to tell. Like when I was in . . . 'Shut up, Spooky, or I'll rip your tongue out,' said Kit.

Rijeka is a crappy town, a yellowish industrial haze full of bad vibes. Rows of dirty, rust-encrusted cranes littered the skyline, with sea-stained tankers jostling each other for position in the cluttered port. Transit city Balkan style. And the place stank of sulphur! We passed the National Museum, heading for the Jadrolinija Ferry Wharf, only to find the ticket booth closed. Panic ... until we saw a scribbled sign, '*Otvoreno podne*' – Open noon. Further panic; it was now four o'clock!

Kit read the timetable with a bit of help.

'Christ, the ferry to Split only runs at night!'

'What time's night?' enquired Pete, still sitting in the car.

'Six o'clock!' Kit replied in a voice of doom.

'How long does it take?' Pete asked, leaning through the open window and coughing from the sulphur fumes.

'I don't bloody know. It's about three hundred kilometres or so to Split ... Forever, if the rest of the boats are anything to go by.'

An old man shuffled up to the door, opening it with a cup of coffee balanced in his other hand. He turned to us with an apologetic smile, saying, '*Dobar dan. Otvoreno sada.*' Good afternoon. Open now.

' 'Bout fucking time,' growled Spooky. 'This ain't no way to run a railroad.'

'Railroad?' the old man queried. 'Not railroad. Station that way,' he said, pointing to the left. 'This is ferry.'

'Yeah, yeah, yeah,' replied Spooky, shaking his head. 'I know. It's just an old American saying.'

Kit took out a suspicious wad of money from his back pocket, handing the old man a pile. 'When does the ferry get in?' he asked as he pocketed the change without looking at it – always a sign of a wealthy man.

'*Uskoro*' – soon – replied the old man, before adding, '*mozda*' – maybe.

'What does he mean, maybe?' Pete started to tense.

'Don't fret. They always say maybe. It's like *sutra* – part of the culture,' Nigel said soothingly.

With less than two hours to wait – maybe – there was little we could do but hang around the harbour and pour scorn upon sailors leaning over the rails of their ships, flicking cigarette butts into the filthy, oil-slicked water. It seemed like another world. No sounds of battle, just the scream of seagulls and Kit and the lads yelling obscenities at marooned seamen, who were happy to shout back in languages none of us understood, although the gestures were universal.

The blast of a horn focused our interest seaward, just in time to see a scruffy old ferryboat rounding the inner harbour, reversing its screws dramatically as it slid into berthing position alongside the wharf. Luxury it wasn't, and I could see Nigel's face drop at the thought of spending the next seventeen hours aboard the tub without the facility of a cocktail bar.

'You gotta look on the bright side,' Kit told him. 'At least nobody is gonna be shooting at you. Unless the ceasefire is broken again.' He paused for a moment before adding thoughtfully, 'course if it is, we're really in the shit. Serb gunboats patrol these waters and we'll be sitting ducks with these uniforms on.' If looks could kill . . .

Mike edged his Range Rover cautiously on board with no help from the crew, who were busy chatting to one another as they watched, no doubt hoping he would blow it and end up in the drink. Other vehicles followed equally carefully, and within half an hour we and dozens of refugees were heading out to sea and past the island of Krk. We couldn't see it in the darkness of course, but we knew it was there – Pete told us so.

The monotonous chug of the engine combined with a bone-juddering vibration soon lulled us into a stuporous desire for sleep. We were easily seduced, crawling into uncomfortable positions on deck before engaging neutral brain activity and getting our heads down, like all good soldiers on active duty.

Most of us were awakened throughout the night by directional shifts, engine fluctuations and plain discomfort, grunting at one another like old drunks on bomb sites before slipping back into fitful sleep. The lullaby from Spooky's orbital sander simulation didn't help, until silenced by a flying size twelve.

Zadar came and went, the brief stop allowing more passengers to embark upon this voyage of discovery. Chains clanked, floodlights glared in our eyes and a group of soldiers noisily booted their way past us. One stopped, looking down at Steve before poking him in the ribs with his AK.

'Wassamatter?' Steve rubbed his eyes sleepily, squinting up at the man angrily.

'You Steve Brown?' he asked curtly.

'Yeah. Do I owe you some money or what?' Steve climbed to his feet, not wanting to be in a prone position if aggravation loomed.

'Nah. I'm Bill Willis. We was together in the mob at Goose Green. Don't you remember me?'

Steve looked closely at the man, clad in black from head to foot with a giant cross at his neck.

He shook his head. 'Sorry, mate.'

'Come on, you gotta remember me. They called me Preacher.'

Steve kept shaking his head, but trying to appear friendly asked, 'What are you doing here?'

'With Dobroslav Paraga's lot. The HOS. Still savin' souls. The bastard Chetniks'll keep me busy for a while yet.'

Steve smiled and shook the man's hand. 'Nice to see you again, Bill. Perhaps it'll all come back when I'm properly awake.'

'Yeah. Catch you later.' He handed Steve a playing card before walking away to join his comrades now disappearing towards the bow.

'Do you know him?' asked a curious Pete.

'Yeah, I know him all right. He's a fucking religious maniac. Sees himself as an angel of death or something, bringing destruction on the devil's disciples. First it was the Argies. Then Colombian drug-dealers. Now it's the Chetniks. He leaves a cross on the bodies of men he kills. They ought to have binned the guy at Aldershot. He's a nut!'

'Who's Dobroslav Paraga?' Pete turned to Kit for an answer.

'He runs the paramilitary wing of the Hrvatska Stranka Prava – HOS. They're against almost everything in this country; extremist bastards, best left well alone.'

Steve flicked the playing card in his fingers absent-mindedly before catching sight of the inscription. 'Look at this!' In the dim bulkhead light a black ace of spades surrounding a smiling death's-head skull stared at us; behind it was a blood-dripping scythe and the words 'WE KILL FOR PEACE'.

'Lemme see that.' Spooky snatched it away. 'These are like the cards they used in 'Nam. The guys left them on bodies after an attack to frighten the gooks.'

'Like I said, the man's a nut.' Steve sighed. 'I'm off this boat before he comes back. That's for sure.'

It was getting light now as the ferry manoeuvred its way past the larger scattered islands of Kaprije, Zmajan and Zlarin, lost somewhere in the inevitable cold morning mist. Sibenik was hidden completely from view, if not memory. 'Remember that bloody road block before Sibenik?' Nigel reminded us with ill-concealed venom.

It all came back in a flash of humiliation – thanks, Nigel, we needed that – the frisking fingers of ZNG scumbags diving into our pockets, bad breath making us gag as they looted our few possessions, their smiles of pleasure at our impotence as they waved goodbye. Some things you don't want to remember; feeling like shit is one of them.

We rounded the coastline, kicking in tightly to Ciovo island before bearing left for a first welcome sight of Split harbour. Civilised, modern and above all peaceful. Not a tank or artillery piece could be seen anywhere; even the roads were unmined! We grabbed our gear feeling like holiday-makers and trundled to the ship's rail, leaving Mike the task of driving his Range Rover ashore.

'Breakfast! Anybody for breakfast?' Kit headed towards the Bastion self-service restaurant, leaving Mike to find somewhere to park the car. Back in minutes with a 'sod em' look on his face, he told us he had left it in a space reserved for officials with a note stuck on the windscreen saying 'Doktor'.

'Doctor! A British-plated Range Rover, full of olive bergans, webbing and military equipment?' Pop questioned.

'Could be an army doctor,' Mike reasoned with a shrug.

Through mouthfuls of breakfast we discussed our next move, deciding against spending time looking around Split in favour of a direct drive to Imotski, then Posusje. The journey, of around fifty kilometres, should take about an hour. But ominous news coming from the café radio indicated that Croatian intelligence had detected Serbian troop movement in the area, meaning only one thing: as far as the JNA were concerned, the ceasefire had run its natural course.

'Look, lads.' Kit turned in his seat to face us. 'I don't know what to expect on this trip, so keep your weapons at the ready and be prepared for anything. It should be easy, but if the war kicks off again, no one knows where it'll start and it's just our luck that it'll be right here on the road to Posusje.'

We decided to chance our luck with the main northern route out of town, turning right to eventually pick up the Cista Prova road and reaching Imotski without difficulty. Posusje was only ten kilometres away and we were optimistic about reaching it before trouble started. We should have known better.

A distant thud, muffled but distinct, dragged our listless minds back to reality. Mike turned the radio off as we listened, hoping we'd been mistaken. We looked at one another with challenging eyes. 'Nah,' said Peter hopefully. 'It was thunder.' Mike pulled over and switched off the engine; in silence we waited for confirmation. Long minutes ticked silently past before another dull sound gently shook the earth, soon followed by others, until they merged into one. Heavy artillery fire to the north, in the direction of Duvno. No doubt about it this time – the spell had been broken.

'Let's go,' Kit said quietly. 'Another ten minutes and we'll be in Posusje.'

We crossed the border from Croatia into Bosnia-Herzegovina with a leaden feeling in the pits of our stomachs. What were we letting ourselves in for this time?

A narrow lane, bushes on both sides, no clear view. Around the corner a group of burly, fierce-looking armed men. Hay bales across the road. 'Fuck it.' Steve breathed, clicking off his safety. The others followed suit.

'Relax,' Kit soothed. 'It's bound to be Drago's men this close to town.'

Logical. Nobody had thought of that. As Kit opened the door they looked at him with undisguised suspicion, old hunting rifles at the ready and not a Kalashnikov in sight.

'Looks like trouble,' whispered Steve, wiping revealing beads of sweat from his eyes.

'*Da li govorite engleski?*' Kit held his hands high, just in case.

'*Da.*' A giant walked from the rear of the group, dressed in bandoliers of shotgun cartridges and an old side-by-side twelve-gauge.

'We have come to meet Governor Drago,' Kit told him.

'He is expecting you?' The man's lips didn't move.

'Yes, we are here at his request to train your men to fight the Serbs.'

The giant moved back, instructing a young woman to return to the village and check out the story. She reappeared after what seemed an awfully long time, and whispered sweet nothings into his beard. He nodded, then they all went into a huddle before turning with smiles of welcome.

'You are Freeman, yes?' the woman asked coyly, fluttering her eyes, farm-girl style. 'The Governor said he is looking forward to meeting you again. Please follow us to the village for refreshment where he will join you shortly.'

Kit nodded and began to climb back in the car, pausing for a moment as the sound of artillery fire started up again in the distance. It was closer this time, with nearby high-pitched auto fire providing a rhythm accompaniment. Somebody was getting a thorough going-over out there in the hills, and it sounded like the action was heading our way.

Chapter Eleven

Don't worry about it. Just learn from the rest of us
and remember that each day is different. Some days
you can be courageous and some days you can't.
Some days you can kill and others . . .

The part-time soldiers of Posusje clambered on to the Range Rover, gleefully straddling bonnet, roof and running boards as the bearded pied piper led us through increasingly narrow lanes, finally reaching the outskirts of the scarred village. Deep craters and a cottage with its roof demolished by shellfire proved – if proof were needed – that enemy action had taken its toll, even in this unstrategic place. The lane curved gently to the left, bringing us alongside the damaged building where we could see a sobbing middle-aged woman hunched against crumbling walls, grief racking her body in juddering spasms. A child of six or seven foraged through the rubble for a doll, a game, a ball . . . any kind of toy to bring comfort.

We'd seen it many times before in villages all over the country. But like the sight of your own blood, you never really get used to it.

'Are we gonna stop and help?' Pete asked.

'What good would it do?' We can't rebuild her house for her, can we? We can't bring back her possessions. What's the point?' Kit wasn't being cruel, just practical. 'Forget it, Pete, there's worse to come.'

We drove on, wondering who was right, until we reached Posusje, which looked a little like an old town from the American West, spread out loosely, with empty streets, and small cafes and bars substituting for saloons.

'Easy pickings for the JNA, innit?' Steve muttered.

The beard pointed us to a small house with '*Otvoreno*' painted on a board above the door. No sign saying 'Bar', 'Café' or 'Lil's' Place'; just 'Open'. In we went, getting hit by a solid wall of lung-destroying smoke from a million Turkish cigarettes.

'Drago come soon,' the big guy grunted. 'You wait, have rest.

Drink *kafu, pivo* – coffee, beer. Goodbye.' He was gone, back to the farm and his cows and pigs, his soldiering over for the day.

We waited for an hour, feeling sick on endless cups of battery-acid coffee and nicotine air. The locals, not bothering to hide their curiosity, stared at us as if we were aliens from some distant planet.

'Take me to your leader.' Spooky tried to communicate with two wizened turban-wearing faces; blank stares showed no sign of humour.

Drago arrived, looking tough and capable, two henchmen backing him up. Curt but charismatic, he shook hands with everyone before getting down to business.

'This is the deal,' he said brusquely. 'I want a unit trained and equipped for the defence of my town. Funding is readily available for these things.' Kit listened attentively, the word 'funding' being especially attractive.

He continued, 'In addition to training the men of Posusje, I want you to operate a special operations force contracted out to any village or township unable to afford their own defence and requiring your brand of military expertise. The work will involve blowing bridges, attacking convoys, driving back JNA and Chetnik offensives. You will travel around the country firefighting and return to base for your weekly wage and bonus. Do you understand?' Well rehearsed, without taking a breath.

Kit nodded, his lips pursed in concentration, as Drago lowered his voice to a whisper.

'You will be paid two thousand Deutschmarks per week, plus a bonus for every task you perform successfully. These men with you will receive a lesser but still generous sum which we will discuss later. Is this acceptable?'

Kit looked around the table at hopeful expressions, nodding his head.

'Come with me now. I have a farmhouse about fourteen kilometres outside of town for you to live and train in.'

We trailed him like lemmings from the bar and clambered into the Range Rover, following his Toyota Land Cruiser through lifeless streets, past occasional empty shops and out into the barren countryside.

So this was private enterprise Bosnian style. Shades of The Magnificent Seven ... Drago's hired guns. All this and a farmhouse to live in; a mercenary's wildest dreams come true.

Drago's Cruiser did a fast right, bumping over hardened mud tracks before lurching to a halt. We stayed put for a few moments, taking it all in. The farm sprawled its way over a peaceful valley surrounded by acres of mixed countryside – ideal training land. Snow-tipped mountains overlooked us, the bright winter sun glinting off jutting peaks. 'I can do with some of this,' Pete sighed, his head somewhere in the Swiss Alps.

We off-loaded the gear as Kit joined Drago, discussing the business arrangement in greater detail, we presumed. Lots of arm-waving, pointing and animated conversation ensued; some laughter and a manly hug. Drago passed Kit a wad of money and slapped him on the back. All was well.

The Cruiser reversed out into the road, and Drago gave us a brief wave before accelerating back in the direction of town. Kit headed straight for Mike.

'Here's some money. I've told him you're the logistics expert and he wants gear for about twenty men.'

'What does he want and how much did he give you?' Mike asked anxiously.

'Boots, DPM clobber, webbing. He gave me a hundred and sixty thousand Deutschmarks. Is that enough?'

Mike nodded. 'I'll have to go back to the UK for most of it, though. There's nothing in this country.'

'I told him that and he said OK. How long do you think it'll take you to get back?'

Mike grimaced, 'Depends on how long it takes to get to Split airport. Depends on available flights. Depends . . .'

'Cut the crap, Mike. How long?'

'There's a fucking war going on here, Kit, and a lot of ifs, buts and maybes.' He paused. 'Say two to three weeks.'

'OK. You'd better get a few hours' kip before you leave.'

Finding somewhere to bed down was easy in this rambling old building; the large rooms afforded space, comfort and a relaxed atmosphere – apart from a strange *Marie Celeste* feeling about the place which we couldn't quite put our finger on.

Cold soup stood in pots on a dead fire, cut bread and rancid butter on plates, covered in grime, mildew and mouse droppings. Coarse woollen clothing hung in cupboards and a ginger cat examined us suspiciously from its window perch. Something strange had happened here, you could sense it with the short hairs at the back of your neck. We checked outside, searching through outhouses for signs of an attack, a struggle, bodies; anything to give us a clue about the previous inhabitants. Nothing, not a sign of violence anywhere.

As Spooky said, 'It looks like they just upped and went.'

We slept like logs, snored like pigs and woke to the familiar sound of the greater cropped Geordie warbling its daybreak melody.

'Let's get the fucking show on the road!' Kit coaxed us into life after our first good night's sleep for quite a while. 'Come on, you idle bastards. The FNGs – fucking new guys – are gonna be here soon and we want to show them what hot shots we are. Don't we?' He shook Spooky's bed, yelling, 'Hustle, hustle, hustle,' deep into his vibrating right ear.

'Sergeant Bilko or what!' Spooky groaned, rolling over in agony, his eyes blinking rapidly in the morning light.

'I fucking hate it when you're like this, Kit,' moaned Steve, stretching as he looked out of the window at the backdrop of mountains.

Breakfast wasn't the normal blow-out. Supplies had been forgotten and the mouse droppings on what remained in the larder didn't make cheese and scraps of meat appealing. So it was coffee, coffee and then more coffee, before a brisk warm-up jog around the farm buildings.

At eight o'clock the first group of trainees arrived by horse and cart, followed in quick succession by others in lorries and beat-up old cars and on foot. Ages ranged from sixteen to sixty: Mountain men with gnarled faces and toughened bodies, kids with bum-fluff beards. All carrying proudly their obsolete but well-cared-for weapons: battered long-barrelled hunting rifles, one shot and reload, deadly accurate at long range but useless against the metallic vomit of an AK-47; shotguns, elaborately etched, beautifully maintained, at short range devastating, but who wants to get that close?; knives, large-bladed, rusty and pitted. Kit was going to have his work cut out. Discipline? Forget it!

'OK, you bunch of deadbeats, get in line!' Kit yelled at the top of his voice. Ranko, an ex-London waiter, translated. They shuffled, giggling, into a column.

'Shut the fuck up!' Kit was in a hurry. These men had a long way to go and only two weeks to get there.

The day flew past in a blur of running bodies. Up and down hills, through dense woodland. Hare and hounds, push-ups, sit-ups. The whole para bit. At the end of the day the poor bastards were totally knackered and Kit was hoarse from screaming orders.

For the next ten days it was train, train, train. Instil agression. Preach tactics. Inspire loyalty. Run, jump, scream, KILL! They had bottle, these men, none dropping out from injury or fatigue. Their eyes gave out a clear message, alive with hope, burning with fever: they were the saviours of their town – it was written in the wind.

Mike returned with the consignment of British DPM clothing, boots and webbing – most of which had been obtained from the Survival Shop in Bristol. He stayed just long enough to say hello-goodbye, as other pressing business matters demanded his attention; especially since the war was hotting up again after its fourteenth ceasefire.

A further week of arms familiarisation and drill followed, the farmers adjusting to their new automatic weapons, grenades and Zolyas like schoolkids with computers. Now fully kitted out and dressed like soldiers, they were beginning to behave like soldiers too – even saluting!

Kit Freeman, in less than a month, had transformed these unprogressive country folk into a small but effective army with the most important attribute available to any general – balls!

Drago was more than impressed as he watched the squad perform in fields around the farm, blasting trees and cardboard cut-outs, screaming as they attacked piles of inanimate hay bales and blowing huts to matchwood. All great fun. He shook Kit by the hand, demonstrating his pleasure by passing over wads of paper in large denominations to a smiling training officer.

Serbian MiG fighter/bombers attempting low-level strikes on Imotski had caused problems over the past few days. Mountainous peaks virtually surrounding the town made the run-in difficult, and getting out without slamming into the rock face was even more hazardous for inexperienced pilots. Posusje, some ten kilometres to the east, was getting the jettisoned cluster bombs and rockets instead, and the unpredictability of raids, combined with the odd hit, made for a nervous existence in the town. Without suitable weapons, there was little Kit and his team could do about the air strikes until a word in the ear of someone high up provoked positive reaction, and SAMs – surface-to-air missiles – were deployed high up on the hills, soon starting to discourage the attacks, which we assumed were designed to soften up defences before a ground assault by JNA forces.

With training complete and the Posusje commando force raring to go, Drago and Kit spent many late nights poring over maps, making telephone calls and generally trying to drum up some business – not difficult with a unique product.

Duvno, twenty kilometres north, was worried about a marauding Chetnik band attacking villages west of the town, and offered 100,000 Deutschmarks for the group to sweep the area clean. Horror stories made the gig even more interesting and Kit accepted it without question.

'Bastards. I'm gonna just love giving them a good kicking,' he told us after his meeting with Drago.

Twenty men in three Rovers, loaded to the springs with nice new gear and just itching to see action. Up at dawn and on the road, passing Ostrac, Mesihovina and Cebara, before going in-country to the left of Duvno, where Kit sent out a scout car to survey the land before proceeding north. We waited for its return, chewing grass and thinking great thoughts.

Steve returned with an all-clear wave from three hundred metres ahead. We rapidly caught up with him before passing the Busko Jezero lake, reminding us of our earlier grenade fishing episode. Pete looked at Kit with a how-about-it expression.

'Nah, can't mess around on our first op, can we? Maybe on the way back. A fish supper would go down nicely.'

A brief stop at Prisoje for a B&B – brew and briefing. The map was laid out and the current village causing concern indicated with a red grease pen.

'We'll drive in to this point, park up and go the rest of the way on foot. This village was hit last night according to reports, so with a bit of luck they'll still be in the vicinity.' Kit pointed to a small hamlet of maybe forty houses. 'No Chetnik prisoners, mind you. Kill them all!'

Tobacco-chewing Ranko, the leader of the Bosnian volunteers, spat a stream of evil brown fluid, adjusted his eye patch and translated in machine-gun Serbo Croat. Smiles widened and the men exchanged vengeful glances, adopting aggressive postures copied from film posters.

Pete felt compelled to take the piss. He handed an eager-looking kid his scrim scarf to wear as a bandanna, saying, 'Rambo.

You look like Rambo.' The youngster understood only one word, but it was enough.

Another five kilometres and we parked the Rovers, stuffing them into a copse and covering them with bracken. Vladimir, the pock-marked slob of the group, and bespectacled Milenko were left on guard, much to their annoyance, until Kit explained just how important their role was. We moved off slowly, unsure of the terrain or the accuracy of our map, heading towards the trig point with little idea of the strength of our quarry but with a strong, almost obsessive desire to make contact.

Keeping close to the edge of the field, with bushes helping to conceal our movement, we loped towards a nearby woodland, crawled under a barbed-wire fence and formed two groups, spreading out in the direction of the village a few kilometres beyond the northern edge. Spooky, leading 'B' group, stopped almost immediately, spinning around and dropping to his knees, then crawling back a few metres as he waved us to him.

'There's a woodsman's hut down there,' he whispered. 'It looks like they're using it as a base.'

Kit moved forward on his belly, fumbling for his binoculars as he went. Back he came after only a few moments, face flushed with excitement. 'Looks like you're right, Spook. I could only see two of them. The others could be inside the hut or out pillaging. We'd better move back a bit and wait until nightfall.'

Steve dropped back to the vehicles to prepare Vladimir and Milenko for hostile proximity and probable conflict. Their exclusion from an impending confrontation with Chetniks pissed them off even more!

With each man taking a turn at watch, we lolled and snoozed in the rough bracken as the hours ticked away. Like the man said, it's ninety per cent boredom and ten per cent panic – this was the boredom bit.

'What happened to the people who lived in our farm?' Pete, never one to beat around the bush, asked Ranko.

'*Ne razumem.*' I don't understand. He looked perplexed at the question.

'Bollocks! You can speak and understand English better than I can.'

Ranko stared at Pete for a moment, gradually moving his gaze to the rest of us waiting for an answer. 'They went away,' he

shrugged, lifting his palms upwards in an expression of uncon-
cern.

'They went away. Just like that?' Kit repeated suspiciously.

'They were Serbian pigs.'

He had answered the question, and no further discussion was
necessary or forthcoming. No doubt their bodies were buried
somewhere on the hundred-acre farm, never to be seen again.

Nigel slid back. 'There's movement from over there.' He
pointed to the edge of the wood, where crashing sounds and
laughter could now be heard.

Slithering forward, we inched to the edge of the brush-covered
rim and peered through dense foliage at a group of twelve men
carrying radios, clothes and various household appliances. They
were back-slapping one another, jostling and bellowing with
laughter. It must have been a hell of a joke; some could barely
stand as they rolled drunkenly against one another.

'They have raided the village,' Ranko translated unnecessarily.
'What shall we do?'

'Wait until they are inside the hut,' Kit replied. 'Then we'll go
and do the bastards.'

The Chetniks, dressed typically in their heavily armed mixture
of military and civilian guerrilla-fighter apparel, played around
in the clearing as their two comrades came out of the hut to join
them, grabbing oddments from bulging pockets and pouring
wine and beer down open gullets. I could feel Ranko, Toni and
Obrad tighten beside me as they watched. Kit, realising that they
were poised to go off with a bang, said quickly, 'Cool it . . . wait.
You'll get your chance soon.'

The horseplay continued as the Chetniks became more intoxi-
cated throwing bottles in the air for haphazard shooting practice
before finally staggering into the hut. 'Sloppy gits!' murmured
Steve, turning to Kit for the go sign.

There was little need for sophisticated military strategy under
the circumstances. Kit stood and the rest followed. Crouching
low, they headed for the hut, paused, looked at one another. Kit
nodded his head, and with a technique reminiscent of Chicago's
St Valentine's Day massacre they simply blasted the hut to
smithereens. Shell casings buzzed through the air and thirty-
round magazines were exchanged without pause. Long after the
mercs quit, the Bosnians continued blasting away, anger, frustration and pain freezing their trigger fingers on hold. The AK-47 has

a cyclical rate of 600rpm; a rough calculation indicated that well over one thousand rounds went into that hut in the space of a minute. It's difficult to believe that anyone could have survived the onslaught, but a low moan disproved that theory.

'Fuck it, someone's still alive,' Steve groaned. 'Who's gonna go in and find him?'

Kit snatched a grenade from his webbing, thumbed the men back and lobbed it into the pile of shattered wood, the explosion buffeting the leaves around him as he walked away. 'That solves the problem. 'Course, we could have used grenades in the first place, but it wouldn't have been so much fun.' With the deafening sounds of gunfire still ringing in our ears we trailed behind him as he headed for the village, knowing in our gut that killing the Chetniks was the easy bit.

Stepping from the gloomy wood into bright blue sky and crisp autumn light we passed through a field of corn stubble overlooking a valley. Below lay a village, frost-covered red-tiled roofs glittering in the brittle sunshine. Cobbled streets intertwined, winding their way past brightly painted bow-fronted shops. Recollections of storybook tales, castles in the air and fairy-tale princesses . . . we were in a time warp. Approaching the outskirts we had every reason to expect a grateful king to grant our every wish.

There's a clear visual distinction between ethnic cleansing and attacks which involve mortar or shellfire – easy to detect from almost any distance. In the former there are no holes blasted in the earth, walls or roofs. No signs of major explosions. It's difficult to describe, but we knew that this was a village of the living dead as we patrolled slowly down the empty cobbled street, staring at once neat front gardens now littered with household possessions, discarded as looters lost interest in their quest for something better. Shattered windows showed strips of charred curtain. Walls were blown outward from dynamite, roof tiles scattered everywhere. The reversed 'C' was sprayed on white walls, often covered in dried execution blood.

Nobody spoke. We wandered tense and expectant from one side of the road to the other, looking up and down with jerky head movements. Checking for snipers, maybe. No. Just blocking the mind. Keep moving . . . stay on the ball. Whatever you do, *don't think!*

We heard a cracking sound, and dived in a heap behind the

cover of a garden wall, feeling stupid as a charred roof beam fell behind us, followed by part of a ceiling crashing into the room below.

'Getting jumpy, lads, aren't we?' Kit clambered out first, just to prove a point.

We were getting closer to the village centre, waving AK's at the sky, looking good, feeling sharp. An old man appeared from nowhere, carrying a tray full of something that looked oddly familiar.

'Oh Christ,' whimpered Nigel, white as a virgin's wedding dress.

The old guy just stood there silently, his gaze disappearing into infinity as he held the tray for our inspection.

'What is it?' Pete called, moving closer. 'Breakfast?'

He wished he hadn't said it, blanching at the sight of about thirty men's testicles, settling in congealed blood.

'Fuckin' hell!' he managed to choke, before repeatedly vomiting over his boots. 'Fucking bloody hell.' What else could he say?

The old man beckoned, shuffling silently through narrow lanes until we arrived at a large grey-stone building in a side street on the far side of the village. Ranko translated the sign above the door so quietly that he just mouthed the word: 'Abattoir.' The old man pushed the door open, standing aside for us to pass.

More than fifty naked corpses lay on the grey slate floor, thick with blood in various stages of coagulation. Men and boys with arms tied behind their backs, scrotums ripped from their bodies, gaping black holes where their manhood once lay. Blood and stomach contents oozed thickly through open, toothless mouths with bloated lips.

The body postures were grotesque – impossible unless all major bones had been broken before death. Cigarette burns were livid on waxen, pockmarked skin, eyes gouged from sockets, fingers smashed to a bloody pulp. They had been left bleeding to death with their faces reflecting an incomprehensible agony. Lifeless, they begged with hands like claws, clutching at lost hope. *'No more, please God, no more!'*

I suppose in moments of extreme shock senses operate in sequence, allowing the brain to determine which function dominates. In this instance our eyes recorded the scene, ensuring that the picture would forever stay in our subconscious. The shutter clicked on motor drive, taking it all in – later we would flick through the photographs in the privacy of our minds.

The smell came next, a cloying stench of death. Sweet, sickly, gaseous, it clung to the skin, burned the eyes, tearing at the throat. We could taste it deep down in our bowels.

'Let's get out of here, lads,' Kit choked, slipping as he turned on the smooth, blood-washed floor.

The old man whimpered from the doorway like an animal in pain unable to express its emotion. He was still holding the tray of testicles, unable or unwilling to put them down.

'Zasto?' he sobbed. Why? 'Zasto, Zasto, Zasto?'

We didn't know why, but we did know who. And they wouldn't be doing it again.

Breathing deeply in the clean air, we followed the old guy back into the village. Ranko tried to talk to him, without success. Conversation seemed inappropriate anyway, so we trailed behind in silence, often catching sight of bundles of clothing in the streets which turned out to be crumpled bodies, wondering what came next. . . with not long to wait.

The schoolhouse was our next stop; this time the old man just pointed, leaving us to walk up to the entrance alone.

They had tried to barricade themselves in. Trestle tables, chairs and bookcases littered the floor, blown away by dynamite. Women and girls lay in untidy heaps, some still alive . . . just. We lit cigarettes for comfort, moving gently around the bodies, unsure of how to behave with young girls of eleven or so who had been raped and buggered before merciful death, their naked bodies slashed with a cross and the Chetnik reversed 'C'.

Many of the older women had been blown apart internally, a charge inserted into the vagina and detonated. Broken glass was found in the bowels of numerous bodies, breasts were sliced off, pregnant women bayonetted in the stomach. We did the best we could for the thirty battered, blood-soaked and traumatised living and left them to mourn their friends, lurching into the open air to suck more fresh oxygen deep into our lungs. I don't recall more than ten words being spoken by any of us in the hour we were there.

The old man had disappeared and we were left to continue our search of the village alone, choosing houses at random. The first was empty and untouched – another sign of selective ethnic cleansing. The second had been ransacked and burned. Two children, no more than nine months old, were found decapitated in a corner with their arms and legs hacked off. They had been set on fire and looked like charred black statues. Kit picked one up, later saying, 'I wasn't wearing gloves and my fingers went straight through the body with a crisp, crackling sound. I felt sick and threw it away in disgust . . .'

Apart from the old man and the few survivors in the school, we saw no other form of life in the village as we methodically searched each house, just recurring scenes of despair and inhumanity. Most of us wished that the Chetniks had not died so easily in the wood, other forms of death seeming much more appropriate.

There was little else we could do to help the injured, and nothing for the dead -- apart from burying them, an impossible task with so many bodies. Kit organised a work detail and an abandoned truck was located and the bodies collected and taken to the edge of the village, where they were piled unceremoniously into a tarpaulin-lined pit, doused in petrol and set alight. We walked away, the Bosnian soldiers moving their lips in silent prayer, not wishing to see the searing flames engulf the remains of nearly one hundred and fifty defenceless people.

Emotions were exchanged without speech as we skirted the wood on our return to the RV point, gaunt expressions clearly indicating those mental processes working inside the skull. The men stumbled across the cornfield, tired and haggard, with hate blazing in their faces, substituted in an instant by pain, vengeance, horror and finally helplessness. They kept shaking their heads as if being bothered by flies.

Wispy smoke greeted us as we approached our hidden vehicles. After a few seconds of anxiety we were greeted by Milenko with steaming mugs of coffee.

'Put that fire out, you wanker,' Kit snarled. 'Haven't I taught you? No smoke on patrols!'

It didn't need translating. Milenko got the message loud and clear as Kit snatched his coffee from him, downing it in one gulp.

The Bosnians narrated the story to their countrymen as we removed the bracken from the Land Rover, tears forming in many eyes as the final chapter was related. All the way back to Posusje they sang deep, mournful folk songs, swaying in grief as they gazed into the middle distance with their arms intertwined.

Drago took the news of the atrocities with grim acceptance,

immediately contacting his client in Dunvo. He took Kit aside, and after emotional appreciation told us of another band of Chetniks operating in a commando group in the Zenica area, about ninety kilometres north-east of Posusje. They were moving fast and had terrorised seven villages in one night; killing, burning and looting. The problem was guessing their next target. A quick look at the map, marking villages already hit, seemed to indicate a pattern, and it was agreed that they were moving south-west in our general direction.

'Which village are we gonna go for, then?' Pop asked.

'Dunno, it's difficult to judge. Other reports have been coming in of Chetnik attacks further south, around Bukovica and Kresevo.' Kit shrugged. 'Your guess is as good as mine.'

Further map-poring, notes and telephone conversations with English-speaking Bosnians led Kit to finally make a decision. 'We'll head for Matorac, it's about fifty kilometres north-east. Maybe we'll get some clearer indication there.'

An early night, plagued with dreams. We were awakened by MiGs on another dawn raid over Imotski. 'Sod them! I thought you told me the SAMs had stopped it,' moaned Pete, lying frog-eyed in his big farmhouse bed.

'Sorry about that, Pete. I'll make sure it doesn't happen again,' Kit replied sarcastically. 'Now you're awake you can get break-fast!'

We gobbled fast, carrying cups of coffee out to the waiting Rovers, loading RPGs, 88s, claymores, AKMs and 47s in readiness for whatever. 'Sling in the bivvy bags. We'll be out all night. Maybe more,' Kit pointed out. 'And don't forget your teddy bear, Pete.'

This was mountainous country, with winding lanes overlooked by grey scrubland. Here we were, exposed again. Still, there were nearly thirty of us this time, an army no less. Ready to be wiped out in seconds by a few well-placed mortars.

We bypassed Mostar and its memories of exploding MiGs, heading north on the main route before cutting off with nervous tension to less hazardous roads. Kit's calculation of distance was based upon a direct route to Matorac; this wasn't direct, adding about fifty kilometres to the trip.

We arrived at a small hamlet near Kresevo in two hours, familiar signs of looting everywhere. The villagers, gathered in groups, didn't want to talk about it. 'Chetniks?' they queried, fearing reprisals. 'Not Chetniks ... bandits!' They shook their heads and smiled, saying, 'They have gone now, all is well.'

'Miserable, lying, gutless bastards!' Pop spat. 'How the fuck can anyone help them if they won't tell the truth?'

'It is not for you to judge,' replied Ranko. 'These people have to live here tomorrow ... many tomorrows. Long after you have gone home to your peaceful English country.'

Pop calmed down instantly, knowing that Ranko had spoken the truth and realising at the same instant that Chetnik raiders could live in this village or the next. Someone's cousin, uncle, brother, husband ... anyone!

We stopped at other chattering groups, who paused in their animated conversation to stare at us suspiciously and give the same vacant response. The shutters had come down. We were wasting our time here.

Dusina was the same, so we drove on, questioning anyone prepared to talk to us, stopping in bars and cafés *en route*, not for refreshment, just information. Many people hurried away as our camouflaged vehicles pulled up beside them, not wanting to get involved, not wanting to be seen talking to foreign soldiers.

'This is a waste of time,' Kit said impatiently after our twelfth attempt. 'Nobody's gonna tell us fuck all.'

Matorac was little better, although some children, eager to show how adult they were, told us of lorries coming in the night and dragging men off to be shot. One, whose grandfather had been taken away, pointed north, saying, 'That way. They went that way.' At last we had a lead, however tenuous.

After five hours' road dust and a million one-sided conversations, and well pissed off at mute Bosnians, we stopped for a well-earned brew. No milk. 'Shit!' You could hear Steve's anguished tone echo through the valley.

'Not worry. I'll get some from over there.' Ranko spoke to Nikola, no more than a kid, who took off at a trot in the direction of a nearby farm.

It wasn't a good place to stop, surrounded as we were by mountainous country. But then the whole place was the same, so there was little choice. Steve and Nigel unloaded the 'hexy' stoves, filling billy cans with water in readiness. Cold beans spooned from cans and dry rolls munched with little enthusiasm, we waited.

A yell from the farm made us jump to our feet. Nikola was

running back, waving wildly, '*Dodjite ovamo!*' he screamed. Come here! He was babbling away so rapidly that only his countrymen could understand.

Ranko listened, turning to Kit, his face grim. 'The farm has been looted and burned. Nikola says the family are dead inside. Come.'

Without waiting for approval, he and the other Bosnians raced back to the building. Kit ordered Pete, Nigel and Pop to stay with the vehicles, and the rest of us followed, chickens flying everywhere as we thundered through the cobbled yard, not knowing what we would find.

'White Eagles,' Ranko choked before entering.

'How can you tell?' Steve asked. 'There are no symbols this time.'

'I just know,' replied Ranko, becoming agitated at the questioning. 'It's either White Eagles or Arkanoci.'

Through the low doorway we could just make out the shape of an inverted figure, strung by its ankles from a roof beam. The dim light made it impossible to judge age or sex. We followed Kit as he led the way cautiously into the house, seeing the body of a man, stripped naked, with his stomach ripped open. Grey intestinal matter flowed freely from the gaping wound and slid down his body into a pool on the stone floor. The stench of open drains filled the room, making us gag in uncontrollable spasms. Nikola coughed once, cleared his throat and ran outside, retching as he hit the air.

Rapidly averting our gaze, we caught sight of another body. A young woman in her early twenties lay sprawled against the ledge of an open window as if trying to escape, her face contorted and a strange grey mist covering blank, protruding eyes. Her head had been smashed to a pulverised mash, an iron bar still lying by her side; she had one ear missing.

The house had been looted, soft furniture set on fire. Charred and still smoking it gave off the pungent smell of an incinerator.

'I'm getting pissed off with this, it's doing my head in,' Kit muttered to himself. Moving towards the stairs, he instructed the rest to check the outbuildings.

He headed upstairs, banging and clattering around the bedrooms before suddenly stopping. The creak of sliding furniture gave way to a yell.

'Up here. Now!' he barked.

We leapt up the stairs in time to see him lift the limp body of a uniformed young man, a pitchfork jammed firmly in his chest, blood bubbling from his mouth as he pleaded with Kit for mercy. Ranko stared at the boy, spitting in his face. 'Chetnik scum!' The kid babbled, his eyes mesmerised with fear as Ranko tore a pink ear from a thong around his neck.

Kit dropped the shaking figure to the floor and walked out, beckoning us to follow, leaving the Bosnian alone to interrogate the boy.

We waited in the open for the inevitable single shot. Ranko joined us moments later.

'They killed the woman first, thinking she was alone,' he whispered as we walked slowly back to the vehicles. 'Her husband was working outside and hurled the pitchfork through the window before they overpowered him. I asked him where his friends had gone and why they had left him, but he wouldn't tell me . . . so I shot him.'

Ranko looked at Kit as we pushed the farm gate open, searching his face for answers, but there were none. Kit had long forgotten the question.

A dog barked behind us, and a flash of black and brown sent the chickens scurrying once again as a large Alsatian ran at us, growling displeasure at our intrusion on its territory. Too late; we were beyond the gate and safe from its snarling teeth. Another hound to join the ever-increasing packs of hungry domestic pets seen scavenging in most small towns and villages these days.

Kit stopped us for a moment and in a confused tone explained his predicament. 'I don't know what to do now. We can't keep driving around the country in the blind hope we'll find them, and nobody's telling us nothing.'

Ranko nodded his head in silent agreement as we reached the cars.

'Where's the fucking milk then?' Pete roared. 'We're bloody gasping here.'

Kit looked at him for a full thirty seconds, his mouth beginning to twitch into a smile. Pop giggled, and both collapsed in a heap, their bodies convulsing with a laughter so infectious that we found ourselves joining in. Tears ran down their faces in waves as they rolled hysterically on the ground, holding their sides in gleeful agony. Difficult to understand? Ask any combat soldier for the answer.

We finally managed to get them aboard, still chuckling, and

headed north for a final attempt at tracking down the raiding party. The whole thing was developing into a futile operation. Morale, especially among the vengeful Bosnians, had reached an all-time low.

'I've had enough,' Kit moaned from the passenger seat. 'We'll loop around Merdzanici and head back. There's no point in wasting any more time on this. Drago's got loads more jobs for us to do.'

For the next two hours we kept stopping, kept asking, kept getting blanks. The people were frightened, refusing to be involved. 'Fuck 'em,' commented Steve after another failure to communicate.

Out on the open road he put his foot down, swaying round corners with the other two Rovers doing their best to keep up. A puff of smoke from a green pine-studded hillside opposite made him slam on the brakes, skidding to a halt. The other cars slid sideways behind us, one rolling into a water-filled ditch. The first puff was followed by another; this time a mortar shell hit the gully, sending a plume of stagnant liquid high in the air. We were out like rabbits, diving headlong into the bushes beyond. Small-arms fire kicked into action almost immediately, stitching the grass five metres to the right, getting closer. Another mortar hit the gully, seconds before a rifle grenade slammed into the ditched Rover, blasting it to scrap metal before our eyes. It went quiet suddenly, before the fuel tank exploded, sending metallic fragments high into the air.

'Who the fuck's that?' Steve groaned. 'Can't be the JNA, they're not in this area yet.'

Kit checked for injury amongst the men; they were OK, none hit by gunfire or flying metal.

We were pinned down, any movement drawing fire from a very accurate sniper.

'Betcha it's the fucking Chetnik patrol,' growled Nigel. 'We found them at last.'

'They found us,' Kit added quietly. 'And now we're in the shit.'

Another mortar shell landed way off course, followed once again by sustained bursts of small-arms fire, splashing into the ditch and ricocheting off our vehicles. A prolonged burst, seemingly from a single source, tailed off and silence fell. Twenty minutes passed slowly. Kit edged his head above the bush . . . no sniper fire.

'We can't stay here all day. Spooky, you come with me. We'll flank them and see what's going on.'

Crawling along the bush line, they made a dash across the road and into the opposite field, clambering exposed up the hill before reaching the pine wood with not a single shot being fired at them. Less than five minutes later they were waving from the top. The attackers were gone, leaving piles of spent ammo cases as souvenirs.

'Just hit and run. Seems familiar,' Kit mused on their return. 'Gimme the map.'

He and Ranko pored over it for ten minutes, discussing alternatives and possibilities before arriving at a decision.

'Here!' Kit pointed. 'The Chetniks are heading for this village.'

'You sure?' Nigel asked doubtfully.

'Definitely. Absolutely.' His tone was positive before pausing. 'Mmmm . . . Maybe. They'd better be, because that's where we're going.'

With almost an hour's delay, there was no way we could follow on foot, choosing instead the tortuous route through tricky, winding lanes.

Now down to two cars, overcrowding and lack of manoeuvrability caused a few problems, especially on tight corners, so we ditched the vehicles and struck out across the fields as fast as our legs could carry us. We reached the hilltop overlooking Kit's trig point . . . too late. Smoke was pouring from a barn, uniformed men running in our direction.

'Down!' Kit ordered. We hit the earth hard, grunting in pain.

Steve eased himself up, peering through the scrub. 'They look pissed. They're staggering all over the place.'

'Are they still heading our way?' Kit asked, keeping his head low.

'Yeah, in fact they're climbing the hill now.' Steve ducked down to meaningful glances. Safety catches were released in readiness.

It was all over in seconds as thunderous gunfire echoed across the open valley and bodies rolled untidily back down the slope, looted property falling from lifeless hands. Drunk and incapable, the Chetniks had made a final and stupid mistake. They should have wiped us out at the ambush or at least legged it; instead greed drove them on to more killing and looting.

'Ranko, you and your lads go down and check the place out.

I've seen enough to keep me going for a long, long time,' Kit said wearily, sinking to his knees.

'Amen to that,' was the silent but universal response.

Vladimir returned first, with the news that Ranko wanted to bury the victims, asking if we minded waiting. Eight this time, hurriedly shot and decapitated. Sick as it was, we all smiled when Spooky suggested that this particular band of Chetniks were on piecework – payment on body count.

The Bosnian peasant-soldiers dragged themselves up the hill towards us with blackened, tear-stained faces. Sullen and uncommunicative, they told us nothing of what horrors they'd found in the hamlet, and we didn't ask. Who needs more pictures in an already overcrowded scrapbook? Once again they hummed mournful tunes on the long trip back to Posusje.

Two days' rest turned into three, permitting some serious loafing to be practised in the many small taverns dotted about the place. We took this opportunity to check out the town and meet the inhabitants, who knew nothing about our reason for being there, and couldn't understand why this group of unshaven wild men kept touring the streets each day, often with painted faces. Muttering groups of men and women stared with undisguised suspicion at our every move, often scurrying indoors as our Range Rovers pulled into the main street.

'Makes you feel like a Hell's Angel, dunnit? The way they disappear like that, dragging their daughters behind them.' Pete clambered out of the Rover, dropping into his outlaw swagger.

On our third day, Kit, with two other lads, took a trip into Split for some well-earned irresponsibility. They were gone all day, returning with bad news learned from an old friend Kit had met wandering in the Varos district. Sprog – seventeen-year-old Paul Eugene Thomas from Warrington – having left Osijek for Vinkovci, had decided upon a final bit of action in Sarajevo before returning home to a life of normality. As the sun set on his first day there, a journalist from the Reuter's agency found his body curled up in an alley, a neat hole drilled dead centre in his forehead. Still clutching his beloved folding-stock AK–47, his cherubic face registered confusion. The brief article and photograph, torn from a magazine Kit had been given, dampened our spirits as we recalled Sprog's speech by the Drava bridge a few short weeks before: 'I'm pissed off with people I don't know trying to kill me . . . I'm going home.'

Another day, another Deutschmark. Trig point 1916, close to Jablanica. A radio station passing information on troop movements back to the JNA. 'Needs silencing,' said Kit. Only half the team went this time, leaving most of the Bosnians behind to guard the village. White Eagles still roamed unabated. Atrocity stories were coming in daily. It was only a matter of time before they got around to Posusje.

It took a day to reach the place and another hour to find a suitable stop to stash the Rover. That done satisfactorily, we climbed the steep hill, found a hollow to hide away in and played poker with an old, greasy forty-two-card deck, waiting for dusk and a last-light attack to ease our escape in the subsequent darkness. Cold food, little movement, no conversation. The long afternoon dragged into a bitter, damp evening.

Five men climbed the final three hundred metres, finding the exterior of the building unguarded. Inside, men could be seen drinking, reading and lounging. Careless. . . it would be the death of them.

Kit and Steve went in first, crashing through the door, yelling like banshees from hell, with Nigel following and Spooky bringing up the rear. The Serbs stood no chance. They froze, gaping at the wild-eyed intruders for a millisecond before dying for their cause without a movement in defence. An overkill of thirty kilos of explosive finished the job and the lads were back at our sides in less than fifteen minutes.

'Textbook operation, that was. Easy money for a change.' Kit whistled a tuneless melody most of the way back.

Chapter Twelve

It's like . . . it's like . . . a sledgehammer. You hold it
low, at your hip, and create a wall of devastation in
front of you. Squeeze, bam! Everyone's scared of a
shotgun. You can't miss and they know it.

Serbian MiGs screamed low over Mostar airfield, landing gear
locked in readiness for a touchdown kiss. In the grey dawn light
the orange glow from roaring afterburners sent luminous threads
shimmering through the damp morning sky. On the ground all
was confusion; noise, dirt and the familiar terrain of burnt-out
houses and burnt-out people, living for what remained of their
lives in Shit Street, ex-Yugoslavia.

One by one the MiGs bounced on the tarmac, smoke belching
from tortured tyres, slowly taxiing to a comforting breakfast and a
few embellished stories. Kit fidgeted as he watched, itching for his
beloved RPG-7 and a hundred HEAT warheads, no doubt
remembering the last time we were here in the dead of night,
leaving just before the place erupted in a blaze of writhing metal.

We'd pulled over on our way back from Jablanica just to stare at
them thundering over our heads like fiery birds of prey.
Gruesomely beautiful killers, never to see the face of their enemy
in death. It was a risky stop, but in relative darkness well worth
the gamble.

'Bleedin' wankers! Look at them strutting about the place.'
Pete's petulant voice grated on our ears as he stared jealously at
the pilots, climbing down to jokes from their crews.

'I bet they've been bombing Imotski again,' he added. 'Don't
know how they can kill innocent people.'

'Not like us then,' Nigel muttered sarcastically, crunching the
Rover into gear and slamming his foot on the accelerator. Thirty-
five kilometres and we'd be home. The rest of the guys were
snoring by the time we hit Knespolje.

Posusje slept as we cruised through the main street, odd
windows showing light from early-morning risers. A lone dog
barked, starting others. Within minutes howls echoed around the
village, and by the time we turned left towards our farm, anxious

faces were appearing at half-open doorways in anticipation of invasion.

Nigel flipped the wheel like a professional parking attendant, showering red dust as we skidded to a halt. Engine off, chirping crickets . . . silence. 'We're home,' to a whispered chorus of 'Thank God.' Milenko nodded from his lonely guard position on the roof, but seeing weary faces he said nothing. We left the gear on board, going straight to bed in our filthy clothes. Dirty boots dropped noisily on the floor, and we were out of it in seconds.

The squeal of brakes and loud voices dragged us back through a haze of sleep. Drago's Land Cruiser stood in the yard, polished and shiny.

'*Dobro jutro*,' he greeted us, face beaming, grey hair combed, a picture of health and vitality. Why the hell couldn't he speak English at this time of the morning?

'*Dobro jutro*,' we chorused back, like children being greeted by a schoolteacher.

'I'd like you to meet someone.' He stood back to reveal the shapely figure of a member of the other sex; known in polite society as a woman.

We rubbed our eyes sleepily. A gift perhaps, as thanks for services rendered? Take her away for now, we're too tired. Later, maybe.

'This is Freda Valk,' he continued, smiling at Pop's attempt to finger-comb his thinning hair. 'She's a journalist from Holland and wants to get through the blockade into Sarajevo. Can you do it?'

In late 1992 there were only two ways to get into Sarajevo – still are, for that matter: one with a United Nations relief flight – hairy and unpredictable; the other even less certain – overland, with or without the kind permission of the less than inviting Bosnian Serbs surrounding the place with large-scale shooters.

Drago had asked a complicated question simply, and waited for the answer. Kit sighed deeply, his breath coming in a drawn-out gasp.

'How much?' He looked at the girl.

She shrugged her shoulders, gesturing helplessly. 'I will pay what it costs. Can you get me there?'

'Of course,' he replied, confidence oozing from every pore. 'When do you want to go?'

217

'Right now!' she answered, brittle-voiced, trying the butch war correspondent bit. Kate Adie eat your heart out.

'No. Not now. I'll need some time to sort out the route. Come back later.'

'I'm in a hurry.' Her voice rose in petulant frustration at Kit's apparent lack of interest.

She had a look about her. *Haute couture* in the face of flying bullets, never a hair out of place. You could bet even money that she wouldn't get creased on the trip.

'I've told you. Come back later or not at all. I'm not attempting it unless I can get some information on the opposition in the area.'

She fell silent, shuffling from foot to foot. The hard-nose act hadn't worked. Should she try the soft approach?

'I'd be really grateful.' Eyelashes fluttered, mournful, little girl conning daddy.

Kit turned dismissively, reaching for his telephone as Steve scrabbled around for maps.

'We gonna take her, ole buddy?' Spooky asked, watching them through the window as they drove away.

Kit was phoning contacts, checking odds, throwing dice. 'Yeah, we'll take her if the money's right.'

Twenty minutes of phone calls followed, with long gaps in the conversation. Lots of 'yeah, yeah' and 'bollocks!'. Friends in the UN offered advice. Trig points and likely problem areas were checked out. Kit left to give her the good news – returning with the bad.

'Sarajevo's under heavy siege. The Serbs have knocked out a Hercules supply plane on its way out and they're moving in more heavy artillery.' He handed us a tattered British newspaper, heavily into the phrase 'Strangulation of Sarajevo' – repeating it three times in as many paragraphs. 'They're holding Mount Igman and Mount Bjelasnica, bombarding the town day and night. It's gonna be a right bastard to get in and an even bigger bastard to get out.' As he rambled on, we just knew that the price was going up for poor old Freda.

Sarajevo was about one hundred and ten kilometres from Posusje – as the crow flies. But as I've said before, crows we weren't.

Maps had begun to mean very little over the past months. Towns and villages indicated often no longer existed. And if they did, they were often given different names by their new land-lords. Over the past week Duvno had been renamed Tomislav-grad by dominant Bosnian-Serb forces. The whole thing was getting very confusing for lads brought up on rigid British army chart discipline, and was made even worse by the fact that few people knew which town was held by which force. With about eight to choose from, it was a hazardous guessing game.

After due consultation, and with the Mostar road now closed by police, Kit chose the main UN supply route from Tomislavgrad to Vitez, through Kiseljak then eastwards into Sarajevo. This way we would get some support if necessary from passing UN convoys . . . maybe!

Freda was packed and ready as we pulled up at her digs. Toshiba laptop, khaki holdall and crisp olive battledress . . . straight out of *Cosmopolitan*. She looked like a pro all right, mirror Ray-Bans coolly reflecting our image as she waited for Pete to load her gear while taking pictures with a shiny, motor-driven Nikon.

'Ready?' Kit slid in beside her, smiling back at us like a Cheshire cat. We just knew the trip was going to be – well, interesting.

With only a trace of an accent she asked about the mercenary role in the country, nodding as the odd note was inscribed in her alligator-skin-covered Filofax. We learned that this was her first overseas assignment and she meant to do well, regardless of the risk to herself. 'Commendable,' Nigel pompously agreed in his best Oxford accent. 'I'm sure you will do excellently in all your endeavours . . . especially with all that posh gear.' The sarcasm went unnoticed and she continued with her mechanical question-ing for the next hour until we pulled into Vitez for some refreshment and a piss – us, not her. She'd never do that sort of thing.

Blue-helmeted UN everywhere and a camera in overdrive, Freda snapped their every move. God knows why; they weren't doing anything vaguely interesting. But with smart, unused uniforms they had a lot of style.

Fifteen minutes later we were back on the road, heading east before the loop into Kiseljak. All was well in the world, no road blocks, no unpleasant sounds and the smell of Chanel No. 5 up our snouts. It seemed that the Serbs were, at least temporarily, keeping their word and allowing aid to pass unhindered into Sarajevo.

219

Kiseljac looked a bit iffy. With houses still burning, roads with deep craters and little movement from the inhabitants, an atmosphere of brooding anticipation hovered about the place. Like they used to say in the old Western films, 'It's quiet. Too damned quiet.'

'I don't like the look of this,' Kit murmured, right on cue.

Slowing down to negotiate the potholes, he glanced at Freda, whose lipstick was beginning to smear from repeatedly nervous licking as she wriggled in her seat, a damp patch of sweat showing beneath her armpits.

A group of young men lounged against the wall of a café, unarmed but tense. One ambled across and seeing the woman called to his friends, who broke into macho laughter. He sidled up to the car and stuck his head through her window, leering at her. '*Da li ste slobodni veceras?*' Are you free this evening? Freda didn't understand the words or the implication. Kit, who had tried it himself in the past, did.

'Fuck off!' He glared at the kid, who understood the method of delivery, if not the expression.

We were so intently focused on the interaction between them that for a moment other matters were forgotten. Serious miscalculation! A flurry of peripheral movement in the café entrance attracted our attention; hooded figures with Kalashnikovs raised were running in our direction. Sharp staccato bursts from their gun barrels made it clear that this was exit time.

Kit hit the pedal and with a vigorous roar the diesel-engine Land Rover hesitated before a sick cough sent it into spasm, jerking twenty metres before expiring with a hiss.

'SHIT!' Spooky was out, spraying the road before the last splutter, Kit feverishly turning the key. The engine snorted, died, coughed like an early-morning smoker and started again, lurching away as Spooky threw his final burst, which downed two and frightened the rest into confused retreat. Pete joined him on the final chorus with short bursts of farewell.

'What on earth were they after?' the incredulous newshound breathed, in a fair imitation of Marilyn Monroe.

'Your Gucci watch. Jewellery. Your body . . . Whatever.'

'Were they Chetniks?' She was excited now that we were away and safe.

'Nah, just kids on the make. The country's full of them.'

Her face glowing with delight, she stopped chattering, instead making feverish, exaggerated notes.

I'd just love to see the article on this event: 'Ambush! Journalist close to death. Our intrepid reporter in Bosnia lives to tell the tale.' Like the man said: 'Never let the truth ruin a good story' – or something like that.

The town of Brnjaci had been tormented a bit, although nothing to speak of. The inhabitants peered through windows, fearing the worst and pleased to see a single vehicle speed on its way without stopping. We waved enthusiastically at the apprehensive faces, trying to transmit hope, receiving a vacant response. A crying child at the roadside induced Kit to pull over. He handed her a bar of chocolate which she snatched from his hand, soundlessly shuffling away without a smile or a backward glance. Traumatised by executions, bombs and unspeakable horrors, the kid had the hollow look of a twisted tree once struck by lightning.

Rakovica came next, and with it the decision to slip off the main route on to smaller, less obvious roads for the final leg of our trip. With less than twenty kilometres to travel, the sounds of incoming shells had become commonplace, dust from their explosive impact rising above the town, high-pitched whistling drowning odd attempts at jittery conversation. Freda hadn't said a word for the past half-hour, but her lipstick was immaculate again.

First stop Sarajevo airfield. Serbs at one end, Bosnians the other. One group defending aircraft, the other attacking them – steady employment for all. Freda had a brief chat with Sky TV journalists at the Bosnian section, swapping stories, telling jokes, doing their thing. We waited in the Rover like unwanted chauffeurs until she'd sucked her information sources dry and exhausted her welcome.

Climbing back in and settling herself down, she told us to head for the centre of town and find Vojvode Punika 6a – the Sarajevo Holiday Inn. Once the home of journalists covering the 1984 Winter Olympics, it was now satellite city and meeting place for the world's top media vultures.

The western side of the city was no mans land, patrolled by gun-toting Serbs who stomped about the place as if they owned it, peering into slow-moving cars, just itching for a reason to open up on the occupants. Freda waved her press card to insolent comments from subnormal gun freaks. They glanced in our direction, focusing on the blonde, ignoring her companions.

Driving slowly away, we looked back; three were arguing and pointing angrily in our direction. They should have checked us out, but it was too late. We were out of range and speeding into the film set of *Demolition Man*.

The town was in absolute and total chaos. An acrid stench of burning filled the streets, sweetened by the sickly odour of death. Shattered glass crunched underfoot as people ran singly and in groups across open spaces, waiting for a sound they would never hear. Graffiti-scrawled walls proclaiming 'HELP BOSNIA NOW' and 'STOP GENOCIDE . . . ARM BOSNIA' gave out a message to the world's TV cameras, who cared more about ratings than restitution. Roy had been right when he'd told his mum that he was going to work in Disneyland; for this was indeed the land of wicked fairy tales.

On our left a queue had formed at one of the few water collection points. Ragged people bent warily to fill their plastic cans and bottles, ears tuned to the slightest sound. Groups such as these, waiting for bread, meat or medical supplies, had been wiped out many times before when lined up like targets for bored snipers or indiscriminate shellfire.

You can imagine the conversation in towering office blocks as marksmen scan the streets below for a random target: 'I bet you a hundred dinar I can hit that woman in the red dress,' one might mutter to his equally apathetic spotter. An abrupt crack, a blue puff of smoke from his barrel and she falls lifeless. He smiles contentedly, pocketing the money. Later in the morning he misses and hands it back. This goes on all day. Some you win . . .

Masonry, already loose from a recent bombardment, fell crashing to the ground, shattering in the road before us. Kit swerved, cursing in pure Geordie at its impertinence. We couldn't understand a word he said so Freda was not offended by the outburst.

'Left. Turn left!' Kit had driven past the hotel, hurling the Rover into a curve down Bulevar Borisa Kidrica. Now he reversed out in gear-crunching irritation.

Freda sat for a moment as Kit kept the motor running. 'Aren't you coming in for a drink?' she almost begged, eyelashes flapping like butterfly wings.

'No thanks, we've done our job and delivered the package,' he replied a little too abruptly.

'Fine ... Well, uh ... thanks for getting me here safely.' She handed him a package which he pocketed without checking. 'I'll see you around, maybe?'

'Doubt it. We'll only be here for one night, then we head back to Posusje.'

Suddenly changing his mind, he offered to take her gear in. We tagged behind, curious to see media-land for ourselves. Polished chrome, tinted glass – piles of it splintered on the floor – and sounds of frenetic activity. Crazy people with foreign voices yelled into satellite phones, fingers jammed into ears to stop incoming abuse from impatient colleagues waiting their turn.

'Goddamn it! My battery's gone dead. Send me a new one ... no, make it two. Wait ... wait ... more disks,' the CNN guy screamed, puce-faced. Next to him an ITN journalist spoke in a rapid but unemotional tone about thirty people killed by mortar fire while standing in a bread line. 'Yes, of course we have pictures,' he answered icily, eyes raised skywards. 'These copy people ...'

We followed Freda to the third floor – BBC territory – where she had been told to make contact with another Dutch journalist. He wasn't there and hadn't been seen all day. Whirling figures threw options at her, none appealing to her sense of adventure. So we went to the bar, always the hub for newspaper hacks.

She ordered vodka after checking with calculating eyes for the 'in' drink as she posed on the only vacant stool. We went for beer and brandy.

The drone of conversation diminished slightly at our arrival. Curious eyes penetrated dense cigarette smoke, then were averted as we stared back. They were no smiles of welcome, no warmth in their eyes. We were mercenaries; lepers with no cause, no country and no place to hide. Hyenas in a fresh-meat factory called Bosnia. Shunned even by other predators.

Although it was bright daylight the bar was dull. Lights flickered from occasional power failures and the room had an uncomfortable, oppressive atmosphere. Most of the window openings were covered in plastic sheeting – the glass having been blown away – making it impossible to see out of the building. Whispered conversation from an adjoining table informed us that a major offensive was expected very soon. Freda looked uncomfortable at the thought.

'Thanks for the drink. We'd better be off.' Kit shook her hand. 'Best of luck.'

'Oh, you're going now?' It was a question and an appeal. She didn't want to be left alone . . . not yet.

'Yeah, we want to have a look around before we go back.'

Nigel lagged behind, kissing her hand. Always the gentleman, was Nigel.

We pulled away from the hotel, counting windows. Out of ninety on one side of the building only five glazed ones remained; plastic sheeting flapped in the wind but there were no direct hits. Lucky so far, but it was only a matter of time.

We drove in silence past the Miljacka river, strewn with floating debris, and headed towards the centre of Sarajevo. They called it Sniper Alley, this direct route to the airfield, and it was easy to see why. High buildings with unobstructed views would make the job a doddle for anyone with a steady hand and a telescopic sight. Ex-Corporal Freeman, second at Bisley 1979, would just love the job if the money was right.

'Wonder where Sprog got it.' Nigel was thinking aloud.

'Dunno,' Kit replied in a distant voice. 'Does it matter?'

'No, I guess not. Just curious, that's all.'

'Did they send his body home?' Spooky asked.

'Dunno that either.' Kit wasn't interested in continuing the conversation, lapsing into thoughtful silence.

As we reached the National Theatre building a shell roared in from the direction of Mount Igman, sounding more like a train than a warhead. The noise they make is different in the confined space of a town – more thunderous than whistling. It crashed into an already derelict office block and became the straw that broke the camel's back, bringing the entire building down in a slow-motion collapse of dust, glass and masonry.

We stared as Kit slowed. No casualties, apart from a small boy pushing his bicycle across the road. He'd been blown off his feet by the blast and sat gazing at the twisted frame with a mixture of horror and disbelief etched across his puckered face.

'Wanna go for a wander?' Kit asked, turning off the main drag and into a side street by the Young Bosnia Museum.

'Yeah, why not?' we chorused with more bravado than enthusiasm.

With a strange shiver running between our shoulder blades we stepped out of the false security of the Rover, feeling stupid and vulnerable as we picked our way past shattered shop fronts and piles of rubble. Only last year my neighbour came here with his family on holiday, returning with tales of visits to exotic mosques and exciting cable car rides to Mount Trebevic. They'd just got out in time as the rumble of civil war began in earnest after many years of uncertainty.

Soon tiring of target twitch, we ambled into the covered market, stopping long enough to have a welcome coffee. Grey-faced people scurried past with shopping bags on bikes or prams, peering at us questioningly as they headed home with provisions for the next siege.

'Let's go back. I've had enough of this goddamned place.' Spooky didn't like the exposed feeling. He, like Kit, needed a gun in his hand to feel comfortable when under threat.

'Never did like FIBUA,' muttered Kit as we reached the car. 'Prefer the jungle any day.'

Monotonous mortar fire was shaking up the south side and the express-train roar of incoming artillery shells vibrated buildings around us like an earthquake about to happen. It seemed that the predicted offensive had begun. Kit started the engine and reversed into an alleyway, turning until we faced the river and mountains. In the failing light, purple tracers drifted in graceful arcs towards the town, popping with an incandescent glow as they found a target. People ran past us in huddled groups, pushing and shoving their way home. This was no place for us; we were just a taxi service and the meter was running.

With the help of a friendly French UN observer, pissed off with his role as submissive voyeur, we found ourselves suitable shelter for the night – a cellar crawling with rats beneath a burned-out shop. Deciding that shared accommodation was better than none, we discussed territorial boundaries with the original tenants, reaching agreement after long negotiation and a few squashed bodies. Their cannibalistic nibbling and occasional resentful squeaks kept us awake for a while, but our policy of non-involvement finally allowed us to slip into fitful sleep as the siege continued above us.

Choking dust woke us early, filling the entire cellar from floor to ceiling and settling in our open mouths and nostrils. We coughed our lungs up, spluttering for five full minutes before we were able to rise. Desperate to breath fresh air. Desperate to get out of town.

The Serbian artillery had – more by luck than judgement – managed some serious devastation throughout the night-time onslaught. And in the fragile gloom, buildings tottered, waiting for a brisk gust of wind to bring them crashing down. Two bodies lay spreadeagled in the road not twenty metres from our parked motor, battered by the impact of falling stonework. A man ran as we approached, arms filled with spoils taken from their lifeless hands. Survival was more important than any other human emotion.

'Bastard!' yelled Nigel after the fleeing figure of a youth with greased-back hair and a pony tail, who turned with a universal 'up yours' gesture, laughing at Nigel's impotent rage. 'Cheeky sod!' Nigel started after him, picking up speed quickly for a man just awake. The kid turned, surprised at the reaction, and made a dash for an alley. He had almost reached it when a whiplike crack from above split the air, spinning him round before dropping him face down in the road, where he twitched for a moment before lying still. Another shot followed, kicking up cement at Nigel's feet as he lurched to a halt and dived behind a parked car. We could see his face as he crouched, wondering.

'They're up early this morning,' Kit said calmly, not being in the line of fire.

We watched as Nigel took a deep breath and with a bound threw himself back in our direction, weaving as he ran panting to our side. 'Lot of fucking help you were,' he snarled.

'You shouldn't have chased him,' Spooky pointed out. 'What's the point? They're gonna kill one another regardless of our intervention, so let them get on with it.' He was obviously in one of his more philosophical moods.

We now had the hazardous business of getting into the Land Rover in full view of a sniper intent on scoring a hit.

Feeling a little irritable from his lack of a bacon and egg breakfast, Kit was in no mood for messing about with tactical discussion and headed towards the corner of the building, weapon poised and safety off. Crack. Crack. We ducked instinctively. No need. The sniper had targeted a passing cyclist, missing once again. It was easy to imagine him up there cursing as he tried to resight on the target, fumbling with a spare clip as the rounds from Kit's gun found him unprepared. We watched the guy fall forward, clutching at the window frame, before tumbling fifteen floors to the ground with a dull, satisfying thud, just ten metres away from the body of the thief.

'The sooner we're out of this place the better.' Kit turned the key and we headed out of town with no regrets, waving at the Holiday Inn as we passed. Just in case Freda was watching.

Minutes later, moving at top speed, we had passed the trenches and the Bosnian checkpoint and were heading for no man's land once again. This time was different. Without Freda to protect, we weren't stopping for any asshole with a cannon and if necessary would shoot our way out. They must have been telepathic; not one Serb made any attempt to halt us as we whooped our way joyously out of Sarajevo city with its quadraphonic sounds of destruction and its odour of impending doom.

With the open road ahead, our immediate problem was food and a wash and brush-up. Rat droppings in Pete's pants made him and the rest of us wonder where the little bastards had been as we slept. Crotch itch only added to the worry, gathering momentum as our imagination ran riot with visions of infested pubic areas, gnawed dicks and subsequent bodily infestation. The uneasiness plagued us as we scratched our way through Kiseljak, stopping by a UN lorry pulled into a lay-by as two men changed a tyre.

After a quick brew and a splash of water down our trousers, we were on our way again, still convinced that by the time we reached Posusje we would all be speaking in high-pitched voices.

The decision to try the shorter route, turning left after Kiseljak, was made simply to speed our return. Still a UN supply route, it was less used but more prone to haphazard road blocks from just about anyone feeling adventurous. 'Bollocks to 'em,' was Kit's answer to Spooky's doubts. 'I wanna get back and have a bath.' He wound the Rover up, bouncing over rocks and hollows, scratching as if demented and becoming more desperate by the minute.

The countryside was getting mountainous again, with deep folds of earth and sprawling pine forests. 'Great bandit country,' Spooky informed us unnecessarily.

'You're right, Spooky, so keep your bleedin' peepers open. The trouble is, by the time you see something it's always too bloody late to do anything about it!' Kit replied.

The sign said Gornji Vakuf, one of the few British bases in this area and unfortunately also the scene of recent outbreaks of Muslim-Croat fighting. Times they were a-changing. When we had arrived in Yugoslavia it had been a two-way battle. Now it was developing into a three-way fight between Muslims, Croats and Serbs – plus splinter groups in it for themselves. A country that had been dangerous was now becoming DANGEROUS! And it was no longer possible to trust anyone – civilian or military.

Each village we passed through showed some sign of armed conflict: graffiti-covered walls peppered with small-arms fire; windows smashed; odd buildings collapsed or burned – always some left untouched; bodies in neat piles at the cemetery gates awaiting quick burial before they began to decompose. It was as if an epidemic was spreading through the country. A sickness. A plague of ethnic insanity. No one seemed immune.

We had learned to drive through such places, alert but uninvolved. The inhabitants, lost in their own despair, continued the ritual of shopping, gossiping and tidying their homes as if programmed robots. Kids played in bombed-out houses using sticks for guns.

'You be a Serb and I'll be Croatian. Bang, bang, bang. You're dead. Now it's my turn.' They played the same game for hours, changing sides and arguing over who was the winner. 'It wasn't real. Daddy didn't get dragged from our garden last week, he'll be back later on. Mummy told me so.' They have large observant eyes that see all, but their child minds allow for selective comprehension. It's all in there somewhere, though.

The very last house was untouched. White walls with green-painted louvred windows. The family tending their garden waved as we passed, smiling as they no doubt did at coaches crammed with holiday-makers. Less than twenty metres away another home had been levelled by explosives. We waved back, smiling like idiots. As they say here, 'What can we do? This is a war.'

There's a lake about five kilometres south of Makljen, and a rock jetty by the big gorse bush. If you're ever there, the size nine Danner boots left by the side of it belong to Nigel; you'll recognise them because of the bullet hole in the left heel. He'd appreciate their return, but will understand if your need is greater than his.

Kit had become irresponsible yet again – he does that from time to time – a quick dip in the crystal water suddenly becoming essential for his continued well-being. Without a word of explanation, the Rover drifted off the road, plunged slowly down the embankment and halted. Kit was out in seconds, throwing clothes and caution to the winds. We stared at him splashing in the water like a carefree two-year-old, refusing for about five minutes to follow his example. Spooky lost his marbles next, rapidly followed by Nigel and Pete. They played around for fifteen minutes, leaving Nigel sunning himself on a rock as another brew was made and we played picnics with chocolate bars and dried biscuits, joking about the hell-hole called Sarajevo, and about poor Freda, who would no doubt be wishing by now that she was anywhere but in the Holiday Inn.

The tractor sound grew louder, more guttural, heaving itself up a steep gradient and breaking into our snooze.

'Whassat?' Pete groaned, sitting up sleepily.

'Just a farmer. Shut up and go back to sleep,' Spooky chided.

The noise increased, changing tone as gears were engaged.

'That's a fucking tank!' Kit logged it first and was up and into the Rover only seconds before the rest of us. Nigel hurriedly grabbed his clothes and dived head first into the open back. We were on the road and motoring before a T-55 snout appeared over the hill, and it was ten kilometres before Nigel realised he'd left his boots behind. Nobody was going back for them.

A few inevitable police checkpoints and random road blocks hampered our progress after Runboci, but only one had the makings of trouble. Busy listening to Nigel going on about his Danners and laughing at his anguished moans, we rounded a tight right-hander, skidding to a halt as a pile of hay bales barred our path. Seconds later a lout appeared, alone at first, then waving a brand new Czech Skorpion in our direction as his six mates moved to search the car, bad breath and body odour everywhere. Kit wasn't having it this time and told him so in mixed, expletive-punctuated, Croat-English. For a moment it looked nasty. The guns hovered menacingly in our direction before the leader eyeballed Kit's much-abused ID card. He snatched it from Kit's hand and examined it, checking the photograph thoughtfully, then lowered his gun and in a tone of reverent submission waved his men back and bade us goodbye. As we drove away, we could hear him hurling abuse at his companions.

'Why did he do that?' Pete asked as we gathered speed.

'God knows. Perhaps he didn't understand. Maybe he can't

read and thought it was some form of official document,' Kit replied, grateful whatever the reason.

For a while the roads were straight, open-spaced and free of threat. The wheels hummed on the dry asphalt and the sun shone warmly through the windows. We dozed, thinking of home, beer, football matches and sometimes wives – our own and other people's.

'Look at that!' Pete woke us from a stupor, pointing to a commotion in a village side street. 'What the fuck's going on?'

An old lorry was moving toward us in sporadic bursts, slowing then accelerating again. Bursts of raucous laughter came from about a dozen men surrounding it. We stared as it came alongside, the driver waving as he poured beer down his throat with the hand that should have been on the steering wheel.

'Christ! They've got someone tied to a rope from the back. They're dragging the poor bastard behind along the road.'

A man of about fifty, arms and legs tied, was being hauled by his ankles, bouncing and twisting as the lorry gathered speed. His screams of pain were muffled as blood gushed from his smashed gums. Old women stood by their doorways throwing stones as he passed, nudging one another as the rocks struck his body.

Kit slammed the Rover into reverse, pulling ahead of the lorry and causing the driver to brake hurriedly. The laughter stopped as the tight-lipped torturers stared in disbelief at this intrusion into their game. Kit climbed from the car, glaring back at them, moving to help the victim. The group moved forward threateningly as he knelt by the man's side.

'What the fuck's going on?' Kit rose after a brief examination. There was no response to his question.

'I said, what the fuck's going on?'

A young man in his early twenties moved closer, holding his palms upwards. 'It is none of your business, English. Now go before we do the same to you.'

Kit ignored the threat. 'Just tell me what is going on! Then we'll go.'

The reply took some time as the Bosnian thought it over. 'The man is a Serb. They are responsible for all of these outrages against my people.'

'You mean you're doing this just because he's a Serb? Has he done anything against anyone?'

'No.' The reply was curt, inviting no further discussion.

Kit beckoned to Pete and Nigel. 'Pick him up and put him in the motor.' He turned to the young man. 'You're all as bad as one another. Now piss off, the lot of you, before I get nasty.'

The victim was conscious now and lay moaning as Kit started the engine, allowing it to idle for a moment as he instructed Spooky to cover the threatening crowd with his weapon.

'This country is gonna be the biggest fucking graveyard in the world if you don't all learn to live with one another,' he yelled out of the window, angry for all sorts of reasons; some he didn't fully understand himself.

Slowly he let in the clutch, watching the fist-waving throng advance towards us. 'Give 'em a quick blast, Spooky.'

They drew back as the unexpected volley burst above their heads, cowering in understandable terror as we drove away.

Ten kilometres out of town, Kit pulled to the side of the road. The man had suffered roadburns, cuts, bruising and a bad dose of absolute terror. Field dressing took care of the first three problems, twelve slugs of brandy the last. Now it was time for him to fend for himself. He thanked us with tears streaming down his face and we left him walking back to the only life he had known since childhood, in the village in which he had been born.

'Won't he get more of the same?' Pete asked as we watched him disappear through the trees in the direction of his home.

'Probably,' Spooky replied. 'But where else does he have to go?'

We drove on in silence, passing through a strangely normal Lipa, and turned on to the Tomislavgrad-Posusje road, which was crowded with fleeing refugees, oddly travelling in both directions. The usual haggard faces ignored us as they headed, brain dead, towards another sound of gunfire. Another gutted village. More of the same, as Pete had commented earlier.

Our Bosnian semi-pro warriors welcomed us with partisan fighter hugs and exaggerated cheers of joy, appearing from their covert positions in the wood as we approached Posusje through the narrow, twisting lanes. Ranko came forward, his face a mask of sadness.

'They have been here again,' he said sorrowfully.

'Who's been here?' Kit asked, his eyes narrowing.

'The planes,' Ranko replied. 'Come, I will show you.'

MiG bombers from Mostar had visited once again, showering the town indiscriminately with cluster bombs, killing two children and a lone villager and his horse as they toiled in the fields.

Silver canisters could be seen scattered about the earth, 'Made in Britain' prominently stencilled on their sides. This wasn't the first time we'd seen evidence of British weaponry in use by the Serbian army, but it always came as a shock to think that you could be killed by something made in a Midlands factory by your next-door neighbour's brother-in-law or whoever. What made it even worse was the thought that he was safely at home in front of the TV as they exploded around you.

'When did they come?' Spooky asked.

'Early . . . very early this morning.'

'I fucking told you!' Pete screamed. 'It was those bastards we watched landing at Mostar.'

'Yeah well. What can you do? This is a war.' Kit turned to Ranko. 'Anything else happened?'

'Pop has gone.'

'What do you mean, Pop's gone?'

'You'd better ask Steve. That's all I know.'

We left Ranko at the field and drove hurriedly back to the farm, just in time to catch Steve as he was leaving to give the Bosnians mortar instruction. Kit called to him as we pulled into the yard.

'What's happened to Pop?'

'Don't really know. Just after you left he went into a bit of a downer. Didn't hardly talk for most of the day. Then he suddenly appeared with his gear packed and said he was going home.'

'Why?' More an accusation than a question.

'He left you a note,' Steve replied flatly, walking towards the farmhouse.

Kit picked up the small piece of crumpled paper from the table. Only a few lines were scrawled, as if Pop had been in a hurry.

'Sorry about this, Kit, but I've had it here. I should have waited until you got back and told you to your face but I couldn't, so that's it. I think my bottle's gone and I'm going home to sit in a pub and bore people to death for a change. All the best, Rodney.'

'I never knew his name was Rodney.'

'Shut up, Pete!' Kit snapped, reading the note again. 'Sod it. I'm gonna miss the old sod. Now there's only four of us left.'

'How old was he?' Nigel asked, turning to Kit.

'Don't really know. He was always touchy about his age. Late fifties, maybe older.'

'That's that then!' Upbeat Spooky finalised the gloom. 'Better get the gear in, guys.'

With little to stow away we were finished in minutes, slumping by the window and watching Steve put the part-timers through their paces in the distance. Most of these country boys seemed able to pick up the intricacies of professional warfare with ease, enthusiastically blasting hell out of a hut assembled for that specific purpose with loud cheers following each successful hit. A noisy hour passed until the hut was demolished, targets destroyed and there was nothing left to aim at. They marched in formation back to the yard where Steve dismissed them in the time-honoured fashion, waving goodbye as they trudged back to their families for the night.

'They're coming along. You've done well,' Kit praised.

'Yeah. They're still a bit wild,' Steve replied. 'But we're getting there.'

'Who the fuck's that?' Nigel looked out of the window at the sound of an over-revving car engine.

The Land Cruiser had swept in through the gate, its headlights blazing in the evening gloom. Moments later the Governor bounced in, flak jacket open to display a sparkling Zastava Z9 tucked into a black shoulder holster. He held out his hand in welcome, grinning broadly.

'You did well.' Drago handed out their bonus for a successful operation. Steve looked on, a bit pissed off that he'd missed out on what appeared to be a doddle job.

'I know you must be tired, so I will leave and return on Thursday. There is something serious I wish to discuss which will involve you all.'

With a parting pat on the back for Kit he strode towards the door; only then did we notice his new combat boots as they squeaked his exit.

'Oh, what the fuck is he up to now?' Spooky moaned, drinking his first cup of real American coffee for a fortnight. 'Don't you just hate it when he does that mysterious stuff?'

Kit looked at Steve. 'Do you know what's been going on?'

'No, not really. We heard whispers about Kupres while you were away, and a guy turned up in uniform yesterday. He was a colonel I think, maybe a general. I'm never sure of rank with these Yugo outfits. He hung around the place with Drago, making notes and watching the Bosnian soldiers train. That's about it.' Steve paused as Kit pondered, then added, 'I think there's a punch-up brewing, and a big 'un.'

With Velika Pumpa still fresh in our minds, the last thing anyone wanted was another full-scale battle, and Kit, impatient as always, couldn't wait two days for the answer. 'I'm going to see him tomorrow after we've had some shuteye,' he said, heading for his bedroom and some peace and quiet.

We slept badly, kept awake by Kit's recurring nightmare – which he wouldn't discuss – and Steve's snoring. Add to this the thought of another full-scale frontal assault and you've got the recipe for insomnia.

Kit was up early the next morning, disappearing in a cloud of dust before we had time to rub the sleep from our eyes. The sky was grey and humid; lightning flashed once, twice. Then the rain came in a deluge, sweeping across the open fields and battering against the dirty windows. A miserable way to start the day, made even worse by a sad breakfast without Pop's chatter and the overloud rhythm of the Stones in full cry.

Pete grunted, Nigel grunted, Steve grunted. Only Spooky seemed unperturbed by Pop's absence. The morning drifted past as the torrent continued, turning mountain trickles into streams, and finally floods, until the field was a swamp. Steve stopped grunting and cursed; soon it would be training time and he didn't fancy getting wet.

We drank coffee, smoked endless cigarettes and listened to the World Service telling us that the war was escalating. The same old regurgitated stuff on an endless loop tape: 'General Prylac, Commander-in-Chief of all Croatian forces in Bosnia, said ... Radovan Karadzic, the Bosnian Serb leader, replied to UN threats, "Drop one bomb and forget about peace" ... Atrocities ... Serb strangulation of Sarajevo ... Ethnic cleansing...' The voice droned on like a verbal parasite, savouring every adjective.

'I'm pissed off with listening to this.' Steve uncurled himself and looked out of the window at a break in the clouds. 'Think I'll do some weapons practice when they all turn up.' He went outside as the rain finally stopped, sloshing through deep puddles in the yard, and headed for the armoury.

Kit turned up late in the afternoon, looking pleased with himself and avoiding direct questions. He hadn't been to see Drago, choosing instead to do a little business in Split. A neatly typed list of weapons left lying around confirmed our suspicions that he was getting itchy feet, and for the next hour he shuffled paper and made endless phone calls with monosyllabic acknowl-edgements – giving little away. Pete couldn't stand it, hovering around with his ears flapping like a bored neighbour.

'What's going on, Kit?'

'None of your business.'

'Bollocks then.'

Drago rang, complaining that the phone had been engaged. He wanted to come over now instead of Thursday and was bringing someone to meet us.

Tall and gaunt-looking, Kobacevic was every inch a soldier. He strode into the room, followed by the short, dumpy Drago, introducing himself immediately with a brief résumé of his past experience with the French Foreign Legion and other élite groups. Now an officer in the Croatian army, he led an outfit named the Green Berets – what else? The conversation jumped around for a while as he and Kit swapped reminiscences about harsh training techniques and patrols in French Guiana. His manner was cold and abrupt. This friendly routine was all icing before he handed us a slice of the cake.

'I have spoken to Governor Drago at some length and he has agreed to allow you to assist me in the defence of Kupres. My men need reinforcement for what I believe to be a major offensive by the JNA.' He paused, his face taking on a grave expression. 'I must warn you that the Serbian army want Kupres badly for strategic reasons and have every intention of taking it. Therefore, in my opinion they will, no doubt, send professionals like yourselves, and not conscripts.'

'What type of attack do you anticipate?' Kit asked knowingly.

'Tanks and infantry.'

'How many?'

'Impossible to judge. An educated guess would be a dozen tanks at the most. Probably T-55s, with foot soldiers in support, of course.'

'What's your strength in Kupres?'

'I have two hundred men.' Kobacevic's voice had developed an irritated edge; he was not inclined to accept cross-questioning from subordinate officers.

Kit nodded, taking it all in. Drago hadn't said a word and seemed uncomfortable with Kobacevic controlling the action.

'OK, seems feasible. When do you want us?'

'I'm sorry it is such short notice, but I think the attack is imminent so we cannot afford delay. It must be tomorrow.'

'We'll leave soon after dawn.' Kit stood and shook his head, watching the pair leave with a sigh of here-we-go-again.

'Do you suppose Pop knew this was coming?' Steve asked. 'It's a bloody good time to pull out, innit?'

Kit didn't reply, already instructing the excited Bosnian soldiers to sort out equipment and load the Land Rovers ready for an early off.

Dawn was four a.m. Thunder once again rolled across the mountains from a moody sky, rattling us into life as it shook the windows. Heavy rain following in short torrential bursts only added to the gloom. Kit was edgy. Pete silent for a change. Nigel, Steve and Spooky moved like men possessed by Valium. We drove through the village in convoy, while sleepy villagers stood by their doors in hushed approval, waving farewell.

Chapter Thirteen

Retire? I'll never retire. Even when I'm sixty I'll
wanna keep my hand in somewhere. To me a soldier
doesn't mature until he's about forty anyway, and
that's when you start to earn your big bucks . . .

Kit Freeman, 16 February 1994

The Land Rover bucked, wheezed and rattled. Trees shook and
howling rain flowed down the windows in liquid curtains. Zero
visibility for Kit, crouched at the wheel singing about long and
winding roads until, bored by the repetition of the first lines,
lapsing into brooding silence. Dark houses passed silently. The
occasional cock crowed. Butterflies flapped in our stomachs. I
watched the second Rover slide around tight bends, hanging on to
our tail with Ranko grappling with the wheel as he tried
desperately to keep up.

Pete started to snore. A low, mournful sound from deep down
in his chest, with odd whimpers from his throat, dreaming like a
fireside dog in a winter's evening.

'Shut him up!' snarled Spooky, curled up in the rear cargo
space.

'Let him sleep,' Kit snapped.

Spooky mumbled something threatening, then turned over and
covered his head with a poncho. Silence, except for tyre hiss and
diesel drone.

Tomislavgrad came and went in the first flash of fork lightning,
illuminating the stark outline of destroyed buildings and reminding us of our last visit, when it was called Duvno.

Pete woke with a start, muttering, 'Incoming?' Steve told him it
was only lightning.

'Ours or theirs?'

'Ours.'

'You sure? It seemed bloody close.'

'Go back to sleep, you prick.'

'Road block ahead . . . I think.' Kit pressed his face to the
windscreen, clearing the misted surface with his nose. Sure

enough, two cars were barring our way as we slowed to a halt, nervous and expectant; at this time in the morning it was unlikely to be an official checkpoint.

'Don't get out!' Kit screamed as Steve started to open the door. 'Wait, and keep you eyes peeled.'

Expecting the worst, we waited. Nothing happened. No hooded figure. No hyped-up psycho with a Skorpion. No gun-chewing freak with attitude. We were starting to feel silly, like when you're waiting for roadwork lights to change and they don't. Kit finally inched the Rover forward and pushed the vehicles from our path, waiting for gunfire to open up from the bushes.

'That was strange,' murmured Pete as we accelerated through the gap, followed by a confused Ranko with his front bumper up our ass.

Suica was yawning itself awake as we slowed to enter the main street, stopping for a quick one in the local café and shaking the morning cramp from our bodies. People did their usual furtive appraisals, smiling tight-lipped at our *dobro jutro*s, moving quickly on as Steve tried to expand his knowledge of the language with conversation. 'Miserable sods,' he muttered as they left him mid-flow.

Twenty minutes and we were on our way again, passing a sign saying 'Kupres 30 km'. The final leg of a journey, like the last steps at the dentist, is invariably the worst: in this instance none of us wanted to arrive.

We met Kobacevic on the southern plateau, surveying the landscape with huge naval binoculars. His skeletal face, now hooded in the driving rain, was set in granite as he turned to meet us with awake-all-night slits where his eyes should have been. A curt nod, a barely perceptible facial twitch, a brief handshake. It was easy to understand his preoccupation. Vast open areas spread around us with few trees to offer infantry cover. This was fast-track country – tanks rule OK!

Visibility was tight in the dense, rolling mist, making the Commander's bino-scan more prophetic than practical; but he looked good, silhouetted against the skyline, watching his men flounder in the thick mud as they attempted the impossible task of trench excavation with folding shovels.

Kit ran his experienced eyeballs across the scene, shaking his head as he walked towards a group of struggling soldiers for a quick natter. He returned still shaking his head; now grim-fraced and muttering beneath his breath.

'Line up over there!' he suddenly barked at the lads, pointing to a position several metres away. 'Now listen. This may be the only chance I get to talk to you alone and you ought to know that I think we're in trouble here. These guys don't know what the fuck's going on, and what's worse, they've got no artillery or training in tank warfare.' He paused and looked across at the lonely figure of Kobacevic, nodding in his direction. 'He isn't much better than his men although he pretends to be. Keep close to me at all times, and when the shit hits, follow my lead. Understand what I'm saying?'

They nodded, hesitant and agitated at Kit's concerned tone.

'Gather round.' He spread a map out on the grass, jabbing his finger at grease-pencilled crosses to the south-west of Kupres. 'If it all goes belly up, these are the RV points, so commit them to memory.'

We scribbled hurried notes on fag packets, returning to our lines for a vigorously bellowed 'Fall out!' just to impress the natives.

Kobacevic climbed on to the roof of a supply wagon, tottering precariously for a few moments, lifting his magic binos for a sweep of the misty horizon beyond the town.

His lips moved. '*Da . . . ima tanks.*' Yes . . . there are tanks.

'*Koliko?*' asked his sergeant. How many?

Kobacevic shook his head. '*Ka daleko.*' Too far. He shrugged, his voice trailing away into silence as he continued his watch over the roofs of the town, focusing on several bright lights coming from the north some twenty metres behind a tree line. Something was moving but the mist obscured vision, and only shadowy figures and the muffled roar of throaty engines gave any clue to what was going on in the distance.

'What do you want us to do?' Kit asked. 'Apart from wave a magic wand.'

The dubious mixture of sarcasm and humour made no impact on the statue. Kit huffed a bit, repeating the request.

'Dig in and wait. That's all we can do,' Kobacevic muttered absently.

'No it isn't.' Kit's voice took on a cutting edge; waiting wasn't his style. Preparation, now that was something else.

'What if we dig some berms or lay out some mines on the road into town?'

'Berms?' Kobacevic enquired lazily, as if the word had momentarily slipped his mind.

'Yeah berms. So the tanks have to climb them, exposing their bellies as they come over the top. They make an easy target and the underside has less protection ... as I'm sure you know, Commander.' Tact was never one of Kit's strong points, and his voice was beginning to quiver with frustration.

'No, we haven't the manpower or the time to do either.'

It was like talking to a sponge. Kit gave up with a shrug and led the lads down the hill, instructing them to dig vertical tube foxholes in the positions he indicated.

'Narrow as possible, mind, with just enough room to snuggle into. The tanks will just roll right over your heads without crushing you. Then you're behind them and it's a piece of piss.'

Nigel and Steve led one team, Pete and Ranko the other, digging away furiously as the revving sounds in the distance increased in volume.

Kit left them working and returned to Kobacevic. 'Have you got forward listening posts ... Commander?' He was still asking questions and still trying to get some constructive answers.

'No. We do not need them.'

'How you gonna tell how many tanks are approaching, for Chrissakes?'

Kobacevic ignored the challenge, without warning jumping down from the truck and walking away to his second-in-command, who was running from trench to trench, gesticulating wildly.

Lorries were bringing in supplies from town, with the odd villager to boost numbers and help with the laborious digging. Most were old and weary; the young were already slaving away in the mire. An air of despondency hovered over the field, gnawing at any slight optimism that may have once existed in the troops. No one laughed, cursed or moaned. Only the sound of distant engines broke the silence. Shovels slurped as they sank into the wet earth.

'Will they come today?' Pete asked quietly.

'There's a lot of activity over there, but with this driving rain and the mist, visibility is shit for both armies ...' Kit's voice tailed off with an 'I dunno' shrug.

Flares were starting to pop, showering an eerie orange-white light over the town. The clunk of heavy machinery and rattling chains drifted through the soggy air, building in a crescendo before dying abruptly into a deathly hush. Everyone stopped work, staring into the distance. Watching faces asked the question. Were they leaving? Had they aborted the attack? Can we go home now . . . please? Bumph, bumph, more flares; closer this time. We could just make out running figures as they burst at their peak, drifting lazily downwards and sizzling on the wet earth.

Kobacevic ordered his men back to work as he continued his medieval king routine of scrutinising the landscape at a safe distance. Kit joined him briefly for what seemed a heated exchange of views on how to tackle the impending attack. The Commander wasn't going to listen.

An hour passed in almost perfect silence, as the lull continued with only distant sounds of clicking from the JNA encampment. Rain water was collecting in the trenches and men were feverishly bailing with their helmets. We waited hungrily at the mess tent for something wet, warm and comforting.

'Bloody Kobacevic, he just won't listen . . .' Kit's voice tailed away as he turned towards the town.

At first it was just a dull rumble from a single point to our left; then it spread across the horizon in waves and built in intensity until the earth quite literally trembled, becoming a sound so overpowering that we were at the same time paralysed with fear and ready to run, hide, dig a hole and bury ourselves; anything to stop that noise. The Croats dived into their water-filled trenches in panic, crouching low and doubtless cringing with understandable fear. We stayed on the hill, watching as huge monsters surrounded by heavily armed infantry crawled through the mist, puffs of grey smoke pouring from their vertical exhaust pipes.

They moved slowly at first, coming straight through the town centre, hesitating as they climbed the slope, then deploying in a line before us. A second and third wave appeared in the classic pincer movement from the right and left sides of the houses, easing into an unhurried staggered line. Engines idled, guns creaked into position, as well-tooled infantry soldiers leapt from their APCs and took position behind them.

The roar diminished to an ominous drone, steady, hypnotic, awesome. Twenty-five tanks idled, each with a platoon crouched at its rear – seven hundred men against two hundred ill-equipped country boys and a handful of vagabond mercenaries.

'Sod this for a game of soldiers! Innit time for a sharp exit, Kit?' Pete stared goggle-eyed as we waited with churning stomachs and dry lips for the referee to blow the whistle and start the game. Kobacevic had put his binoculars away and stood beside us, already beaten.

First came the clunk of engaging gears; then engines revved as the tanks inched forward on some invisible command, stopping to re-elevate with clanking chains and hissing exhausts. Without warning the whoop of shells turned into an earsplitting blast as they crunched into the earth, blowing shattered bodies from shallow trenches to slide on the muddy surface like fallen skaters.

The lads looked at Kit for guidance. He grabbed his AK, muttered something to himself, and waved them down into the field below, where he drew them into a group. They fired at shadows as they ran blindly into the battle area, yelling to psych themselves and deaden their hearing to the clank of tracks and the roar of V-12 engines.

The first row of tanks were T-72s, firing HEAT-FRAG. Behind came the older T-55s, losing ground a little as the faster leaders wound themselves up to full speed, grinding the first line of shallowly entrenched soldiers into the mud.

Using flares to confuse thermal detection devices, Kit, six British mercs and the toughened men from Posusje did their best to halt the rolling terror, dashing around like madmen with the Bosnian soldiers, who fought bravely with the little armament they had at their disposal. It was a battle without any chance of victory. Men ran from their trenches in terror, falling under the tracks of advancing machinery. Screams echoed across the battlefield, lost in the roar of explosions and the chatter of Serbian machine-gun fire.

The JNA took Kupres that night. It was a massacre, as the untrained men ran around the battlefield, confused and disorientated. Kobacevic lost over fifty men and the Serbs gained another small piece of real estate to add to their mounting territorial expansion.

We legged it . . . simple as that. 'He that fights and runs away may live to fight another day.' *Musarum Deliciae* said it first, but Kit repeated it – almost accurately – as we stumbled, gasping, over a ridge three kilometres away from the evaporating sound of conflict.

'Everybody here?' Kit counted twenty-two. 'Who's missing?'

Ranko did a double check. 'Nikola, Milan and Milenko.'

'Shit!' They know the RV, don't they?'

Ranko nodded slowly, with doubt flickering in his dark eyes.

'It's stupid travelling in the dark, so we'll wait until dawn. If they're not here by then we'll have to go on without them.' Kit's tone was irritated and final.

Five a.m. No sign of the missing men. Kit was getting fidgety, peering anxiously over the gully edge in all directions and glancing at his watch as each minute ticked by. A helicopter chopped its way overhead, swooping low as we crouched in the hollow. They were obviously searching for something, turning in a steep climb to clear the hedges by inches and hovering as the spotter leaned out and searched the ground around us with a scoped M76 sniper rifle. We could feel the down draught from the rotor blades as Kit lined his weapon on the man only two hundred metres away, rolling back with a sigh of relief as the pilot climbed vertically and disappeared over the pine trees in a puff of blue exhaust smoke.

'Looks like an old Bell UH-1H.' Spooky stared over the ridge at the receding helicopter.

'Bell fucking what?' Steve queried.

'A Huey . . . American chopper used in 'Nam. Look, you can just make out the oversprayed markings on the tail.'

'Wonder where the Serbs got that from?'

'That's the business to be in,' Kit muttered from his map search.

'What business?' Steve looked at him blankly.

'Arms dealing. That's where the money is. Not lying here in this crappy hole waiting to be shot at.' He looked at his watch. 'Fifteen minutes and we're off. Somebody go out and look for them. Maybe they've got lost.'

Nigel and Pete crawled over the ridge in the direction of Kupres with a warning not to go far, leaving Kit plotting a course through mountains to the nearest town, Livno, about thirty kilometres south-west.

With just two minutes before the allotted time, all five men returned, Milan looking sheepish as he explained to an irritated Ranko that they had gone to the wrong RV point and had been waiting a kilometre to the east. Ranko translated for Kit, who gave them both a shrivelling look of disbelief before returning to his route planning.

It took three days and two nights to reach Livno, scavenging food from houses, farms and waste bins, sleeping in barns and hedges, ducking and diving at the slightest sound. A welcome light moment was seeing Nigel run across a farmyard pursued by an angry old lady waving a brush at him as he tried, unsuccessfully, to carry two plates of cakes stolen from her kitchen. She actually caught up with him as he clambered over a gate, hammering him into submission with witch-like screams and curses.

Serbian patrols hampered our progress, appearing at the most unlikely places and causing moments of alarm. We dived for cover, holding our breath, as they passed, sometimes only a metre away. Mountains often formed impossible barriers, making tortuous detours necessary, forcing us to backtrack for hours over rugged terrain until we were dirty, hungry and exhausted.

Nikola sprained an ankle after a fall that could have injured him severely. He tumbled twenty metres as the rocky path gave beneath his feet and plunged headfirst into a river, staying under until Kit, in a moment of *Baywatch* heroism, dived in and rescued him. He wished he hadn't bothered. In the bitter cold they both shivered, fearing hypothermia, until blankets were liberated from a clothes line and a risky fire warmed them back to normal temperature.

Day three, with less than five kilometres to travel. A GPMG rattled as we crossed a road, dirt kicking at our feet. A copse on the hill was providing cover, smoke filtering from the trees. We couldn't run with Nikola hobbling on lashed-together crutches; anyway we were all too bloody knackered.

'Who's gonna go and do 'em?' Kit asked wearily from yet another water-filled ditch.

Ranko volunteered, taking Milenko and Milan as punishment for their crime of misdirection. We watched them flank the emplacement, flagging slightly as they reached the top, then crawling around the rear of the copse. One detonation blast and a few seconds of auto fire, then Ranko appeared, fist waving in triumph.

We tried singing to boost morale, joining in choruses of Bosnian folk songs. Then we attempted to remember our own, learned at school and since forgotten. We gave up after a few short verses of 'Hi Lily Hi Low', feeling stupid and not sure if it was a traditional folk song or not.

Kit held up his arm, still covered in the blanket. Through the trees we could see a town; people stood talking casually and wandered aimlessly across the square. The whole scene was one of relaxed informality.

'It looks clear, but go and check it out first,' Kit instructed Steve and Ranko.

Watching through binoculars, we could see them skirt the nearest houses before slipping through a gap and disappearing from sight behind a warehouse. Twenty agonising minutes passed before they reappeared, smiling, with a group of Bosnian soldiers in tow. Lots of greetings, hugs and even kisses, then a hearty meal of some kind of stew, ladled down our welcoming throats with large spoons that nearly choked us in our enthusiasm to fill our bellies.

We were in no hurry to return in defeat to Posusje, and spent the day in relaxed contentment, telling porkies to the Bosnian soldiers and listening politely to their stories in return. Jungle drums had passed the Kupres fiasco down the line, complete with tales of rape, torture and pillaging. One of the soldiers lived there; his family remained. The bullshitting stopped as tears ran down his cheeks and he left to cry alone.

That evening, dirty and stinking, we were invited to a party at the town hall. Cries of '*Zivela!*' – Cheers! – greeted us, and the night blurred with generous helpings of *viski*, *votku* and the local drink of *vinjak* – work it out! At three a.m. we'd had it, staggering back to the army camp in no fit state for nothin'.

'Come on . . . wakey wakey.' Kit was up before us, face clean-shaven and sparkling. Don't you just hate it when you feel like shit and there's this guy looking fresh and energetic with a clean uniform and creases in his trousers?

'Where did you get that gear, you old bastard?' asked Pete, lying in a pool of vomit.

Kit touched the side of his nose with his forefinger. 'Never you mind, my son. Better get up and wash, I've got us a lift back to Posusje and it's leaving in ten minutes.'

Half an hour later, after chewing endless cups of the treacle they called coffee, we clambered on to a military truck bound for Split, but detouring for our benefit. The ride was bumpy but the fresh air useful to our rebelling stomachs. Many stops were required as nausea and a bad case of the Indian curries made regular bush trips necessary. Glad we were to see our village, and gladder still to arrive at the farm.

Drago took it well, listening to our tales of woe with sympathy and understanding, the loss of his Land Rovers seeming more important than the fall of Kupres. Then he and Kit had a heated exchange out of earshot, which Kit refused to discuss when he returned, but his manner was overcast, remaining that way for the next two days as we recovered from our ordeal.

The Kupres episode cast a veil of gloom over everyone which refused to lift as the days passed in further patrols and training periods for new volunteers. The few remaining members of the original group had been in Yugoslavia for over a year now and were becoming weary of the catch-as-catch-can existence, the constant insecurity and the life of perpetual motion. At one time Bosnians and Croatians were allies in a common cause; now things had changed. Friends and neighbours were torturing and killing one another, murdering the children they'd once played with. Agreement couldn't be reached on the matter of territorial rights and government leaders bickered constantly; the country was at war with itself.

Pop sent us a postcard from Blackpool, signed with a flourish and the immortal words 'Wish you were here', to which he'd added, 'Don't you?' He was right; we'd have done almost anything for a ride on a roller-coaster and a pint on the seafront. We pinned the card to the kitchen wall, gazing at the picture of relaxed, sunlit beaches. It just made things worse.

Reports of small skirmishes in neighbouring villages had introduced a new daily routine: clock on, grab your gun, jump in the Rover, off for a brief firefight and back home for tea; remembering to clock off again. 'It's like working in a bleedin' factory,' moaned Pete after the seventh trip in three days.

Kit was spending most of his free time on the telephone these days, or off on business trips in Split; always returning with lists which necessitated yet more phone calls. Mysterious boxes with indecipherable labels appeared in the stores, and Mike returned, staying for a few nights of animated and secretive conversation. Money changed hands and Kit chuckled himself to sleep.

On Wednesday morning, Drago came in with another 'job sheet'. This time we were off on a trip to a now nonexistent village near Mamici where the governors felt they were under threat from a marauding band of irregulars.

Intermittent attacks over the past few nights had led them to conclude that an invasion was imminent, and they wanted it crushed. We arrived as dusk was settling in. Mortar explosions had flattened six houses on the perimeter and sporadic small-arms fire rattled the still air, as people huddled in shop doorways in what had become the universal condition of fear. It was too late in the day to start patrolling the hills and we were given an empty house as a control centre, unloading our gear for an early start.

By dawn the mortar and small-arms fire had stilled to a blissful peace, as we lay on our beds wondering what had woken us from our dream-filled sleep. 'That's a baby crying!' Steve whispered. 'Sounds like it's just been born.'

In a house still blackened by recent hits, a child was born to eighteen-year-old Zenca Erchak. Her husband, a part-time soldier away in the hills somewhere, had become a father for the first time. He was never to share in her joy, never to hold his crying baby or see his wife's contented smile. For at 8.48 that morning the first Serbian shell of the day landed on the house, killing them both. The second landed on our command building, causing little damage and no casualties.

Steve, big tough Steve, cried that day as he helped clear away the debris, finding little Zenca still clutching her child, a look of disbelief on her pale, lifeless face. Steve was a hard man; some would say cruel, even callous. He was after all a mercenary.

Carrying her body into a neighbour's house, he cursed the world and all the bastards in it, pacing up and down as he clicked his AK safety catch on and off in impotent rage. He was going to kill the bastards one by one . . . he swore it.

Kit tried to reason with him, taking the practical view that this sort of thing happened all the time. But for some reason, years of simmering frustration finally erupted and Steve was unable to accept the pointless death of one unknown young girl. Perhaps in his mind she represented all the helpless deaths he had witnessed in countries all over the world.

Steve kept his word. Over the next few days he and Kit led endless patrols, finally locating the mortar position responsible for the attacks on the village. A brief firefight ensued and the men stormed the position without casualties. Nigel and Pete dragged Steve off two Serbian prisoners as they sobbed in terror at his brutal beating, but they were unable to stop him kneeling them down and emptying a magazine into their bodies.

The next day we were due to return to Posusje. We woke in the morning to find Steve's bed empty and his gear missing. He'd disappeared in the early hours without even leaving a note of explanation. Kit did some checking when we got back, coming up with zilch. Rumours of aid work in Rwanda filtered back through the network but were never confirmed. Steve had simply vanished from the circuit and has never been seen or heard of again.

Morale went from bad to worse. The Kupres cock-up and now Steve leaving; Kit was pissed off with the whole thing. Enough was enough. You could see it in his eyes and the way he moved around the place, dispirited and preoccupied.

On Saturday he said he was going into town for a quick pint and a natter with some of his old mates from Mostar. He stayed away for three full days without any form of communication, sliding back through the farm gates in a civilian Range Rover with British plates.

'I'm out of here!' were his first words, before explaining to a crestfallen Nigel and Pete his new role as an arms and equipment dealer. We helped him load the mysterious boxes into his car and watched him hurriedly stuff his belongings into a black holdall: 'Forget the bergan, that's for squaddies.' A quick handshake with the Bosnian soldiers and a manly hug for Pete, Nigel and Spooky.

'See you around, lads,' and he was off into the wild blue yonder and a new life of wheeling and dealing with the big boys.

'Ethnic cleansing' was the buzz phrase these days, making the Muslims a worthy cause and media underdogs in just about every magazine and television report. Persecution, genocide, subjugation: great copy for the newspaper parasites. Kit was to become a saviour to the oppressed, for once able to take the moral high ground, and it felt good for a change.

Zagreb was his first port of call; tricky with a car full of bent gear and no mates to back you up at police checkpoints. Bribes worked better than bullets in most cases and the trip was uneventful if nervous. First stop, police headquarters and a lengthy meeting with old friend Inspector Urirch. A deal involving transportation and storage of military equipment was top of the agenda. Kit needed someone he could trust while he was on whistle-stop tours or out of the country, and Urirch was happy to oblige with offers of a safe house on the outskirts of town. A police inspector's salary needs the occasional transfusion.

Next call was Colonel Tony Abranovich. As always, he was

pleased to see Kit, especially scrubbed and in civvies. This was the new model Christopher Freeman, fast-talking and hyperactive. An entrepreneur/mercenary, a different breed of cat. No longer did his life depend upon the AK-47. For the warrior turned businessman the ultimate weapon had become the HR8A-BK continuous-paper-roll-fed, non-jamming, full-auto-memory, F-5.4-cut Casio calculator, complete with universal currency compensator as an optional extra and usually worn in its fast-draw position in the left armpit inside pocket, cocked and ready at all times, day or night. When in combat mode the calculator went into its familiar chuga, chuga, chuga rhythm, laying down some heavy bright-green stencil numbers across a black display panel as the paper jerked from its mouth in an endless stream. Deutschmarks, dollars, sterling, and of course the Swiss franc – bam! bam! the machine barked its answer. 'When? Where? OK, fifty per cent up front, trust me!' Abranovich was impressed and the meeting was enlightening, profitable and cordial for both. After a slap-up meal in a four-star, Kit left Zagreb to travel south and set up shop at a deserted farm near Suica; filling the outhouses with MG-42 GPMGs, M-53 GPMGs, AKMs, 47s, ARMSCOR MGL grenade launchers and a variety of Soviet pistols, many still in waxed paper wrappers. In a small copse adjacent to the farm he stashed his major investment, a heavily camouflaged fifty-two-year-old Soviet T-55 tank, just waiting for the highest bidder.

Building up this stock had been a long-term project, starting months before Kit had made the final decision to pull out of the shooting war.

'What set me off on the trail were my visits to Bosnia. I started collecting gear and selling it as a job lot. This went on for a few months, with me getting better and better at it and making a few bob without getting shot at. Then one day I was having a drink in Split and a group of Muslims approached me – word gets around – asking for certain items of equipment, which I agreed to supply. Some of it was difficult, but I managed with a little help from my friends. The black market is very active here and it's not breaking any arms embargo because the stuff's already in the country . . . and if it isn't, it soon will be. You can buy an RPG-7 from a barman in Split – no problem!'

The procurement of weapons has never been a problem for those with specialist knowledge, contacts and cash . . . lots of cash.

Kit Freeman was now in possession of these three essential ingredients for success in his new role. Plus the fortunate set of circumstances that had made his turf Yugoslavia, which along with Spain, Portugal and Czechoslovakia was one of the easiest countries in the world in which to buy and transport arms. End-user certificates are considered to be something of a burden to the businessman dealing in military hardware.

'They're all at it in Yugoslavia; it's become a bloody red-hot business these days. Selling pistols and small arms and smuggling them back to Britain to flog to squaddies in Aldershot pubs for about two hundred Deutschmarks . . . Makarovs, CZs, Berettas, Tokarevs, the lot. Not only is the gear coming out, it's also going in. British pilots are flying stuff into the Croatian island of Krk. Iranian 747s are bringing weapons into Zagreb airport under the very nose of the United Nations Protection Force and nothing can be done about it. Croatia is free to import arms but not pass them on to Bosnia . . . Disgusting it is!'

Trips back home to the UK became necessary as business expanded. And after a two-week break in the Lake District to finally cleanse his pores of camouflage cream and his ears of the shriek of battle, he drove south to set up deals with the Muslim parliament in London. Using his code names Mustapha (Christopher) and Yahaha (John), he made covert arrangements in the luxury of top hotels where advice was given on the most suitable weaponry, its availability and, most significantly, its price. Promises were made and broken, deals teetering on the edge of completion collapsed. But he continued ducking and diving until a million pounds changed hands; bringing it back to his home in Wales in a cheap nylon rucksack costing £4.75 from the Army and Navy store.

There are a lot of expenses in the supplies business. Bribes, overland delivery and storage eat up a great chunk of the money, and associates in Bosnia expect part payment upfront, with the balance on delivery. They are at the sharp end, where things can, and often do, go desperately wrong.

You can question the morality of Kit's chosen profession – many do. But is the man who pulls the trigger any different from the man who supplies the weapon, or the politicians who plan the war?

Chapter Fourteen

> I've shot blokes right in front of me . . . Not just once
> or twice but many times – but that's work.

You can't help but like him, this amiable bear of a man. Shaven head, enormous grin and snappy Geordie dialogue peppered with expletives. It's difficult to believe that he's a killer, difficult to believe he has seen and done those things. Almost impossible to picture him prowling through the jungle on a recce or crouched in a tree, cradling a sniper rifle.

It all changes, however, when he tiger-stripes his face and hands with black/olive/brown camouflage paint and dons his well used DPM para smock with the subdued Foreign Legion wings on his right breast. His eyes change to smouldering slits as the jaw line sets in concrete, and he becomes everyone's nightmare . . . right before your eyes.

I first met Kit through a mutual associate, also a mercenary, and we talked of the old days well into the night: of 'Mad Mike' Hoare and his exploits in the Seychelles; 'Colonel' Callan in Angola; John Banks and his own brand of SAS – Security Advisory Service; and of course his own exploits with the DEA in Colombia, before his more recent and final gig in Bosnia/Croatia. Two weeks later I met him again, this time to suggest a book on his life as a Soldier of Fortune, a Dog of War . . . whatever the media call freelance soldiers these days. Kit was keen on the idea, saying that he'd thought of trying to write one himself, one day.

The initial chats were the easy part. Getting him pinned down to a specific time and date for an in-depth interview was something else, a bit like trying to catch a fly with chopsticks; difficult and requiring some patience and skill. Numerous arrangements were made and broken, although courtesy phone calls were received from colleagues using ambiguous phrases such as 'Kit is unavailable at the moment but will contact you in a few days'. Sometimes he just didn't turn up; then the phone would ring and his cheery voice would apologise yet again and a further meeting would be arranged. I finally got him, nailing his feet to the floor and beating him into submission with the butt of an AK-47. This is Kit's story . . .

From the tender age of seven Kit knew that he was bound for a military career. His father had served with the British army for much of his adult life and his grandfather before him. Kit would continue the family tradition; of that there was little doubt.

'Me dad was a right friggin' hard case, he was. I remember when I came home on leave for the first time, thinking I was bit of a Jack the lad. I was a bit pissed and said some things which were bang out of order. He waited until I'd finished ranting, and said, "I suppose you think you're a man now – outside!" Then he battered seven pillars of shit of me . . . Good old boy. I miss him dearly.'

Kit's memory of his father was very clear, and it was obvious from his tone and moistening eyes that his death at fifty-four still affected him in those quiet moments.

Christopher Freeman is an enigma: loyal to his friends, benevolent with his time and money, loving, caring, warm and friendly; he is also callous, cruel, dangerous and of course a cold-blooded contract killer! That's his job and the reason that many governments, including our own, pay him and people like him large sums of money to help them. Especially when things could go embarrassingly wrong.

Why does he do it? The simple fact is that he just loves his work and is very competent at what he does, taking great pride in doing a job well for itself alone. Monetary reward doesn't seem to be a factor in his desire to excel, although it is the prime motivator in his involvement with any overseas conflict. He readily admits to having little regard for territorial rights, political leanings or moral viewpoints, and would, if necessary, work for any government offering a bigger pay cheque.

'It's a simple economic fact. Where there's a war there's a pile of loot just waiting. Sod the cause, that's for somebody else to worry about. We're in it for the dosh!'

Kit and his colleagues have their own morals, and the unpredictable governments of the world offer business and large amounts of money to those prepared to die for them in some distant land. At the moment Bosnia is the marketplace, but when this income source dries up it could be any of the twenty or so countries that have internal conflicts and need experienced military advisers unhampered by rules and regulations.

Security consultants are always in demand on those little islands controlled by dictators with little or no military skills. Weapons are – due to the fall of Eastern Bloc countries – easy and cheap to obtain. It's a growth industry, it seems, and Kit is shrewd enough to take advantage of this fact and exploit it for his own ends, unlike many mercenary soldiers who are happy with a gun and a fistful of dollars.

Kit's military career has now spanned a period of twenty years, starting at the tender age of thirteen when he joined the Royal Fusiliers as a cadet. Later he entered the junior Parachute Regiment and found that he possessed a natural talent with SLR, producing one-inch groupings with a high degree of consistency. This intuitive skill led to his selection for the shooting team, and after six months of dedicated practice on the Aldershot firing range he achieved a second at the junior Bisley, giving him a taste of success when interviewed and photographed for the military magazine, *Pegasus*.

But he was not a happy man.

'The prospect of battalion life stuck at Ash Rangers, with each day spent on the rifle range shooting at targets, really did my fucking head in! What I wanted was a trade.'

With several options open to him, he transferred to the Royal Artillery 29th Commando Regiment, RA, in Plymouth, undertaking the medic's course before being posted to the Citadel Medical Centre at 29 CDO. Still not settled, he moved yet again, this time to 148 Battery (Para Commando, forward observation battery for the RN) where he undertook and passed the OP course/Signals. Within a very short period he had a personality clash with one of the second lieutenants and did twenty-eight days for striking an officer, leading to a further transfer to the 4th Field Airborne Artillery at North Camp, Aldershot.

A change of direction seemed worthy of consideration at this career juncture, and Kit chose the SAS selection route, but failed and got RTU (return to unit). No reason was given, apart from 'Too immature' scrawled on the bottom of his application form. It was suggested by the commanding officer that he might like to try again in eighteen months.

'Failed. I couldn't believe it.' Kit uttered the words in a flat, unemotional voice, intentionally creating a barrier against further questioning on the subject. He could still hear judgement being passed by the selection board officer, his cold public school accent echoing around the large unfurnished room, shattering the very essence of his military ambition. Until now he had never truly realised how desperately he had wanted to emulate his father in becoming a member of this most élite corps of fighting men. But he knew in that instant he would never try again.

Back to 4th Field Airborne Artillery – totally gutted, pissed off and dispirited. He was thankfully posted to Belize, where he spent a period training and developing further skills in the art of jungle warfare, which he thoroughly enjoyed. Possessing a natural aptitude for stealth and an affinity for the hot, sticky climate, Kit found that jungle fighting gave him the excitement lacking in his previous role as a sniper, and it was with regret that he was only able to spend six months there before returning to the UK and routine military tasks.

It was this period of enforced inactivity that led him into an incident that would change his life . . .

'What I thought was a dressing-down for the theft of petrol was in fact rather more serious. I'd been having an affair for six months with a woman who was married to an army captain. I swear I didn't know she was married, but nobody believed me. There was nothing to indicate that there was a man living in that house . . . nothing. It was bare of any masculine furnishing of any kind. There were no military photos, men's clothing or objects of any kind. They had me by the balls and that was me finished. The bastards gave me "Services no longer required" and I was out of the army. Discharged due to an error of judgement!'

So that was that! An ignominious conclusion to an interesting career in Her Majesty's forces: an uninspiring meander through various training establishments, a few trips overseas, some experience of action in the jungle and a little urban conflict. The zigzag course through the minefield of army training was over – it was the end of everything. Childhood memories lingered; tales of battles and heroes, death and glory. Tell me some more, Dad, it's over, it's over, it's over!

Back home, in civilian life, the months drifted by aimlessly. Odd jobs, a bit of this and a bit of that. No career, no direction, no sergeant barking orders. Nothing quite filled the gap; how could it? Thoughts of other forms of military service began to invade his mind, popping in and out, taunting and teasing, until one stayed and flourished. The French Foreign Legion; they would surely take him on with his experience. This was the answer to his predicament. In November 1984, after five months in the wilderness, Kit made his decision.

'It was easy. I simply went to Paris by coach, got on the Métro and then walked to the top of the hill where I just knew the fort was. I didn't have a map but I knew instinctively that it was there. I knocked on the huge door and a distant little voice answered in French, and like a prat, I said, I've come to join the Legion. The door opened and the voice told me to come in. He was an American guy, nice and friendly. He searched me first and then fed me loads of food and drink – then I had to do all the dishes!'

Without realising it, Christopher 'Kit' Freeman was about to embark upon his first step into the world of mercenary soldiering. The Legion constitutes perhaps the most élite form of mercenary, certainly the most glamorous and professional, undeniably the most formidable.

The first week in this grey, utilitarian building was spent on endless interviews, tests and medical examinations. It's tough to get into the Foreign Legion these days; only about one third of the applicants are selected. But the chance of starting life anew remains one of the principal objectives of the new recruit ... exactly the reason that Kit was there. Morale is high on the list of essential requirements, a quality often absent from the erratic character of many entrants. Unsuitable people are not an asset to a unit with an international reputation for military efficiency; gone are the days when drop-outs, vagrants and misfits gravitated to the Legion. Interpol computers are used extensively to screen out undesirables and those with proven criminal records. If a man is wanted anywhere in the world for a major crime he is immediately arrested and detained until the relevant authority can claim him.

With the initial selection procedure complete, the fortunate few are dispatched overnight to L'étranger at Aubagne, a suburb of Marseilles, which serves as the Legion's main induction and administration centre. The document of allegiance is signed, but only after further medicals, tests and checks into criminal activity have been performed by the Legion's military police. The 'chosen ones' are then taken to Castelnaudary in southern France, home of the training regiment 4e étranger.

'We didn't stay at the barracks for long, shipping out the next day in our respective companies. I belonged to 1st Company (Premier) and we were sent to a farm in the hills to do four weeks' basic to earn our kepi. After the initial training period, the final test was the ninety-kilometre kepi march, which was not a lot of fun. All failures were back-squadded to the oncoming group, repeating the whole vicious process. Success meant a further six weeks at Castelnaudary barracks.'

A large part of this final training period included learning all of the Legion's marching songs – in French! Le bleux, to instil esprit de corps, raise morale and bind men from differing nationalities.

The top three trainees at Castelnaudary barracks normally stay behind and attend the NCO course, finally becoming instructors themselves. Kit managed a distinguished second place, 'but they couldn't wait to get rid of me! I was out on the piss at every opportunity and they didn't want me to stay behind as an NCO.' The failure to respond to Legion discipline meant that he and three others were selected for parachute training – and he won his para wings, yet again!

Posted to the 1st Company of the Regiment Etranger Parachutiste (commando and anti-tank), Kit started to make some real progress at last and was elevated to Premier Class (lance-corporal), prior to being dispatched overseas to the traditional Foreign Legion hunting grounds in Chad, Djibouti and French Guiana. He undertook and successfully completed his French commando course and was now fully trained at killing people – in two languages!

Kit spent nearly four years with the Foreign Legion, a great deal of which was in many ways similar to his life in the British army. Repetition and rigid discipline, however, started to eat away at him until terminal boredom set in and a way out was sought. Not easy, especially when you consider the stories of brutality and death served upon deserters. But it was time for a change, and with a fellow malcontent named Simon he boarded a bus from Marseilles to Paris, hopped on a ferry to London – all without passports – and sold his Legion gear to a little shop in Victoria. Thus ended another phase in his military career.

London . . . broke and on the run from the Foreign Legion! Not an enviable position to be in, even for the ever-resourceful Kit Freeman. A well-paid job seemed an appropriate goal and he easily obtained one as a bouncer, living in the twilight world of late-night revellers and potential physical abuse. It was a living, but fate and the way of the warrior beckoned him yet again. This time it was the classic man-in-a-pub situation and an opportunity to return to the thing he does best.

'Mozambique. That's where the action is,' the man explained, telling Kit what to do when he arrived, who to contact and what would be expected of him. It all seemed a hell of a lot more interesting and profitable than his job as a bouncer – what could he lose? His first five-week contract brought him £4,500 working with the guerrilla forces; he didn't kill anyone, didn't have to put up with military crap, and he came home jubilant and moderately wealthy. He was given a second contract, returning to Mozambique for nine weeks. On this trip he met and became firm friends with a leading figure in the mercenary world who would later become his guru, learning from him everything about survival in this dangerous and often treacherous game.

Now that Kit was 'on the circuit', offers of work were readily available to him, and he spent much of his time in the area of Islington known as the Angel, where rooms are taken for short periods to set up mercenary contracts. Here he picked up a nice little earner in Colombia, working for the American DEA – Drug Enforcement Administration – where his specialist jungle training came in handy on search-and-destroy missions. He was enjoying this freedom lacking in discipline with high financial reward. He was at last truly a 'freeman', and that suited him just fine . . . until Khadija came along.

The romance turned quickly into marriage, temporarily changing his life into one with softer edges, less frantic, more deliberate. Kit quit the roving life and became a bodyguard to the rich and famous, only occasionally leaving her for work overseas in Colombia. They made plans for their future together – only there wasn't one.

Within two years Khadija had died of encephalitis, a disease of the brain for which there is no cure. Kit was devastated. She had touched him and found the vulnerable boy beneath the tough northern soldier, made him want something more than artillery fire and the sound of marching feet; but she had gone, and part of him and his dream had gone with her.

'Madness overtook me, I'd had enough. Nothing mattered any more and I became a nasty piece of work, battering people at the slightest provocation.' Trouble with the law inevitably ensued, with drunken pub brawls and the theft of a police car leading to brief periods in Bedford and Durham jails on remand for theft, fraud, and a charge of armed robbery, which was finally not proven.

Kit knew he could not continue with this destructive lifestyle, and with the help of close friends gradually hauled himself back from the edge.

Then a war called to caress his wounds, to dry his eyes and salve his tortured soul. The war was Yugoslavia, then in 1991 broken and fragmented into Bosnia/Herzegovina, Montenegro, Macedonia, Slovenia, Croatia and Serbia. Not a Geneva Convention war. A killing, torturing, dirty war – just the kind of war a man like Kit needed right now. What could they do to him? He was already dead.

This time he went without contacts or thought of financial gain. Overland to Zagreb, then to Gospich, easily finding allies to help him in his cause. A taxi driver who fought part-time with the Croatian Tiger Brigade against the dominant Serbians introduced him to the action. In his first conflict he was injured by a detonation blast while retaking Gospich; but he had performed well, ducking, diving, killing and maiming with a total disregard for his own safety. They were impressed by this crazy Englishman, but they didn't know the reason for this outward display of courage and daring . . . not that they would have cared.

The events at Gospich had raised Kit's standing with his newfound friends to such an extent that he was offered the rank of *zapovjednik voda* (lieutenant) and given an official Croatian soldier's ID under the assumed name of Darren Abbey. His salary was 47,000 dinar per month (£250). Now he was legit!

For a while Yugoslavia became his stamping ground, where he could rebuild his shattered life and utilise the skills kindly taught by the British army and the French Foreign Legion. He came home on the odd occasion, returning at the request of an associate for a recce on Mostar airfield which led to his final year as an active mercenary.

Kit returned triumphant to the Welsh town that had become his home for a well-earned period of rest and recuperation, only occasionally interrupted by visits from Special Branch concerned about his intentions and future objectives now he was back in the UK. They needn't have worried; the gypsy life had temporarily lost its appeal. Time passed pleasantly, as the camo-tinted pores cleansed themselves of olive dye and memories were locked away.

Haunted still by the death of his wife, and romance the last thing on his mind, fate did a strange thing. At a Swansea discothèque he met a pretty Welsh girl named Rose – strange because the word 'rose' is the English translation of the Arabic word *khadija*. Kit still finds this eerie. 'It made the hairs on me neck prickle.' The chance meeting developed into courtship; long drives into the Welsh hills, dinners in darkened restaurants and an interesting trip to Brighton . . .

'When I returned to Britain I was using my Darren Abbey alias because of police problems before I left for Yugoslavia. I didn't need any aggro at the time, deciding to turn myself in at a later date. It was Rose's birthday and we went away for the weekend, booking into the Oakwood Hotel in Brighton. Without my knowledge the place was very close to where they were holding the Conservative Party Conference that year. Big mistake! I was signing the forms at the reception desk and noticed that one of the police on security duty was clocking me a bit funny. About fifteen minutes later, as we were unpacking, somebody started battering on the door. I went to see who it was, only to find a police team kitted out with Heckler and Kochs waiting outside. Fucking crazy; they were crouched against the walls, bulletproof vests . . . the lot! I told them they could put all that stuff away because Rose wasn't used to that sort of thing and she was doing her nut.

'They had me on the floor, did the body-search routine and stuck cuffs on, before arresting me as a suspected terrorist. I ask you. Me a bleedin' terrorist! Then I was taken to the Brighton nick and kept waiting for someone from the intelligence service. A guy finally turned up and told me that they knew who I was; the copper in reception had recognised me from the TV programme *Dogs of War*. The intelligence bloke went on a bit, threatening all sorts of things before saying that they thought I was here to do some damage to the party conference for the IRA . . . Me motor, left in the NCP car park, was torn apart as they searched, without any luck, for something incriminating. I was finally taken to Brixton Prison and kept for a week until visited by some Special Branch guys and some other people who brought maps with them. For two days we had these meetings about Osijek. They wanted to know where the Serbian mines were placed so British Royal Engineers could deal with them. Later I was up before the judge for past crimes and fined £4,000 and given a two-year probation.'

Rose wasn't going to put up with any of this mercenary stuff and made it clear that for Kit it was time to settle down and get a proper job.

Using his ill-gotten gains he started a legitimate business venture which briefly prospered, then exploded, leaving him broke and for a while dejected. This was not an acceptable position for a warrior. His military training, coupled with his positive mental attitude, rapidly locked on to automatic fire, seeking a way out – fast.

'I didn't know what to do for a while. I owed money with nothing coming in and it was desperate times. First I thought of going back to the front line in Bosnia but Rose put her foot down, so that was that. Then I decided to contact the Muslim parliament in London again; so I rang with the old Mustapha routine and they were very pleased to hear from me. At the time the whole war was going down the tubes because they didn't have enough gear for their troops. So I jumped in the car and headed for Gotham City and was back in the supplies business.

'When a meeting was being arranged, a coded destination was given – "I'll meet you outside Buckingham Palace at 10.30" would mean something totally different, a location prearranged at an earlier discussion. The Muslim buyer would say, "I have x amount to spend", and I would provide equipment to this sum – making allowance for my commission, of course!'

Ivan Urirch remained the contact in Bosnia, arranging storage in sheds and outbuildings in the Zagreb area. It had to be this way; Kit wasn't going back against Rose's wishes. He was in love and his new family came first.

For such an outwardly gregarious man, he was lonely, desperately needing the new family who had backed and supported him. He wasn't about to let them down.

Kit spent ten weeks in and around London, meeting new people and arranging for delivery of goods by Australian mercs in Bosnia; once again coming home with enough money to repay his debts and start another business venture.

'Fighting's a risk I don't want to take any more. I've been shot before, but next time it might be for real and I could be dead . . . I've got something now that I've never had before and I want to keep it.'

So . . . Christopher Freeman had emerged, relatively unscathed, from the traumas of his mercenary and military past, and his path right now is clearly, if not irrevocably, directed at the business end of the game.

He has recently moved away from South Wales and is now living in a quiet suburb somewhere in the north of England. He's still a young man in his early thirties, but a lot of blood has passed under the bridge in the past few years. It's going to be difficult to settle into a conventional existence, with a wife, dog and 2.4 children . . . Hell! It's going to be impossible.